EDMONTON

PICTURE RESEARCH BY JOHN E. McISAAC
"PARTNERS IN PROGRESS"
BY STANLEY ARTHUR WILLIAMS

PRODUCED IN COOPERATION WITH THE
AMISK WASKAHEGAN CHAPTER, HISTORICAL SOCIETY OF ALBERTA

WINDSOR PUBLICATIONS

EDMONTON
Gateway to the North

An Illustrated History by John F. Gilpin

Windsor Publications
History Books Division
Publisher: John M. Phillips
Editorial Director: Lissa Sanders
Senior Picture Editor: Teri Davis Greenberg
Editorial Director, Corporate Biographies: Karen Story
Assistant Director, Corporate Biographies: Phyllis Gray
Marketing Director: Ellen Kettenbeil
Production Coordinator: Gladys McKnight
Design Director: Alexander D'Anca
Production Supervisor: Katherine Cooper
Production Manager: Dee Cooper
Typesetting Manager: E. Beryl Myers
Proofreading Manager: Doris R. Malkin

Staff for *Edmonton: Gateway to the North*
Editor: Annette Igra
Assistant Editor: Sarah Tringali
Picture Editors: Julie Jaskol, Jim Mather
Corporate Biographies Editor: Judith Hunter
Editorial Assistants: Kathy Brown, Patricia Buzard,
    Ethel Karez, Lonnie Pham, Pat Pittman
Sales Manager: Bartholomew Barica
Sales Representative: Beverly Cornell
Layout Artists: Ellen Ifrah, Chris McKibbin
Production Artists: Lynn Agosti, Connie Blaisdell
Proofreader: David Simmons
Typographer: Barbara Neiman

Designer: Alexander D'Anca

FC
3696.4
.G48
1984 / 45,183

Frontispiece: *A.J. McDermid's 1933 oil painting vividly illustrates the autumn beauty of the Saskatchewan River Valley at dusk. He utilizes the well-known landmarks of the Walterdale Bridge, also known as the 5th Street Bridge, and the High Level Bridge to lead the viewer's eye to the Provincial Legislature, which dominated Edmonton's skyline for decades. Courtesy, City of Edmonton Archives (COEA), Hubert Hollingworth Collection*

To
Katherine Kirkpatrick

CONTENTS

Autumn is a very special time in Edmonton. The crisp air and cloudless sky are a perfect complement to the stunning colours found all along the riverbanks. Courtesy, Alberta Photograph Library, Public Affairs Bureau

FOREWORD

Great cities grow only when resources of many sorts abound and when people, filled with faith, stretch out their hands to couple them with works. Such has been Edmonton's luck on both accounts.

When in 1795 Duncan McGillivray built the first fur trade post at Edmonton, he declared, "This is described to be a rich and plentiful country, abounding with all kinds of animals especially Beavers and Otters which are said to be so numerous that the women and children kill them with sticks and hatchets." From that day forth, in revealing so many of its surrounding riches, Edmonton has justified his faith and attracted so many enterprising business people that by now it is the country's seventh-largest metropolitan area and has a population of some 560,000 souls.

Edmonton did not become a city until 1904 and during its early stages depended largely upon exploiting its vast area of rich soil, assisted by its valuable coal and timber resources and by the coming of the railways. Moreover, even then and ever since, it continued to be the gateway to Canada's rich northland.

By 1905 Edmonton had become the capital of the newly created Province of Alberta and soon thereafter went on to develop into a great educational centre. The city served in these capacities for three decades or so, playing its part in two world wars and becoming the crossroads of international air routes. It continued to grow gradually until in 1947 its fairy godmother proved it to be in the midst of great oil and gas fields. These new and unexpected resources carried the city's population to well over the half-million mark.

So with sundry speculative booms succeeded by several spectacular busts, Edmonton has become the great city fortunate enough to have John Gilpin as its historian. He, with his scholarly competence, conscientious care, and a few caresses, along with the help of many of the city's leading business people, has succeeded in showing how by their combined efforts the fur traders, farmers, and financiers made Edmonton the successful city it is.

J.G. MacGregor

PREFACE

Edmonton as a fort, town, and city has played a diverse role in the history of Canada. Initially it emerged as a result of the transcontinental search for furs that began in the early 18th century. The fur trade as the basis of its existence was replaced in the 19th and 20th centuries by the search for agricultural land, mineral resources, and national security.

In addition to its role on a variety of frontiers, Edmonton's history also reflects the advantages and disadvantages of being a river valley city. The North Saskatchewan River, which permitted the rapid extension of the fur trade westward from Hudson Bay, would on occasion threaten the lives and property of the people who lived in the valley.

A source of diversity in Edmonton's history has been its people. Chief Factor John Rowand, pioneer businessmen Richard Secord, John A. McDougall, and Frank Oliver, bush pilots Wop May and Leigh Brintnell, and sports promoter Deacon White are some of the individuals who have contributed to the building of a strong sense of community with distinctive social traditions.

Overriding these aspects of Edmonton's history has been its consistent role as a boundary community, a role that has had anthropological, geographical, and historical dimensions. Edmonton stands between the boreal forest and the plains, the Cree and the Blackfoot, and the Canadian Northern Railway and the Canadian Pacific Railway. Edmonton, as a result, has been a

focus for the clash of these northern and southern interests. Either by necessity during the fur trade era or by choice after 1881, Edmonton has embraced the north as its hinterland unlike any other community in Canada.

Many Klondikers travelled in groups to the goldfields. Captain Purdy, who led one such party, shown here outfitted and ready to go, bade Edmonton a final farewell in 1898. (COEA)

CHAPTER I

FUR TRADERS, MISSIONARIES, AND GOLD MINERS

1795 - 1870

Edmonton's location on the upper portion of the North Saskatchewan River is distinguished by steep river banks and a series of flood plains or flats on the valley floor. These flats have been given names, such as Walterdale, Rossdale, Cloverdale, and Riverdale, which in some cases reflect their early associations with specific individuals. The river's most significant impact on the residents of the city has resulted from its great seasonal fluctuations in flow and its seasonal progression from break-up in the spring to freeze-up in the fall. The river has brought catastrophe in the form of floods, protection against hostile natives to the south, and economic progress through its role as a vital transportation link crucial in the founding of Edmonton. Major springtime floods of the valley have taken place in 1820, 1898, and 1915. From November to December the river freezes over, permitting travel between the north and south sides over the ice bridge. The ice bridge was used until 1902 when the Low Level Bridge was completed.

The North Saskatchewan River, which has its headwaters in the Rocky Mountains, was a vital part of a river system

Paul Kane's 1850 watercolour depicts Métis, descendants of French trappers and Indian women, "running buffalo." Though the shooting of buffalo did occur, it was more productive to stampede the animals over an embankment. This type of hunting contributed to the near extinction of buffalo on the prairies. Courtesy, Provincial Archives of Alberta (PAA)

connecting Western Canada with Hudson Bay. The valley of the Saskatchewan River at Edmonton was complemented on both sides by a series of ravines that had been created by the drainage of sloughs located on the upland surface. Those destined to play a major role in Edmonton's history included Mill Creek, Rat Creek, Groat, and White Mud Creek ravines. The grass and shrub covered south-facing slope of the valley contrasts sharply with the relatively heavily forested north-facing slope.

The land to the north and south of the river is generally flat and only partially forested. This aspect of the landscape is a legacy of the occupation of this region by glaciers. The retreat of the glaciers approximately 10,000 to 11,000 years ago created glacial Lake Edmonton, which had the effect of smoothing out the area it occupied. Beaver Hills, a region of small lakes and heavy forest located in the eastern section of the Edmonton district, is another legacy of the glacial retreat. In the context of the overall geography of the Province of Alberta, the Edmonton area is part of a transitional zone between the grasslands of the south and the forests of the north.

Evidence of human occupation dates back 5,000 years when people began visiting a site in the area of what is now Strathcona Science Park on a seasonal basis for the purpose of manufacturing tools. The quartzite rocks used to make tools were plentiful at the river's edge. Other advantages of this site as a temporary camp included the availability of water and game, which could be observed from a protective lookout. The Edmonton district was rich in wildlife, most significantly buffalo, which continued to be a vital food source for inhabitants of the region well into the latter part of the 19th century. The bison bones, hearth stones, and scraping tools found at this site attest to the success of the area's first residents.

The most significant group in the Edmonton area by the end of prehistoric times was the Cree. The Cree had originally inhabited an area surrounding Hudson Bay and were thus one of the first native groups to come into contact with the Hudson's Bay Company when it established Western trading posts in the latter part of the 17th century. As a result of contact with the Europeans, the Cree shifted from food gathering to fur trapping for part of the year and also acquired firearms.

The Hudson's Bay Company was chartered on May 2, 1670, by Charles II of England. The Governor and Company of Adventurers of England Trading Into Hudson's Bay (the company's official title) was given the monopoly on trade through Hudson Strait and exclusive possession of any territory to be reached through the strait. This land grant would ultimately extend the authority of the Hudson's Bay Company to the Rocky Mountains. The principal post on Hudson Bay used by the company was York Factory, established in 1685. The areas covered by the Cree in search of furs to supply the Hudson's Bay Company expanded in the constant quest for new areas that had not yet been overtrapped. The role of the Cree as middlemen in the fur trade was further enhanced by the failure of the Hudson's Bay Company's efforts to attract native people from further inland

Right: *This painting by Edmonton artist Ella May Walker depicts Father Lacombe arriving from St. Albert to celebrate Christmas at Fort Edmonton in 1858. (COEA, Richard Y. Secord Collection)*

Below: *Ella May Walker painted this watercolour scene of Fort Edmonton as it was in 1860. (COEA Hubert Hollingworth Collection)*

Left: Fort Edmonton re-creates the days of 1846, when the fort was home to the fur traders of the Hudson's Bay Company. Courtesy, Travel Alberta

Below: Visitors enjoy pioneer-era sights, sounds, flavors, and activities on 1885 Street at Fort Edmonton Park. The historical park features a farmer's market and authentic crafts. Courtesy, George Hunter, Masterfile

to come to the bay to trade. The fur trade would have to expand further inland if the increasing demand for furs was to be met. By 1740 the westward migration of the Cree that would bring them to the Edmonton area had begun.

The western penetration of the Cree was rapid since their weapons were superior to those used by the tribes located further west. In their westward march the Cree moved up the Saskatchewan, sending the indigenous tribes retreating to the north and south. The Beaver Indians moved northwest to the Peace River Country, while the Blackfoot tribes were pushed south from the North Saskatchewan River. The westward migration of the Cree laid the basis for generations of intertribal warfare between the Cree and the Blackfoot, which would remain an aspect of Edmonton's history until the 1870s. A further result of the westward movement of the Cree was their division into two groups: the Plains Cree, who occupied the region south and west of Edmonton, and the Woodland Cree, who were located further north. By the 19th century the Plains Cree were further divided into eight loosely organized bands. The group associated with the Edmonton district were referred to as the Upstream or Beaver Hills people. This band ranged along the North Saskatchewan River in the neighbourhood of Edmonton and south to the Battle River.

The westward migration of the Cree was duplicated by that of the Hudson's Bay Company, which began the construction of a series of trading posts along the Saskatchewan River in 1774 when it established Cumberland House near the Saskatchewan-Manitoba border. The construction of these inland posts by the Hudson's Bay Company was necessitated by the invasion of this region by independent traders from Montreal following the capture of Quebec in 1759. These "pedlars" were organized into a number of companies, the most important of which was the North West Company. A period of intense and often violent competition ensued between the two companies, which would only end with their amalgamation in 1821. This intense competition accelerated the rate at which fur-bearing animals were systematically hunted to extinction around each post. New posts were thus constantly being built upstream in an effort to tap new sources of supply. In order to observe the activities of their rivals as well as to offer some degree of protection, the Hudson's Bay Company and North West Company posts were generally located close together.

By the mid-1790s this constant search for new furs had brought the Edmonton district to the attention of Angus Shaw, chief factor at Buckingham House. He had received reports that beaver and otter existed in such numbers that women and children were killing them with sticks and hatchets. This first recorded evaluation of the resources of the Edmonton district led the North West Company to construct Fort Augustus in 1795 at a site some 20 miles downstream from the present city of Edmonton. William Tomison of the Hudson's Bay Company built Edmonton House "within a musket shot" of the North West Company post in the same year. By 1799 this region was depleted of its furs with the result that plans were made to remove the two forts to the present site of Edmonton. The relocation of Fort Augustus and Fort Edmonton to Ross Flats was completed in 1802. The Rossdale site was occupied on a continuous basis until 1830, with the exception of the three years between 1810 and 1813. Despite the violence perpetrated by the North West Company and the Hudson's Bay Company at other locations in the West, the two companies at Edmonton achieved some degree of cooperation. They used a common palisade to separate the two forts and agreed to rules governing trade in order to prevent the Indians from playing one company off against the other.

The union of the two companies in 1821 would ultimately bring an era of stability and progress to the fur trade in the Edmonton area. This turn of events reflected the intervention of Sir George Simpson and John Rowand. Sir George Simpson was appointed governor of the Northern Department of the reorganized Hudson's Bay Company in 1821. His initial responsibility was to integrate the operations of the two companies into one effective organization. One suggestion to achieve the absorption of the excess of manpower created by the union was provided by James Bird to Nicholas Gary in 1821. It involved an expedition to the Bow River to open up trade with the Upper Missouri. The first Bow River expedition was supported by the Northern Department Council meeting held on June 24, 1822. Chief Factor Donald McKenzie and Chief Trader John Rowand were placed in charge of "twelve young gentlemen" and 80 servants. If the expedition proved successful, Simpson planned to abandon the north branch of the Saskatchewan in 1823. In anticipation of the success of the expedition, John Rowand was appointed chief trader for the south branch of the Saskatchewan. On March 1, 1823, however, the leaders of the expedition, Donald McKenzie, John Rowand, Francis Heron, and J.E. Harriott, reported that it had been a failure and urged that the establishments on the North Saskatchewan River be maintained. This gave Fort Edmonton a degree of importance that it had lacked during the earlier years.

Sir George Simpson chose John Rowand to rehabilitate the fur trade in the Edmonton area. Rowand, the son of a surgeon at the Montreal General Hospital, had entered the service of the North West Company in 1803 as an apprentice at the age of 13. In 1823 he was appointed a chief trader in the district, and in 1826 he assumed the position of chief factor of the entire Saskatchewan district. John Rowand would remain the dominant figure in the fur trade in the Edmonton area until his death in 1854.

Soon after Rowand's appointment, the fortunes of Edmonton were given a further boost with the opening of the Fort Assiniboine Trail in the summer of 1824. This led to the emergence of Edmonton as the most important company outpost west of the Red River. Its role expanded from a trading post to a district administrative centre and a station along a vital communications link with the company's other operations on the West Coast. Its new-found permanence was reflected in the final relocation of the fort in 1830 to a bench above Ross Flats. It was hoped that the higher elevation would

JOHN ROWAND: FRONTIER TRADER

John Rowand first arrived in Edmonton in 1803 as a 14-year-old apprentice in the North West Company. Rowand came from Montreal, where his father, an Edinburgh-educated Irish physician, was a surgeon at the Montreal General Hospital. Rowand was stationed at several posts — Fort Augustus, Fort White Earth, Pembina Portage, Rocky Mountain House, and the fort at Bas de la Rivière — during his 18 years of service with the company. While at Bas de la Rivière, he played a marginal role in the battle between the Hudson's Bay Company and the North West Company at Seven Oaks in 1816. This event would ultimately force the union of the two companies in 1821. By 1821 Rowand had become Chief Trader at the company's Rocky Mountain House post. He earned the title "Big Mountain" for his years of trading with the Plains Indians. During these early years on the North Saskatchewan with the North West Company, he married Louise Umfrieville, a native girl who had nursed him back to health after he had fallen from his horse during a hunting trip.

Rowand's conduct during the Bow River Expedition and his pioneering of the Fort Assiniboine-Fort Edmonton Trail led to his advancement in the new company. In 1826 he was appointed Chief Factor of the Saskatchewan district. As Chief Factor, Rowand had to deal with a number of problems at Fort Edmonton. This was primarily due to the fort's role as a centre for administration, transportation, and commerce.

Commercially, for example, Rowand had to deal with the friction between the various tribes that traded

at the post. In a letter to Governor George Simpson, dated January 1, 1840, he described one specific incident and the solution he adopted in this situation.

During our absence last summer a good many of the Slave tribes made their appearance with a little to trade. Had it not been for a rascally Cree Indian, who killed a Peigan Chief at some distance from here, a great many more was to have come on a trade, but were prevented by the unexpected [act] of

From 1826 until his death in 1854, John Rowand was Chief Factor at Fort Edmonton. He is remembered as being a shrewd fur trader, and as the person responsible for the construction of the Big House, or "Rowand's Folly." (COEA, from a painting by D.G. King)

that Indian at a time when they thought all was peace as it was told to them.

On my arrival here from the Red River I had the satisfaction to find everything connected with this place in capital order and what pleased me not a little was to find the rascally Indian who had killed the Peigan Chief well secured in irons, hand and feet. I felt a little at a loss what to do with the rascal and had half a mind to deliver him up to some of the relations of the poor man he had killed to meet the fate he so well deserved. But no, a friend of the deceased was only allowed to shave his head which was accomplished with a large knife quite à la mode. All this took place in the presence of Crees to serve as an example to others not to commit

murder as the rascal did. This kind of punishment was the only means to placate the Peigans, who would have it that the murderer is to be taken down to Canada to be hung.

The same letter also documents the increasing competition from American fur companies for trade with the Plains tribes and Rowand's need to cater to the Indians.

The Peigans who are the worst of all the Slave tribes to please expect a great many things for nothing. They are all Chiefs who must be dressed as such, gratis of course. If not, off they go back to the Americans where they say they are sure of being well received for their few furs, Buffalo Robes, Wolves and their Horses.

The horse trade with the Peigans was of particular significance since it enabled the post "to keep up the number of Horses so much required for the Company's work and for sales to our men and Indians etc." The post needed to replenish its horse supply because of frequent losses to sickness, theft by Stony Indians, and wolves.

Rowand died in the fall of 1854. He was first buried at Fort Pitt, but Governor Simpson, hearing of his wish to be buried in Montreal, had the body disinterred and, according to tradition, rendered down to the bones. A package containing Rowand's bones was delivered to Norway House in the summer of 1856. It was repackaged and sent to Montreal via York Factory and then to London, England.

prevent flooding such as had occurred in 1820. From the mid-1820s to the mid-1850s, Fort Edmonton settled into a routine that revolved around its role as a provisioning post, transcontinental route, and collection and distribution point for subsidiary posts in the Saskatchewan district, including Rocky Mountain House, Lesser Slave Lake, Fort Assiniboine, and Jasper House.

The community of Edmonton was totally encompassed by the walls of the fort. The 20-foot-high palisade described a five-sided figure into which five bastions were incorporated. These bastions housed brass cannons, which were used for ceremonial purposes and which threatened the life of any company servant who fired them. A walkway ran the full length of the palisade. The Big House of John Rowand dominated the interior of the fort. This three-story log structure served as his residence and as the administrative centre for the operation of the fort. The central courtyard directly in front of the Big House was flanked by the married men's quarters, an icehouse used primarily to store buffalo meat, and the Indian House, where the actual trading took place. Entry to the Indian House was controlled by a series of gates and partitions that allowed the natives restricted access to the fort for trading purposes. The remaining portion of the fort was occupied by the blacksmith shop, boat-building yard, and stables.

Despite its designation, the fort was not a military installation. It was designed to protect its inhabitants from the violence that could arise from the use of the fort as a place of trade by both the Cree and their rival, the Blackfoot. The defensive works incorporated into the fort also reflected the fact that it was beyond the protective reach of any other fur trade post or military installation. The kinship ties that developed between the fur traders and the native population of the region provided additional protection. These ties reflected the economic cooperation between native and fur trader that characterized life in Edmonton in the first half of the 19th century.

The trading season at the fort was inaugurated with the arrival in late September or early October of a brigade consisting of some 10 York boats manned by 50 men from York Factory. The goods they brought to trade included such items as guns, powder shot, and metal cooking utensils. Since this was the conclusion of a 1,000-mile trip from York Factory on Hudson Bay and a six-month absence from the fort, the men were anxious to celebrate. Each member of the boat's crew was issued a ration of rum to enhance the celebration — a quart for the steersman, a pint for the men at the bow, and a half-pint to the middle men. A dance followed at the Big House featuring eight- and four-hand reels and single and double jigs. All the residents of the fort took part. The diverse group included French Canadian Voyageurs, Orkney Islanders from Northern Scotland, English Canadians from Montreal, and the Indian wives of the various company servants. Conversations took place in French, Gaelic, Cree, and English.

Any bachelors who arrived with the fall brigade had to obtain the approval of the chief factor for any "marriages"

they wished to establish for the winter with the native women. Such a step was necessary if the bride and later the family were to receive provisions from the fort. These marriages *en façon du nord* were frequently permanent with the result that the fur trader would retire to Red River with his family when his service with the company was over. Conspicuously absent from the society of the fort were European or Canadian women. This situation changed for only a short time in 1808 when Marie-Anne Logimodière accompanied her husband west to Fort Edmonton, where she remained for four years.

When the festivities associated with the brigade's return concluded, the company servants began to organize the goods and transportation to supply the various subsidiary posts with

winter trade goods. The first expedition to leave headed for Jasper House and the Columbian and New Caledonia districts on the Pacific Coast. Although many trade goods for the company's posts on the Pacific Coast came in by the Pacific Ocean and around Cape Horn, and although furs were shipped out the same way, such items as dressed skins, leather thongs, and lacing for snowshoes passed overland to the Pacific via Edmonton. In 1854 twenty-eight horses were required to carry these goods and provisions. During the winter months horses were supplemented by dogs that were controlled by tying pieces of wood to each dog. In 1848 Paul Kane, a painter who travelled the Canadian West, estimated this dog population at 500. The westbound trip of the Columbia Express, the

Hudson's Bay Company's mail canoe between the Pacific and Hudson Bay, supplemented the fall expeditions. The Columbia Express came through the Athabasca Pass and Edmonton in October westbound and in April or May eastbound. It carried yearly instructions, annual reports, officers changing their posts, and new recruits. The next group to leave after the Columbia Express was destined for the post on Lesser Slave Lake. It covered part of the trail on horseback and the remaining portion via the Athabasca and Lesser Slave Lake rivers. The last of the Northern group was the outfit for Fort Assiniboine. The final supply expedition to leave departed by boat for Rocky Mountain House.

With the dispatch of the above brigades, the Woodland Cree and Plains Cree would arrive to trade. The chiefs were received with great ceremony. The chief factor shook hands with them within the main gates, and the flag was raised and a salute fired. In the Indian House the interpreter lit the pipe of peace and passed it around. After a series of speeches, all retired till the next morning when trading began. The bands were given credit in the form of ammunition and other necessities for the hunt and then moved north for furs or south to kill buffalo. The Blackfoot from the south preferred to trade during the summer. They would send a scout on ahead to announce the arrival of the main group. Trading was accomplished as quickly as possible in order to reduce the chance of violence between the Blackfoot and the Cree.

The fall months at the fort were also occupied by the harvesting of the wheat, barley, turnips, and potatoes that were grown in two fields located outside the stockade. The wheat was subsequently milled into flour. By 1847 a windmill, the first west of the Red River Settlement, had been erected at Fort Edmonton to supplement the use of steel hand mills. The windmill could grind both wheat and barley, and under favourable conditions it could handle 15 or 16 bushels of grain per day.

Enormous quantities of fresh meat and fish were required to feed the approximately 150 officers, servants, and their

Dressed in period costumes, the participants at an authentic Paul Kane dinner in 1970 enjoyed the same types of food and drink that Paul Kane and Hudson's Bay Company staff enjoyed in 1845. (COEA)

families who lived at the fort. The killing of buffalo, moose, or deer was the responsibility of the fort hunters and other company employees stationed at Lac Sainte Anne and the Beaver Hills. In addition to the fresh meat required to sustain the fort's inhabitants, there was also the dried meat, the pounded meat, and the grease to be procured for use in the preparation of pemmican. Other resources to be gathered from the area for use in the fort included cordwood for the fires and logs for use in the production of York boats. The blacksmith would also collect lumps of coal for use in his forge.

The winter routine was interrupted by the celebration of Christmas. Paul Kane left a detailed account of the Christmas celebration of 1847. Highlights included a dinner of boiled buffalo hump, boiled buffalo calf, dried moose nose, whitefish browned in buffalo marrow, buffalo tongue, beaver tails, roast wild goose, potatoes, turnips, and bread. All the members of the fort participated in the dance that followed:

Indians whose chief ornament consisted in the paint on their faces, voyageurs with bright sashes and neatly ornamented mocassins, half-breeds glittering in every ornament they could lay their hands on; whether civilized or savage, all were laughing and jabbering in as many different languages as there were styles of dress.

The dancing to a Highland reel tune provided by a fiddler continued through to midnight. The week-long Christmas celebration a decade later expanded to include a meeting of the staff from the various posts. The week ended with New Year's Day sports, which included footraces, toboggan slides on the North Saskatchewan River hill, some competitions for women, and the big dog-train race of three miles on the river.

Each year in the spring preparations were made for the departure of the brigade for York Fort, as residents of the Edmonton district began the season's ploughing and seeding. About the middle of May the brigade was dispatched downriver with most of the men of the fort. A small staff consisting of 12 men, including an interpreter and a clerk, remained behind.

The routine of the fort was also interrupted by the threat of an Indian attack by the Blackfoot. In response to one incident described by Harrison Young in 1870, the staff of the fort created a barricade to repulse a Blackfoot war party that had come to get Takoots, a Cree half-breed, and Big Crow, a Stony who had murdered a Blackfoot and a Sarcee across the river at the forks at the Pigeon Lake Trail. The staff also loaded the two brass cannons. The river, however, prevented the war party from getting close to the fort. One of the brass cannons blew up when it was test-fired after the excitement had

died down.

An integral part of daily life at Fort Edmonton after 1840 was the missionary. The first one to arrive was 29-year-old Robert Rundle, who volunteered to come to Edmonton as part of the agreement between the Hudson's Bay Company and the Methodist Church. This agreement was designed to provide ministers for the Indians and the Hudson's Bay Company staff. Accommodation was provided in a small chapel and residence within the fort. While at Fort Edmonton for the next eight years, Rundle made frequent trips to various outlying posts, such as Rocky Mountain House and Lesser Slave Lake, as well as to the Blackfoot to the south. Rundle was bothered by the laxity of Sabbath observance at the fort. While Sunday was not a workday, it could be interrupted for trading purposes or for horse racing, which was a favorite sport. In addition, most of the staff were Catholics, not Methodists. Also appalled by the violence in the native community, Rundle finally left in 1848. He was succeeded by Thomas Woolsey, who remained from 1855 to 1864.

One of the concerns of the Methodist ministers was the activities of the Catholic priests. Rundle's concern about "popery" was made manifest in 1842 with the arrival of Father Thibault who had come at the request of the Métis. Another Catholic missionary, Father Albert Lacombe, came to Edmonton from Red River on September 19, 1852. A chapel was constructed inside the fort in 1857 and named Saint Joachim's in 1866.

By the late 1850s there was a shift away from the York boat and toward the use of Red River carts. The importance of the North Saskatchewan River and Athabasca Pass as a transcontinental communication system also declined in the mid-1850s as more efficient links to the Pacific Coast were established through the United States. The last recorded use of the Fort Assiniboine Trail was in 1860.

The number of visitors to the fort began to increase, and Edmonton's isolation and the life-style associated with it were coming to an end. The most significant of these visitors were

ROBERT TERRILL RUNDLE: MISSIONARY TRAILBLAZER

Methodist missionary Robert Terrill Rundle arrived in Edmonton during the early hours of October 18, 1840, after a 216-day trip from Liverpool, England. Rundle was sent to Fort Edmonton when the Hudson's Bay Company and the Wesleyan Missionary Society agreed to provide missionaries for three of its Western posts. John Rowand, despite his view that missionaries disrupted the fort's operations, welcomed Rundle and provided him with lodgings and a horse. The lodgings consisted of a cabin that served as both a residence and a chapel.

During his first three months at Fort Edmonton, Rundle served as chaplain to fort personnel and made his initial contacts with natives in the immediate vicinity. His role as chaplain was not an easy one, however. The majority of the fort's personnel were Roman Catholics. He conducted his first English service on October 18 and his first Cree service, through an interpreter, on October 25. Early in November he baptized the infant daughter of John Edward Harriott and six children belonging to the fort. On November 29, 1840, his journal recorded the initial response of the Cree Indians to his ministry: "Several Indians at the Cree Service in evening. One a blind old man came to the Fort expecting to have his sight restored. I believe he was much disappointed on finding that I had only to do with the blindness of the mind."

Rundle began his first extended trip beyond the walls of Fort Edmonton on February 16, 1841, when he left by dog carriole for Rocky Mountain House. While there, he had an opportunity to meet the Blackfoot, Bloods, and Peigans who traded, at this point, from February 22 to 27.

The natives' response to the arrival of Rundle was affected by a tradition among the Stonies that a woman had a vision, predicting the arrival of a white missionary at Rocky Mountain House. Rundle recorded in his journal shortly after arriving at Rocky Mountain House that, "Indians say I came down from heaven in a bit of paper which was opened by one of the Co.'s gentlemen at the Fort & lo!! I came out." From Rocky Mountain House, he travelled as far south as the Bow River before returning to Fort Edmonton in May 1841. Over the next 12 months, he continued to travel to

Robert T. Rundle, the first missionary to reach and settle in the Edmonton district, arrived in 1840 and stayed until 1848. Upon his return to England he married and continued to preach, though he never returned to Canada. (COEA)

various locations in the area, including Lesser Slave Lake and Fort Assiniboine.

When Rundle returned once again to Edmonton on June 22, 1842, he found, to his horror, Father Jean-Baptiste Thibault. Thibault arrived at

Fort Edmonton after a Métis from the area made a personal visit to Bishop Provencher at Saint-Boniface, Manitoba, to request the services of a priest. This Métis, named Piche, had also served as a guide to Rundle during his first trip to the Bow River area in 1841. Henceforth Rundle regarded Fort Edmonton as a "hotbed of popery." Rundle's journal entry for June 22 indicated this concern: "The priest appears to be sweeping everything before him. I preached in the morning, all the English present. Evening Cree Service, only a few present." On July 19, 1842, he expressed hope for divine intervention to save his "poor Indians from the snares of popery." Rundle's abhorrence of Catholics, however, was to mellow in 1845 when he spent some time with Father Du Smet. His journal entry for October 4, 1845, records his changing attitudes:

To my surprise Mr. Du Smet arrived at the Fort. . . . I found him very agreeable and we parted with each other when we left on very friendly terms. He did not interfere with my Indians at all, though he had an opportunity of doing so. I met him again at Edmonton later, where we passed part of the winter together, and before we separated he gave me a letter of introduction to his brother in Belgium. Perhaps a Roman Catholic Priest and a Wesleyan Missionary never before met and parted on such good terms.

In addition to Rundle's concerns about the activities of Roman Catholic priests in and around Fort Edmonton, he also objected to the Hudson's Bay Company's failure to observe the Sabbath. The company continued to trade with the Indians, race horses, and travel on Sunday. These activities displeased the missionary. In a letter to James Evans, superintendent of missions in Western Canada, dated January 6, 1844, he described an incident of avoiding Sunday travel:

I had difficulty in doing this when I went to Lesser Slave Lake in the fall of 1842. We were then in Slave River. The men said that Mr. Rowand had directed them to leave me behind if I stopped on the road. I was not, however, to be frightened with popguns. I know the road (and above all I felt confidence in my heavenly father) and I said I should say nothing to them about stopping but that if they intended to proceed on the Sabbath that I should leave them the Saturday and try to travel as far up the river in one day as they would go in two. I intended starting with my blanket on my back in company with one or two others in the boat (not in the employ of the Company). We all stopped, however, and I believe not a moment was lost by it.

After eight years of enduring the hardships of constant travel, intense loneliness, and a society that did not always respond to his evangelism, Rundle returned to England.

the members of the Palliser expedition. In 1857 Great Britain launched this expedition to evaluate the resources of the Hudson's Bay Company's land. While it would be 20 years before the first homesteader would arrive to fully develop the agricultural potential of the area, the expedition did discover another source of wealth—gold. This discovery coincided with the gold rushes in the United States and British Columbia. The first gold miner, C.A. Love of Wisconsin, arrived in March 1858. In the summer of 1860 Tom Clover, a native of Missouri, arrived. Correspondence between Clover and Love concerning the gold deposits on the Saskatchewan ultimately led to an article in the Toronto *Globe* on the mineral resources of the region. Encouraging reports also appeared in

the *Nor-Wester,* a Winnipeg paper, in the spring of 1862. The discussion of gold in both the West and British Columbia led to the organization that spring of two overland expeditions from Fort Garry (Winnipeg) to the Cariboo in British Columbia. The overlanders of 1862 consisted of about 175 men who set forth in two main parties from Fort Garry in early June. Despite statements by Woolsey that no gold was available, 75 people stayed over, encouraged no doubt by contrary reports that gold existed in large quantities.

The Palliser expedition and the gold miners who arrived in the 1860s brought an end to the fur trade as it had been conducted by the Hudson's Bay Company. The official end of this period in Edmonton's history took place with the transfer of the Northwest Territories to the newly created Dominion of Canada in 1870. The transfer agreement granted the Hudson's Bay Company a 3,000-acre land reserve around some of its Western posts. All other land was available for settlement.

In 1890 "Washee Joe," a well-known Edmonton Indian woman, continued to use the famous Red River cart, long after its use was discontinued by the white population. The Red River cart was an all-purpose vehicle made almost entirely from wood. (PAA, E. Brown Collection)

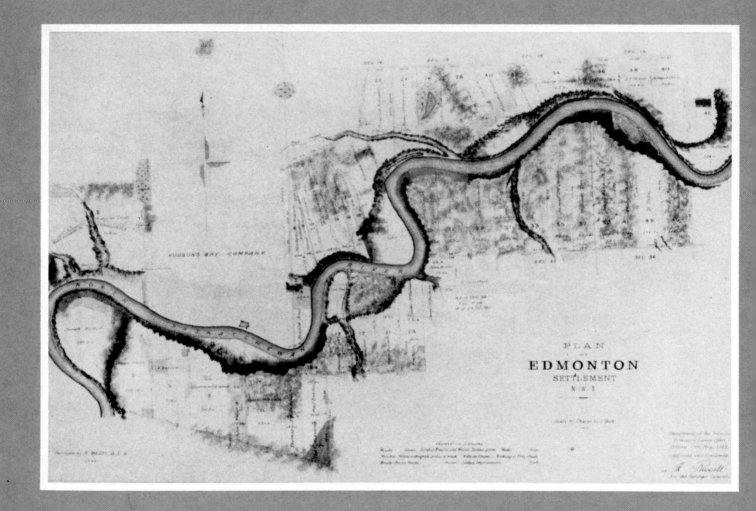

C H A P T E R I I

THE VILLAGE BEYOND THE FORT

1871 - 1890

Facing page: *Until the Dominion Land Survey team reached Edmonton in 1882 the first settlers had only squatters' rights to their land. Once the survey was approved and confirmed in 1883, all those listed on this, the first map of Edmonton Settlement, were assured of ownership of their river lots. (COEA, Hubert Hollingworth Collection)*

The development of a community beyond the protective walls of Fort Edmonton was initiated by the Reverend George McDougall, one of the first individuals to take advantage of the availability of land in the Edmonton area after 1870. In June 1871 McDougall arrived from Fort Victoria, about 50 miles east on the North Saskatchewan River, to take charge of the Methodist mission in Edmonton. Upon his arrival, he claimed land on behalf of the Methodist Church to the east of the anticipated location of the Hudson's Bay Company Reserve while his son, David, claimed the adjacent plot of land. By 1873 a church and manse had been constructed on these properties at a combined cost of $3,000. These were the first buildings constructed adjacent to the fort that were more than simply ancillary to its function as a fur trade post.

The fact that the McDougalls were starting a new chapter in Edmonton's history was emphasized by the location of the mission buildings approximately one mile east of the fort. It had not been McDougall's intention to create the nucleus for the development of a future city but rather to provide the church with land in the absence of any official townsite. Fort

Edmonton continued to be considered by the local citizens as the future location of the city of Edmonton up to 1882.

Other land claims were made at this time by former employees of the Hudson's Bay Company such as Malcolm Groat, John Walter, Joseph McDonald, John Norris, H. Hardisty, R. Hardisty, E. McGillivary, Donald McLeod, James Rowland, William Rowland, and Kenneth Macdonald. As in the case of the church property, the majority of these land claims took the form of river lots located on both sides of the river. The only land claim to receive the benefit of a legal survey in the 1870s was the Hudson's Bay Company Reserve. This survey was carried out by W.S. Gore of the Dominion Land Survey in 1873. The Hudson's Bay Company, however, did not proceed with the creation of a townsite.

The Methodist Church was not the only religious organization to depart from the security of the fort. In 1876, at the request of Chief Factor Christie, St. Joachim's Church was dismantled and relocated to a site provided by Malcolm Groat on the eastern boundary of the reserve. On January 14, 1877, the new building was blessed by Father Henry Grandin. The successful relocation of St. Joachim's ensured that the Catholic Church would continue to act as a vital focal point for the French-speaking community's religious and social activities. Rapid growth in attendance necessitated the appointment of a resident curé in 1883.

A number of the individuals who were claiming land in the 1870s would retain ownership well into the next century and thus would play a significant role in the social, political, and economic development of Edmonton as a town and city. John Walter, a native of the Orkney Islands, claimed land on the south side of the river across from the fort. After working for the Hudson's Bay Company as a boat builder, Walter directed his efforts toward the establishment of Edmonton's first ferry, which began operating in April 1882. John Norris, whose homestead was located on the western boundary of the HBC Reserve, left the employ of the Hudson's Bay Company in 1864 to go into business as an independent freighter. In this

Facing page, top: John Walter, for whom Walterdale district is named, made his mark in Edmonton as a boat builder, first for the Hudson's Bay Company and later as an independent. He holds the distinction of being Edmonton's first ferry operator as well as being a successful pioneer lumber merchant. (COEA)

Facing page, bottom: Donald Ross was the founder of Edmonton's first hotel in 1876. During the next two decades he added to and improved the original structure. By 1907 business was so good that he constructed the Edmonton Hotel Annex, shown here in 1908, to accommodate his many customers. (COEA)

capacity he delivered the first pool table for Donald Ross'
hotel in the Edmonton settlement and the first bell to Father
Lacombe's mission at St. Albert. In 1882 he went into partnership with Edward Carey, forming the well-known general
merchandising firm of Norris & Carey, which operated
until 1894.

A number of the early land claims were relinquished by the
original holders in whole or in part to new arrivals such as
Donald Ross, who acquired River Lot Four from Hudson's
Bay Company employee William Leslie Wood. Prior to his
arrival in Edmonton in 1874, Ross had spent nine years
prospecting for gold in California. After acquiring his land
claim, he constructed the Edmonton Hotel & Feed Stables:
"The pioneer house of accommodation this side of Portage la
Prairie," where a "good game of Billiards or Pool can be

played and a very social evening can be spent in the Billiard Room." In 1883 he began the development of the coal reserves on his land claim. In the summer of 1889 he added an air shaft to his operation, thus creating the first true mine in the Edmonton district.

Frank Oliver, another new arrival, was born near Brampton, Ontario, in 1853. He left home at an early age to work for the Toronto *Globe* and in 1873 moved to Winnipeg where he worked for the *Winnipeg Free Press* until 1876. In the spring of that year he invested his savings in a small freighting outfit and joined an ox-cart brigade bound west for Fort Edmonton. In the summer of 1878 Oliver bought the first town lot to be sold in Edmonton. He purchased it from Colin Fraser, the original owner of River Lot Ten, for $25. On this property he built a log store, the first commercial operation in the settlement outside the fort.

In partnership with Alex Taylor, Oliver started Edmonton's first newspaper in 1880. The creation of the Edmonton *Bulletin* was made possible by the arrival of the Dominion Telegraph in 1879. The "telegraphic news" relating to Western

Canada and the world was supplemented by local news and editorials. Frank Oliver and the *Bulletin* emerged as Edmonton's most ambitious boosters. The future growth of the city as seen by the *Bulletin* was related primarily to northern development. In Oliver's view it was "on the certainty of possessing the trade of this immense region that the more brilliant prospects of Edmonton are principally founded."

Matthew McCauley and John A. McDougall, also native sons of Ontario, followed Frank Oliver to Edmonton. Matthew McCauley, a native of Owen Sound, arrived in the Edmonton area in 1879 and took up farming near Fort Saskatchewan until he sold the farm in 1882. He then relocated to Edmonton, where he established the community's first livery stable (which would eventually develop into the Edmonton Cartage Company) and in 1883 opened the first butcher shop.

John A. McDougall arrived in Edmonton in the spring of 1879 after having spent the previous three years as an independent trader at various points in the Canadian West, including Fort Carlton, Prince Albert, and Fort Victoria. His first store in Edmonton was a big log structure close to the Methodist mission and Frank Oliver's establishment. McDougall built a new store in the summer of 1880, which he occupied until the summer of 1882, when he sold out and returned to Ontario. But later that year McDougall returned from Ontario and built a third store on the northwest corner of Jasper Avenue and 98th Street. The Hudson's Bay Company purchased this building in 1889 for use as its first retail store outside the fort. Up to this date, the company had tried to ignore the activities of the independent businessmen.

The commercial endeavors of Edmonton's early merchants such as Oliver, McDougall, Norris & Carey, Brown & Carey, and W. Johnstone Walker were complemented by the arrival of two of Edmonton's pioneer industrialists: William Humberstone and D.R. Fraser. Born on the Niagara peninsula of Ontario, William Humberstone came to Edmonton from Winnipeg in 1880. Shortly thereafter he started a brickyard and opened a coal mine, and later he acquired an interest in

Without the benefit of safety hats and boots, or even proper coveralls, these two novice workers, circa 1885, discovered how back-breaking, dirty, and tiring coal mining could be. The shaft was supported by poplar trees which by today's standards make this operation look very precarious. (PAA, E. Brown Collection)

the sawmill business with John Walter. His main business interests were in coal mining, which he relocated to the east end of town after the turn of the century as a result of Edmonton's growth. D.R. Fraser, a native of Edinburgh, Scotland, worked for the Hudson's Bay Company on the steamboat *Lilly* and oversaw the operation of flour and sawmills from 1874 to 1881. In 1881 he settled at Edmonton where he purchased the flour and sawmills of Norris, McLeod, and Belcher, and he operated them with Richard Hardisty until 1889.

Ontario was not the only source of entrepreneurial talent in the community. In 1880 Xavier Saint-Jean, a native of Quebec, reached Edmonton, where he established himself as a cabinetmaker with a furniture factory in the rear of Heiminck's store on Main Street. Stanislas LaRue, who was

Teamsters using sleds, which could be converted to wagons in the summer, lined up in 1900 at the coal chute outside William Humberstone's coal mine. Until natural gas started to become popular in the 1950s, coal was the main heating fuel in Edmonton. (PAA, E. Brown Collection)

born at Sainte-Martine, Quebec, in 1860, came to Edmonton in 1883 after a short stay in Winnipeg. Upon arriving in Edmonton he worked as a surveyor for two years and as a store clerk from 1885 to 1889. In 1889 he opened the general merchandise business of LaRue & Picard in partnership with Joseph-Henri Picard. Picard, originally from Saint-Jean-de-Matha, Quebec, came to Edmonton in July 1887 and was engaged in construction for two years prior to entering into partnership with LaRue.

The development of commercial agriculture, an important part of Edmonton's economic diversification, resulted from the demand for flour for the Indian Agency and oats for the North West Mounted Police. Local farmers such as William Cust took advantage of this demand, and facilities such as the Fraser & Company mill provided employment in the grinding

Farmers, traders, and men who were just passing through stopped at LaRue & Picard's store, shown here in 1890, to purchase the basic necessities for life in the West: staple foods, ammunition, and warm clothing. (PAA, E. Brown Collection)

of the farmers' grain into flour. Local merchants also prospered as brokers between the farmers and the Indian Agency. Evidence of the importance of agriculture in the local economy was the 1879 exhibition of the Edmonton Agricultural Society, which by 1890 had become an annual fall event.

The creation of an independent business community in Edmonton and its concerns about the economic development of the area were institutionalized with the creation of the Edmonton Board of Trade in 1889. The organization of the Board of Trade began in April of that year and was strongly supported by the Edmonton *Bulletin,* which argued that:

Besides looking after the commercial interests of the place there are other matters of importance which the organization of the board would furnish a means of dealing with such as the direction of immigration to this locality, and the spread of information regarding our mineral resources so that capital might be attracted as well.

The *Bulletin* went on to suggest that the board could assume certain responsibilities of municipal government, such as "opening new streets and improving old ones, causing the abatement of nuisance and providing assistance in cases of fire." The charter members were S.S. Taylor, P. Daly, Frank Oliver, E. Raymer, J.A. McDougall, W. Johnstone Walker, Alex Taylor, James McDonald, John Cameron, E. Carey, Colin F. Strang, J.H. Picard, and A.D. Osborne.

Edmonton businessmen and area farmers also directed their efforts toward the creation of Edmonton's first school. Although Dr. Verey and Mrs. James McDonald had operated private schools in Edmonton at various times between 1870 and 1881, generally those residents of Edmonton who wished to provide their children with a formal education were obliged to send them to Eastern Canada or to such institutions as Emmanuel College in Prince Albert. In October 1881 the first public meeting to discuss the issue was held. Edmonton residents elected William Rowland, Matthew McCauley, and Malcolm Groat as school trustees and gave them the responsibility of finding a site for the school and preparing the necessary plans and specifications for a building. At the same time a committee of nine residents agreed to contribute $50 each to guarantee the salary of a teacher. The newly elected trustees immediately advertised for tenders for the construction of a frame building to be located on the eastern edge of the Hudson's Bay Company Reserve. Lots had been donated by the Hudson's Bay Company on the condition that the cost of erecting a building would be assumed by the residents of the settlement. The original specifications called for a 12-foot-tall frame building measuring 24 by 30 feet.

The Edmonton *Bulletin* commented favourably on these developments:

Believing that a public school is a public benefit, the promoters of the scheme are organizing it on a free basis to be supported by the public at large, and no greater inducement can be offered to desirable intending settlers than the advantages of a free school. Besides being used as a school house, the building, if of a sufficient size, will answer as a hall to hold public meetings in until the place grows sufficiently to afford a town hall.

Construction of the school began immediately, and by mid-December the keys had been turned over to the trustees. James Harris was hired as the first teacher, and classes officially commenced on January 3, 1882.

With the formal inauguration of a school system, the community was faced with the ongoing problem of providing operational funds. The initial approach was to avoid the imposition of a tax and to continue to rely on voluntary subscription by the local citizens. At first this approach achieved some success. The Edmonton *Bulletin* reported that:

The collection of subscriptions towards the school building fund is making good progress. There is still a balance due on the school exclusive of the mortgage of $26.00, and an unpaid balance on the list yet of $29.00, all of which it is confidently expected will be paid. Besides what is due on the building there is $15.00 to pay for the stove pipes and the putting of them up, besides $10.00 rent for the use of the stove during the winter. The wood is to be supplied voluntarily by parties sending their children to school, and others who are generously inclined.

In order to supplement the funds obtained through public subscription, an "entertainment" was organized in January 1882. The *Bulletin* noted, "should more money be realized than is necessary to clean off the debt at present due on the school it will be used to purchase maps and other school fixtures."

The optimism expressed in January 1882 concerning the school's financial position, however, quickly faded. The board's financial crisis was a product of a decline in public contributions and the lack of substantial financial support from the Territorial Government. At a public meeting held on December 23, 1882, Matt McCauley reported that the board of trustees owed a total of $708. This total included $400 still owed for the construction of the building, $250 for the

teacher's salary, and $10 for the rental of a stove from the Hudson's Bay Company. The solution adopted by the meeting at McCauley's suggestion was the formation of a school district and the appointment of a person to assess the property within the section to the amount of $400 a year, the amount necessary to run the school.

The problems encountered by Edmonton citizens in creating a stable school system clearly demonstrated the need for some kind of initiative by the Territorial Government in the field of education. Such initiative was to come from Edmonton's first elected member on the Territorial Council, Frank Oliver. He had been elected in 1883 on a platform advocating greater support for schools throughout the Territories. Oliver's interest led to the passage of the school ordinance of 1884, which,

As new people came to Edmonton the school-age population grew. To solve the problem of over-crowding, an addition to the original 1882 single-room school was added in 1888. (COEA)

43

among other things, introduced compulsory taxation for the support of schools.

The citizens of Edmonton responded immediately to the requirements of the new act and were the first to petition the Lieutenant-Governor for the creation of a school district. The taxation provisions in the new ordinance, however, generated considerable protest. This opposition came in part from Hudson's Bay Company officials. The plebiscite held to determine the community's opinion on the creation of a school district was hotly contested. Both sides made great efforts to get out the vote. Despite a close election the creation of a school district was approved. Its creation was officially proclaimed in the *North West Territories Gazette* on February 21, 1885. A separate school district was created with much less effort in 1888.

In addition to the public and separate school boards, a number of new social organizations were created in Edmonton

FRANK OLIVER: EARLY EDMONTON PUNDIT

Frank Oliver, as newspaper editor and politician, played a major role in defining Edmonton's identity as a northern community and in defending its interests during Western Canada's evolution from a frontier region to an established part of the Dominion of Canada.

After serving his apprenticeship in the newspaper business with the Toronto *Globe* and the *Winnipeg Free Press*, he came west in 1876 to Fort Edmonton, which he later recalled as being a "place which was particularly marked by the star of empire."

Oliver, however, spent five years as a general merchant in Edmonton before he was able to concentrate fully on his career as a frontier journalist. As in the case of Edmonton's other general merchants

at the time, he had to make annual trips back to Winnipeg to arrange for fresh supplies of groceries, hardware, and dry goods, as well as men's and women's wear. In December 1880 he offered for sale "a yoke of young, well bred Oxen, and 3,000 lbs of the best beef in the country."

The arrival of the Dominion Telegraph in the fall of 1879 was the catalyst for the creation of the Edmonton *Bulletin*. Edmonton's telegraph office was located in John Walter's carpenter shop at the south side ferry landing. Weekly news bulletins were forwarded over the wire from Winnipeg. The cost was covered by private subscription. Alex Taylor, who operated the telegraph office, wrote out these weekly messages or bulletins and sent them

Frank Oliver was the co-founder of Edmonton's first newspaper, The Edmonton Bulletin. After being in the North West Territorial Council he was elected to the House of Commons as Minister of the Interior. (COEA)

in the 1880s, among them two new church organizations, various fraternal societies, and cultural groups. The Anglican Church was established in Edmonton by Canon Newton. The first Anglican church building in Edmonton was constructed on the corner of Jasper Avenue and 121st Street on land purchased from Malcolm Groat for five dollars. The first Presbyterian services were held in the 1873 church constructed by the Methodist Church. In the spring of 1882 the Reverend Baird bought a lot on the Hudson's Bay Company Reserve close to the first school on what is now 104th Street and 99th Avenue, and in November of that year a church was opened on the site. Among the American settlers was Pastor A. McDonald, who would serve the Baptist community. In addition to dealing with the spiritual needs of the community, the various churches contributed to its cultural development.

The Edmonton Glee Club, established in 1887, and the Edmonton Literary Society, formed in 1882, added to the

around to the subscribers. In order to better disseminate this information, Alex Taylor and Frank Oliver combined their resources to purchase a small printing press. They found a small press in Philadelphia that was suitable for their purpose. The press was shipped to Winnipeg in the spring of 1880, and Oliver picked it up during his annual freighting trip that summer. When Oliver returned to Edmonton, the original proposal had been expanded to include not only telegraph news, but also local news, editorials, and advertisements. The Edmonton *Bulletin* had been born, with Oliver and Taylor its proprietors. In the summer of 1881, Oliver returned with additional printing equipment and a bride, the former Harriet Dunlop. The new, improved

Edmonton *Bulletin* made its first appearance on October 29, 1881. The editorial on this occasion stressed Oliver's renewed commitment to the newspaper and its role as a communications link between Edmonton and the rest of Canada:

According to our promise of last spring, we issue the Bulletin in an enlarged form, and we hope, with an improved appearance. No effort will be spared to keep our readers posted on all that is transpiring in the Upper Saskatchewan country. While our telegrams will give all important items of general news, special attention will be paid to matters relating to the North-West. Our opinions in regard to subjects that may claim our attention will be expressed truthfully and fearlessly, with a single

eye to the best interests of this western country.

One of the themes that frequently "claimed" Oliver's attention was Edmonton's future as a northern city.

To possess the trade of such a country, when developed, must build up a great city, and what place more likely to possess that trade than Edmonton? Only two series of rapids interrupt navigation from the Arctic ocean to Athabasca landing, less then ninety miles distant from Edmonton by cart road, which soon will be replaced by a railroad, and from Edmonton to the eastward the Saskatchewan furnishes a freight line independent of railways and giving a competing route when railways are built. It is on the certainty

In the early days a keen eye and a steady hand could mean the difference between having supper on the table or going hungry. The Edmonton Rifle Association, formed in 1886 to encourage marksmanship, posed in 1891 with an unnamed trophy won at a local competition. (PAA, E. Brown Collection)

of possessing prospects of Edmonton are principally founded, and that they are well founded does not admit of the shadow of a doubt.

Oliver was also on guard for what he described as the "rights of the pioneers," which were subject to abuse by the federal government and large corporations, such as railways and land companies that simply speculated rather than invested in the development of the area. In his view settlers who came west and invested their own time and money in the development of the community were progressive elements on the frontier. The land grant to the Edmonton and Saskatchewan Land Company in 1882 produced the following editorial comment from Oliver:

It is galling to think that those who came here long ago, or even lately, who sweated and toiled, faced exposure and danger and hardship of all kinds to make homes for themselves and build up a country, should have now to stand aside and see the land that they hoped would be settled on within the next few years by independent and enterprising pioneers like themselves occupied partly by riffraff from Europe but principally held to be a dead weight around the necks of themselves and others whose exertions in their own behalf will cause it to increase in value, to the profit of the members of this speculative company, many of whom will probably never see the land that their money has cursed and would disdain to notice those by the fruits of whose exertions they live.

Later, as Minister of the Interior in the federal government from 1905 to 1911, Oliver came to appreciate the role that European settlers could play in the development of the West. In 1929, at the 25th anniversary of the building of St. Mary's Church at Shandro, located east of Edmonton, he called on the 5,000 people gathered for the occasion to "not forget your race or your religion; build up this country by building up yourselves; these are the terms on which we took you, and your success will be the success of Canada."

THE VILLAGE BEYOND THE FORT

cultural amenities of the budding village. The very active membership of the literary society held regular bi-monthly meetings that included debates, readings, and musical presentations. A demonstration of swordsmanship was planned for one meeting but had to be cancelled because the cold weather prevented the participants from practicing sufficiently.

The Edmonton Rifle Association was organized in 1886 with Matthew McCauley as president and Colin F. Strang as secretary. Mrs. Hardisty started the first annual fall meeting of the association with a bull's-eye shot. The best aggregate score was made by Walter Scott Robertson who won the Dominion of Canada Rifle Association medal and $10 in cash. Other sporting activities were part of the celebrations of the anniversary of Confederation. The July 1, 1882, activities included horse races, foot races, and lacrosse matches. In anticipation of the events, the *Bulletin* reported:

The prospect for sport today is good, as the race track is in fair condition, and a great deal of interest is manifested in the events to take place. The form of the track has been changed from a circle to an oval in order to get past a wet spot, and is fenced on both sides for about 100 yards from the outcome. No entries had been made up to yesterday morning, but a great many horses have been practising for the past week, intending to take part. For the mile race it is expected that Jim Campbell, W.S. Robertson, S. Cunningham and Elziard Page will enter their horses. For the half mile, A. McNicol, E. McGillivray and J. Sinclair will enter, and for the quarter, A. McNicol, J. Campbell, J. Mowat, and D.M. McDougall.

The prize list amounts to $210 and the subscription towards the sports to $220. The total expenditure will likely run a little over this amount. The entrance money in the horse races will be added to the purses, and will make the amounts quite an object . . . The principal prizes are $15 first and $5 second for the 100 yards foot race, and $35 each for the mile and half mile horse races, for the quarter mile race $20 and for the trot, $15.

The North West Mounted Police detachment, complete with pet dog, posed in front of their home in 1891. The NWMP has contributed to Edmonton's tradition of peaceful development, and to law and order in the West. (COEA)

The sports will take place first and commence at 10 a.m. If all goes well there will be an adjournment for dinner before the horse races take place. Boston Boy, Little Angus, and Vallandlingham which were barred from all but the mile will not appear in any.

Edmonton citizens also participated in the activities of the neighbouring communities of Fort Saskatchewan and St. Albert, such as the sports day held in May 1885 by the Fort Saskatchewan Amateur Athletic Association.

The social and economic developments that occurred in Edmonton in the 1870s and 1880s were in part the result of the transfer of the Northwest Territories to the new Dominion of Canada. The first permanent representatives of the Dominion Government to come to Edmonton were members of the North West Mounted Police, an organization created in 1873 to establish law and order in the Canadian West.

On October 27, 1873, Troop A of the NWMP arrived at Fort Edmonton and remained in Edmonton throughout the winter of 1873-1874. In the spring of 1874 Inspector W.D. Jarvis,

commander of Troop A, received orders from NWMP
Commissioner George A. French for the construction of
barracks on the right or south bank of the Saskatchewan
anywhere between Fort Edmonton and Sturgeon Creek, since
it was anticipated that this would be the location of the railway
crossing. This location avoided the barrier created by Beaver
Hills and the high banks of the river at Edmonton. The
decision about the location precipitated Edmonton's first
meeting to protest a move by the federal government. Donald
Ross, the leader of the protest, recalled, "The location was
ostensibly decided on account of the nearness of a certain pine
bluff which furnished the necessary timber, but really because
Col. Jarvis . . . was bucking against the Hudson's Bay
Company and desired to take the barracks as far away as
possible." The NWMP would not be moved back to Edmonton
until 1913.

The transportation system in the West was revolutionized
by the introduction of steamboats. On July 22, 1875, the
Northcote reached Fort Edmonton with a cargo estimated at
130 tons. The S.S. *Northcote* had been constructed by the
Hudson's Bay Company in the summer of 1874 under the
direction of Captain J. Reeves of Grand Forks, North Dakota,
and by shipwrights recruited in St. Paul, Minnesota. It was a
prototype of steamboats to be seen on the Mississippi and
Missouri rivers. Other boats to serve Edmonton during the
period included the *North West,* the *Lilly,* and the *Manitoba.*
The introduction of steamboats on the North Saskatchewan in
1874 was complemented by the introduction of steamboats on
the Athabasca and the opening of the Athabasca Landing Trail
in 1878.

The first Hudson's Bay Company land boom occurred in
1881-1882. The company, after a decade of ignoring the
development of Edmonton, announced in the *Bulletin* the
creation of the "City of Edmonton." According to the HBC
advertisement, the townsite was:

situated at the head of navigation on the North Saskatchewan

A North West Mounted Policeman visits with some Cree Indians who camped near Edmonton, circa 1891. The Indians have gathered to hold a tea dance, a purely social affair where, not surprisingly, gallons of tea were consumed. Alcohol was strictly forbidden at tea dances. (PAA, E. Brown Collection)

River; the centre of the Gold, Coal, Timber and Mineral region of the great North-West, and surrounded by the richest wheat-producing country in the world.

The four great highways leading from Winnipeg, the great Bow River grazing country, the Peace River country and British Columbia via the Jasper Pass centre on the Town Site.

It is the terminus of the CP telegraph line, the North-West mail route, and the projected Saskatchewan branch of the C.P.R.

The HBC's enthusiasm for its new townsite was initially shared by Frank Oliver, editor of the Edmonton *Bulletin:*

There is a possibility . . . that the syndicate have decided to build the CPR via Edmonton, crossing the river here, and uniting with the H.B. Co. in building upon their property the metropolis of this far North-West. If this surmise should prove correct, and it is at least reasonable, all the booms that have taken place yet in Manitoba or elsewhere will be as nothing compared to that which the tumble-down walls of Fort Edmonton will see during the next year or two.

This announcement was followed by the calling of a public meeting in October at which the company explained its intentions to the citizens and invited their participation in certain aspects of the town's design. Initially 100 lots were created for immediate sale. Terms of the land sales were to be one-third cash down and the balance in two equal annual installments. Land purchasers were also required to erect a building within 18 months from the date of purchase on at least every second lot. Lots would also be given for schools and churches, and "liberal inducements in the shape of lots will be given to parties starting manufactures." The people at the meeting were also requested to select the location of a market square and decide which street on the plan should be Main Street.

Edmonton's first legal subdivision found a ready market

when offered for sale in October 1881. At first company officials in Edmonton conducted the land sales. The Edmonton *Bulletin* reported that "the moment the sale opened there was a rush for lots that would have surprised even a Winnipeg auctioneer, and in three or four days $12,000 worth, or about 400 lots were sold subject to building erections." HBC Land Commissioner Brydges, however, considered the price too low and ordered sales from the Edmonton office stopped four days after they began. Henceforth land sales were to be conducted from Winnipeg.

The S.S. Northcote, the first steamer to reach Edmonton, rests alongside the much smaller S.S. Minnow, while freight is loaded. The S.S. Northcote travelled the North and South Saskatchewan rivers on behalf of the Hudson's Bay Company. It is seen here, circa 1884, on the South Saskatchewan River, near Medicine Hat. (PAA, E. Brown Collection)

Interest in the Edmonton townsite, however, did not endure beyond the spring of 1882. This rapid decline of interest in Edmonton real estate reflected in part the failure of the HBC and the Canadian Pacific Railway to cooperate in the development of the townsite. The CPR chose a route that ran south of the town, thus avoiding the various land speculators who had gathered in anticipation of the CPR's arrival at the Edmonton settlement. The collapse of the land boom in Edmonton also clearly reflected the lack of local participation stemming from the decision to conduct land sales from Winnipeg. As the Edmonton *Bulletin* observed:

Outside of the boom the prospects of Edmonton are second to those of no place in Manitoba or the North West except Winnipeg. The boom as far as it has gone has left a large amount of money here of which every dollar has been invested and if it has burst utterly and lots can not now be sold in Winnipeg for a cent a piece the matter will concern very few of the people here.

They have not been in the real estate business. The boom started suddenly and went ahead too rapidly for them to invest.

Frank Oliver clearly resented the fact that the Winnipeg business community was monopolizing the benefits to be derived from land speculation. The HBC Reserve was no longer given the same deference by the citizens of Edmonton as the logical location for the development of an urban community. While the Hudson's Bay Company land boom did not change the physical development of Edmonton, a number of important land sales were made. For instance, the Catholic Church purchased the land that would eventually develop into the Parish of St. Joachim's.

The Hudson's Bay Company land sale was only one aspect of the land issue agitating the community during the winter of 1881-1882. The other problem was the failure of the Dominion Government to survey the various land claims and issue legal certification of title. The failure of the Dominion Government to carry out these procedures and the prospect of a railway resulted in attempts at claim jumping. In response the citizens formed a land claims association or vigilante committee. On two occasions this association threw "unauthorized" structures over the river bank.

Other potential threats to Edmonton's welfare, in addition to federal government bureaucrats and Winnipeg land speculators, developed in April 1885. When the Indian agency at Saddle Lake was attacked, it was feared that the Indians in the Edmonton area would join the Riel Rebellion. A meeting was held in Luke Kelly's saloon to organize the defence of the community. By April 25 the panic had subsided with the arrival of the relief column from Calgary.

During the 1880s Edmonton had successfully made the transition from a fur trade outpost of London, England, to a commercial and administrative centre for the new Dominion of Canada. It was, however, a relatively isolated outpost of this new nation, and its citizens anxiously awaited their opportunity to be fully integrated into the developing West.

THE RIEL REBELLION

Edmonton in the 1880s consisted, in part, of a relatively small number of white settlers in the midst of a large population of Cree Indians who had been established on reserves created following the signing of Treaty Six in 1876. Four of these reserves were located in the immediate vicinity of Edmonton, while others were located to the north at Lac La Biche and Saddle Lake. A vital communication link between Edmonton and the rest of the prairie West was the Dominion Telegraph.

News of the first battle of the second Riel Rebellion at Duck Lake between the North West Mounted Police and the Métis, under Gabriel Dumont, arrived over the telegraph on March 27, 1885. In response to the news, a meeting for the organization of a volunteer company was held in the schoolhouse. A total of 68 men were enrolled in the company, and nine officers were elected. Senior commanding officer was William

Right: *Born in 1844 at St. Boniface, Manitoba, Louis Riel, leader of the Métis, was hung on November 16, 1885, for his role in the hostilities. The controversy over his participation in the rebellion, and over his execution, continues today, almost 100 years after his death. (PAA, E. Brown Collection)*

Below: *In retrospect, the second Riel Rebellion did not have a chance of long-term success. This scene depicts the surrender of Chief Poundmaker to General Middleton. (PAA, E. Brown Collection)*

Stiff, a local real-estate agent and one-time teacher.

Despite these preparations, the Edmonton *Bulletin* warned against the community taking any drastic action with respect to the rumors of war, and lamented their effects on business.

More men have been killed in flight than ever were in fight, more men have been killed by theatre panics than by theatre fires and it is not hard to see that if a rumor, groundless though it be, is diffused throughout this settlement, more injury will be done to business and the general welfare than might possibly result from an actual raid.

This relative calm, however, changed dramatically when news was received from Saddle Lake. It seemed to indicate that the Indians at this reserve were going to join a general uprising. In response to the news from Saddle Lake, a meeting was held

The government took no chances in quelling the Riel Rebellion; soldiers and police were well-armed and well-trained. These men, camped near Batoche, prepare an artillery piece for an imminent battle against the Métis. (PAA)

in Luke Kelly's saloon at 2 p.m. on April 7. At the meeting:

A proposition was made to send messengers to Calgary at once with the news, but as funds for the trip were not available it was decided to await the arrival of Capt. Griesbach from Ft. Saskatchewan, who would have all necessary authority. A message had already been sent to inform him of the report received and asking him to come to Edmonton. A messenger was also sent out towards the Little Mountain to inform the settlers of what had occurred.

When Griesbach had not arrived by 7 p.m., a second meeting was called, at which a committee of defence was created to take all necessary steps to organize the protection of the district. Captain Stiff of the volunteer company pledged his support. Also, the committee sent a second message to Captain Griesbach, "asking him to take the necessary steps for defending the place or give official sanction to the committee to do so." James Mowat also volunteered to go to Calgary at once "without any agreement as to pay if a horse were furnished him." But prior to the end of the meeting, Griesbach arrived. He

was promptly elected to the defence committee. On April 8 a third meeting was held, and more specific steps for defence were announced. By Saturday, April 11, further indications of an uprising were received. Captain Griesbach's Beaverlake dispatches indicated that the Whitefish Lake, Lac La Biche, and Egg Lake bands were on the way to join the forces of the Bears' Hill oufit. The dispatches also indicated that the Blackfoot had turned out and torn up the railway. That same day the Edmonton *Bulletin* editorial conveyed the new panic that gripped the community: "When the Indians around Edmonton will rise appears now to be only a question of days. What they will do in that case or what numbers they will be joined by is something which can be better decided after the event."

The panic subsided, however, the following day, when more reliable news reported that the Whitefish Lake and Lac La Biche reserves were quiet. The community was further relieved when James Mowat returned on April 20 with news that a relief column was on its way north. This column arrived on May 1 at noon. A number of citizens went several miles out to meet them and accompanied them in on horseback and in buggies. General Strange, who commanded the relief column, crossed the river shortly after noon and was received with a salute of nine guns. The Edmonton Company was drawn up under Captain Stiff and briefly addressed by the general. The mounted men of the force crossed first, followed by the rifles, ammunition, and a supply train of about 200 wagons. As the 65th Regiment formed up on the north side, they were given three hearty cheers by the crowd above them.

Edmonton artist Harry S. Craig worked from an 1871 black and white photograph taken by pioneer photographer Charles G. Horetzky to create this watercolour. Members of the Canadian Pacific Railway survey team are shown resting at their camp located along the North Saskatchewan River. (COEA, Hubert Hollingworth Collection)

A.H. Hider's watercolour illustrates the type of stagecoach that operated between Edmonton and Calgary from 1883 until the arrival of train service in 1891. The stagecoach would take a minimum of five days to make a one-way trip, at a cost of $25 per passenger. (COEA, Hubert Hollingworth Collection)

Left: *Bill Kennedy and his matched team and wagon pause at Fort Edmonton Park, a modern re-creation of pioneer life. Courtesy, George Hunter, Masterfile*

Below: *An Indian village is part of the historic representation of Fort Edmonton in the mid-19th century. Courtesy, Bill Brooks, Masterfile*

The beautiful glaciers of Banff and Jasper national parks have always been a favorite destination of vacationers from nearby Edmonton. Courtesy, Alberta Photograph Library, Public Affairs Bureau

Left: *Banff National Park, near Edmonton, is the oldest and best-known of Canada's national parks. Courtesy, Alberta Photograph Library, Public Affairs Bureau*

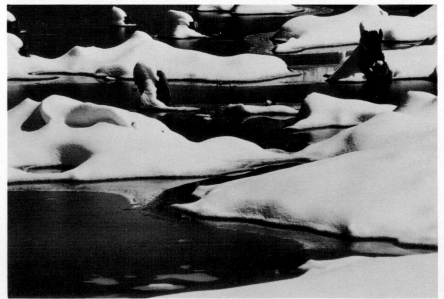

Left: *Spring sculpts beautiful patterns from the ice on the river. Courtesy, Alberta Photograph Library, Public Affairs Bureau*

Left: *Scores of ducks take to flight at Beaverhill Lake, 30 miles to the east of Edmonton. Beaverhill Lake is among the larger lakes in the Beaver Hill area, attracting flocks of birds to its shores.* Courtesy, Alberta Photograph Library, Public Affairs Bureau

Left: *The fields east of Edmonton are rich and fertile for agriculture.* Courtesy, Bill Staley

CHAPTER III

THE BIRTH
OF THE
"TWIN CITIES"
1891 - 1902

Edmontonians began the last decade of the 19th century with the optimistic expectation that railway construction would bring increased economic development. On April 24, 1890, the Calgary & Edmonton Railway was incorporated for the purpose of building a railway from Calgary to "a point at or near Edmonton." The provisional directors of the railway company included James Ross, Edmund B. Osler, Herbert C. Hammond, William Mackenzie, Nicol Kingsmill, Herbert S. Holt, and Donald B. Mann. This group of entrepreneurs had been actively involved in various aspects of railway construction in the Canadian West prior to the construction of the Calgary & Edmonton line. The most significant individuals of the group were Osler and Hammond, who were members of the Toronto and Winnipeg-based investment firm of Osler, Hammond & Nanton. This company was the trustee of the land grant received by the Calgary & Edmonton Railway Company as well as its various townsite properties.

Construction of the line began on July 8, 1890, and was completed to Red Deer by the fall of that year. In the spring of 1891 construction resumed in the direction of Edmonton without any public announcement as to the exact location of the northern terminus. These construction activities were of great interest to the Edmonton *Bulletin*, which provided detailed accounts of how the railway was being built and recorded the comings and goings of various C & E officials in anticipation of the railway's arrival in Edmonton.

These expectations were dashed with the announcement in July 1891 that the terminus of the railway was to be on the south side of the river, across from the existing settlement. The railway company had purchased property at this location earlier in the year, and now it began to survey a townsite and to construct a station, engine shed, water tank, and hotel. In the view of Osler, Hammond & Nanton, it was necessary to locate the new town permanently on the south side because "the banks of the Saskatchewan at that point are about two hundred and fifty feet high." This townsite, which was intended to replace the existing community on the north side, was referred to as South Edmonton until it was incorporated as the Town of Strathcona in 1899. The completion of the line was marked by an impromptu ceremony at which Donald Ross drove in the last spike. Immediately upon its completion the line was leased to the Canadian Pacific Railway, which provided the equipment and crews for its operation. The line had a relatively low priority to the CPR since it was only being operated on a lease. Therefore the railway cut costs by not constructing fences along the right-of-way and by placing the telegraph poles double the normal distance apart.

Edmonton's response to the location of the terminus on the south side of the river was immediate and unequivocal. In a July 18, 1891, editorial Frank Oliver stated his faith in the north side's future growth and prosperity:

Even if there were no town established on the north bank of the river, the fact that four-fifths of the settlement and nine-tenths of the trade of the district is on the north side would naturally tend to establish business on this side. But when there is an old and well established town on the north side, there is no good

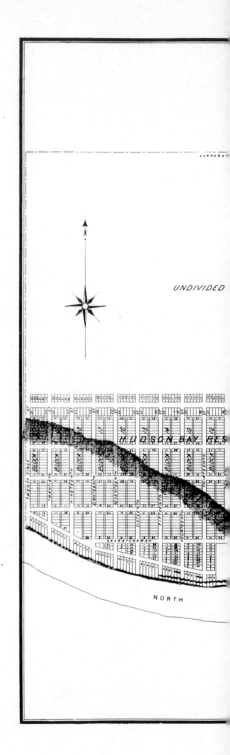

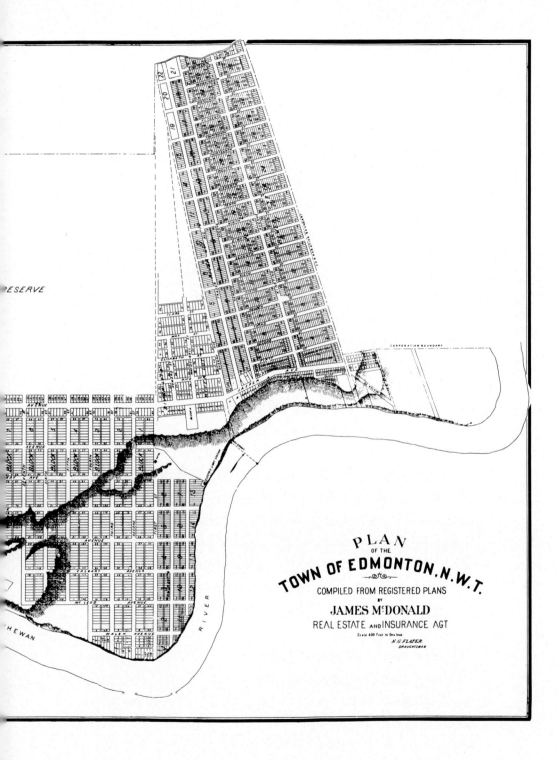

PLAN
OF THE
TOWN OF EDMONTON, N.W.T.
COMPILED FROM REGISTERED PLANS
BY
JAMES McDONALD
REAL ESTATE AND INSURANCE AGT
Scale 400 Feet to One Inch
N.G. FLATER
DRAUGHTSMAN

Created in 1892 by James McDonald, this was the first official map used by the newly created Town of Edmonton. The shaded areas on the map indicate the brow of the Saskatchewan Valley. The borders shown remained intact until 1904, when Edmonton attained the status of a city. (COEA)

reason why it should not continue to grow and prosper even during the few years that are likely to elapse before the railway crosses the river in its future inevitable extensions northward and westward.

Despite his faith in the eventual triumph of Edmonton, Oliver warned his fellow citizens that "it would be altogether unwise for them to adopt a do-nothing policy," since:

The influence of the C. & E. company will undoubtedly be used in favor of their own town site, and their influence—wealthy and astute business men as they are—may count for a great deal. There is no doubt that their interest lies in bringing as much of the business of the district as possible to their own town site to increase the value of their lots, and . . . they will use every means to this end, no matter how disastrous such a result might be to the people whose business and investments are in this town.

The citizens of Edmonton responded immediately to Oliver's call for action. Within four days a meeting was called to discuss incorporation at which a committee was appointed to define the boundaries of the proposed town. The boundaries were chosen deliberately to exclude the railway townsite on the south side. The strongest opposition came from Thomas Anderson, a major south-side landowner. In his view:

The time had not come to incorporate. The town was too scattered and the population too small. When the population had increased to one or two thousand he would favor incorporation but not until then. If incorporation were forced upon now, some poor settlers who had large claims but very little money would have their land eaten up in taxes. He mentioned several large property holders as being opposed to incorporation. If the town were incorporated, salaried officials would have to be employed and taxes would become very burdensome.

He also indicated that Mr. Hamilton of the CPR said the idea of incorporation was nonsense. Despite this objection and a relatively lukewarm response from the HBC, the citizens at this town meeting supported the idea of Edmonton's incorporation as a town. The Territorial Government proclaimed the statute incoporating the Town of Edmonton in 1892, and Matthew McCauley was elected its first mayor.

Frank Oliver's warnings of July 1891 about the actions of the town promoters were also prophetic. In September 1891 A.M. Nanton, writing on behalf of the Calgary & Edmonton Townsite Company to federal Minister of Agriculture John Carling, suggested that the immigration hall and other public buildings proposed for the Edmonton settlement should be constructed on the railway townsite:

From the rapid progress made at the Railway town and because of the advantages of the location and the great improbability of the line ever being carried across the River at what is known as the former Edmonton Settlement, it is altogether likely that the present terminal point will be the business centre of that district. Any Public Buildings to be erected there should, we venture to suggest, in order to meet the requirements of the district and to be conveniently situated, be located within convenient distances of the Railway station and on the South side of the River.

The Dominion Government did not adopt a policy of relocating its offices to the new townsite in response to this request. However, in May 1892 Thomas Anderson, the Dominion Land and Crown Timber Agent in Edmonton, suggested in a letter to Mr. A.M. Burgess, Acting Deputy Minister of the Department of the Interior, that it would be advisable to have the government offices adjoining the immigrant shed at the station "so that the Immigrant when housed in the shed would only have to go next door to make his entry and then remove direct to his land and future home, instead of at present having to go over to the north side 3 miles and cross in a scow and return to his family." Having been authorized to carry out this change, Anderson arranged to have the land office documents loaded into a wagon for relocation to the south side on Saturday, June 20, 1892. Various citizens who noticed this activity immediately surrounded the wagon and sent out a call for reinforcements. They removed the nuts from the wagon axles and unhitched the horses so that the documents already loaded could not be moved. Two Royal Canadian Mounted Police officers from the local detachment arrived but, because the horses had been taken, could not provide any assistance to Mr. Anderson. The angry crowd sent telegrams to Ottawa and formed a citizens' guard to hold the wagon until they received an answer. The guard increased in size when rumors of police reinforcements from Fort Saskatchewan spread. Finally the situation was resolved when the government agreed to establish a sub-office on the south side.

Edmonton's vigilante tradition had thus been successful in ending yet another apparent Winnipeg-originated threat to its future growth and in creating the twin cities of Edmonton and Strathcona. South Edmonton, however, did achieve some degree of progress despite the lack of strong long-term support from the townsite promoters and the Canadian Pacific Railway. Robert Ritchie, a prominent South Edmonton citizen, was one of the principal owners and the manager of the Edmonton Milling Company, which constructed Northern Alberta's first roller process flour mill. Other pioneer businessmen included William and James McLaren, Arthur Davies, James McKernan, Frank Cowles, W.E. Ross, and the Douglas brothers. A prominent member of the legal profession, Alexander Cameron Rutherford, established his practice in South Edmonton in 1895. He became Alberta's first premier in 1905. Property owners in South Edmonton established a school district in 1894, and the South Edmonton *News,* also established in 1894, perpetuated the idea of South Edmonton's future greatness. The position of editor was held by R.P. Pettiepiece between 1894 and 1896 and by J. Hamilton MacDonald between 1896 and 1912. The primary function of

Arriving in 1891 from Perth, Ontario, Robert Ritchie established the Edmonton Milling Company. Well-known and admired for his honesty, integrity, and business acumen, Ritchie was elected mayor of Strathcona in 1901. (COEA)

Above: Frank Cowles came to Strathcona in 1894 and opened his first drugstore in 1895. He served on the Strathcona Town Council and the Public School Board. (COEA)

Left: James and Robert Douglas operated Douglas Brothers in the heart of Strathcona's business district. Their general store sold everything from books to do-it-yourself wills. Courtesy, Glenbow Archives

the newspaper, as stated in the first edition, was to promote the interests of the town:

We are desirous of letting outside people know of our excellent farm lanes, of what kind of grain, vegetables, etc., can be produced, and of the many advantages the farmers in this district have over those in other parts. . . . We are here in the interests of this town and the people of the district.

By the end of the first year of publication, the newspaper was a staunch guardian of and spokesman for Strathcona's civic pride. Having assumed this responsibility, the paper solicited subscriptions from the citizens on the grounds that they would be contributing to the welfare and promotion of their town:

When we cast our lot with this town some thirteen months ago, a good deal of confidence in the place was required as here seemingly was no room for a newspaper. But as before stated in these columns a newspaper does a great deal to promote a town's interests. . . . And by keeping your local newspaper up to the standard you create a feeling to the outside public that you are a progressive and busy people.

Edmonton's dislike of the railway townsite extended to the entire Calgary & Edmonton Railway system throughout the 1890s. The traditional complaints about freight rates and poor service continued. These deficiencies were not only the subject of editorial comment, but also of a poem:

Arthur Davies made his first home in Strathcona in 1895, on the site of what is now the Old Strathcona High School. He co-founded the Commercial Life Assurance Company of Canada. He was the last mayor of Strathcona and played a leading role in the amalgamation of Edmonton and Strathcona in 1912. He is remembered as The Father of Greater Edmonton. (COEA)

OVER THE C. & E.
(by a regular passenger)

Ho! let her go — she's off at last, we aren't
so late to-night.
An hour and forty all you say? By Gad!
that's out of sight.
And here she goes, and there she rolls, a

Alexander Cameron Rutherford arrived in Strathcona in 1895. A lawyer and a Liberal, he became Alberta's first Premier in 1905. His successes are many, including the establishment of the University of Alberta in Strathcona. (COEA)

playing pitch and toss.
While Luggin by the track rides on, and
keeps up with his horse.

The C. & E., you never heard I reckon, who
they are.
The "nicest, dearest lot," I'll bet that ever
run a car.
The C. & E., why bless your heart, the
"catch me easy" line.
That never broke its record yet, by coming
in on time.

You mind how once we ran a race with
Farmer Jones' steer.
And the blessed boiler nearly burst, for the
thing ran like a deer.
How Dan who drove the engine jammed
the valve right open wide.
But couldn't choke the creature off, which
kept close by our side.

The C. & E., that line we love, with love
that does not wear.
Who's rates are low, who's motto, "by,
monopoly we swear."
No don't complain, if things are not, just
suited to your mind.
They'll answer, "you be hanged," or
"then, get out and shove behind."

In addition to Edmonton's constant criticism of the Calgary & Edmonton Railway during the 1890s, the town also made strenuous efforts through both private and public channels to overcome its lack of a railway. In September 1893 the Territorial Government passed an ordinance authorizing the Town of Edmonton to build a tramway that could be extended across the river. The following year some Edmonton

Left: *Constructed by the Dominion Bridge Company, the Low Level Bridge was built primarily to allow the Canadian Northern Railway to cross the North Saskatchewan River. (COEA)*

Below: *Donald Ross, extreme right, swings the sledgehammer that will drive the last rivet into the Low Level Bridge. (PAA, E. Brown Collection)*

businessmen incorporated the Edmonton Street Railway Company, but could not muster the necessary capital to build the tramway. A third and ultimately more successful attempt was the Edmonton District Railway, which was incorporated in 1896. Little progress was made until the acquisition of the charter by Donald Mann and William Mackenzie in 1899 when construction finally began. The company was renamed the Edmonton, Yukon & Pacific Railway, but it was truly part of the Canadian Northern Railway system, which Mackenzie and Mann were creating. The Dominion Government constructed the Low Level Bridge as part of this system.

The completion of the line in October 1902 provided the last opportunity for a clash between the CPR and Edmonton. The CPR attempted to prevent the installation of the switch connecting the Calgary & Edmonton and the Edmonton, Yukon & Pacific by sending two policemen to the construction site to prevent the tracks from being "molested" by Mr. Pace and his Canadian Northern construction crew. When Mr. Pace ignored their order to stop construction, the police produced a warrant for his arrest. This warrant delayed the work long enough to give the CPR an opportunity to park a locomotive on the location of the proposed junction, and it "was evidently intended to remain there all day." Mr. Pace responded to this situation by sending his men to another construction site, anticipating an opportunity to install the switch later that afternoon. He realized that the guard train would have to move out of the way of the regular 5:30 p.m. train from the south, and he could then pull up the appropriate amount of rail. When word of Mr. Pace's problems reached Edmonton, many of its citizens "figured that if it were merely a question of force, there was no reason why the CNR should be at a loss on that account." After dinner several busloads of men drove over to the switch site to offer assistance. However, these reinforcements were apparently not required, since little seemed to be happening.

About a quarter after five Mr. Pace appeared quite casually on

Above: *W.J. Pace risked assault and arrest to connect the Canadian Northern Railway (Edmonton, Yukon & Pacific), and the Calgary & Edmonton Railway. In 1907 he left the CNR to oversee the construction of Edmonton's street railway system. (COEA)*

the scene, and wondered what all the row was about. The regular was soon sighted and the guard train backed slowly up to the Y to let it into the Strathcona station. As soon as the regular had passed the point of connection Mr. Pace gave a sharp whistle, his gang, who had been resting calmly and unobtrusively behind some convenient shrubbery, appeared on the scene and proceeded to lift the C & E rails, at the same time putting out red flags at each side.

Donald Ross, who had driven the "last spike" on the C & E, "had the honor of driving the first spike in the connection and the whole thing was completed in less than an hour."

Edmonton's interest in railway construction was only one aspect of its preoccupation with resource development not only in the immediate Edmonton district but as far away as the Kootenay district of British Columbia and the Klondike in the Yukon. The Klondike gold rush through Edmonton occurred in 1897-1898 when an estimated 1,500 people left Edmonton for the Yukon, although less than half completed the trip.

A less spectacular but ultimately more valuable rush was the settlement of the agricultural land adjacent to the north and west of the town by a variety of people from Ontario, Quebec, and Eastern Europe. The development of a full-scale land rush was noted by Dominion Lands Agent R.A. Ruttan in his 1899 report:

The number of homestead entries granted (866) exceeds that of my former year in the history of the agency; the sales of railway lands for the like period show also a large increase, the number of quarter sections being 320 as compared with 116 for the preceding year; the sales of other farm properties, held by corporations and individuals, make an equally satisfactory showing; the enhancement in farm and the willingness of newcomers, intending permanent occupation, to pay these values is an indication that Northern Alberta has passed the experimental stage, and takes rank among the most prosperous agricultural regions of America.

The settlement of this agricultural land in the Edmonton area provided a long-term demand for goods and services that extended well beyond the period covered by the Klondike rush. It also provided the basis for Edmonton's industrial development, which was based to a large extent on the processing of agricultural goods.

Social activities during the 1891 to 1902 period continued to include the annual fall fair and the Dominion Day celebrations. From 1891 to 1895 the fair was organized by the Edmonton Agricultural Society. Between 1896 and 1900 a fall fair did not take place on the north side since the fairgrounds site was subdivided by the Hudson's Bay Company. The tradition, however, was perpetuated by the South Edmonton Agricultural Society, which had held its first fair in 1894. In 1899 the South Edmonton Agricultural Society changed the fall fair to a summer event, which took place on July 25 and 26 of that year. The advantage of a summer fair was that the "farmers can have the necessary leisure in which to take an active interest in the fair's progress." Strathcona's first summer fair featured exhibits of horses, cattle, and other livestock, poultry, grain, farm produce, handiwork, and arts. Athletic events included a baseball match beween Edmonton and Strathcona as well as horse races. In the 1900 fair a balloon ascension took place from the fairgrounds.

The balloon ascension on Wednesday afternoon from the Strathcona fairgrounds was very successful and brought out strong expressions of approval from all who witnessed it. The balloon, which was inflated with hot air, rose rapidly almost straight up from its moorings. Professor Thompson did a number of acrobatic feats from the trapeze, while the balloon was ascending. When a height had been reached at which he looked like a very small boy he made the descent safely with a parachute. When the balloon had been relieved of his weight, it tilted to one side, allowing the air to escape. Very soon the balloon reversed and as the hot air was forced out by the descent the balloon was soon empty and came down just outside the

The country spirit of the 1908 Edmonton Fair was conveyed by photographer Ernest Brown. (PAA, E. Brown Collection)

THE KLONDIKE GOLD RUSH

When the news about the Klondike gold discoveries arrived in May 1897, Edmontonians were busy organizing a celebration in honour of Queen Victoria's Diamond Jubilee and exploiting the market for agricultural goods created by an earlier gold rush into the Kootenay area of central British Columbia.

The first indication that Edmonton had a potential role to play in the Yukon gold rush came in a letter to the editor dated June 11, 1897.

EDITOR BULLETIN

In a recent conversation with a miner who has been over the ground, from Edmonton to the Yukon, he informs me that for a party of prospectors wanting to reach the latter point, they could start from the Athabasca Landing by boat and travel down the Peel river, on the Mackenzie and thence across the mountains to the Porcupine river, and that the total distance travelled by land between the Peel and Porcupine rivers is only 90 miles, and the balance of course is all river route from Athabasca Landing.

This being so, why should not Northern Alberta divert the traffic and travel, at least during the summer season. The Hudson's Bay company have steamers now running between Athabasca Landing and the Mackenzie river, for its own trade, it is natural to suppose the company would like to increase its revenue, as it undoubtedly would, owing to the immense trade to be done, if the proposed route were once established and advertised, and the company would then have the lion's share of what trade is now being done by American concerns, with much less means, but more enterprise, and with much less facilities.

In addition to the water route an all wagon road, via ruins of Fort Assini-

boine, Lesser Slave Lake and Peace river Landing and on to the Liard river and thence to the head waters of the Yukon can be easily got at a nominal cost, which would prove invaluable to the whole Dominion of Canada, in assisting the development of the resources of what experts claim are the richest gold fields so far discovered in the world.

Are the members of the Edmonton Board of trade aware of the town's important situation in connection with the Yukon?

PROGRESS.

Those fortunate enough to reach the goldfields endured long, hard days of gold panning. This back-breaking process was often made more difficult by the cold water which carried the much sought-after gold dust and nuggets. (PAA, H. Pollard Collection)

The Klondike gold rush of the 1890s was a boon to local merchants. Prospectors on their way to the Klondike stopped in Edmonton for supplies before continuing to Dawson via the Peace, Findlay, and Liard rivers. Courtesy, Glenbow Archives

"The Trail of '98"
Klondikers ascending Chilkoot Pass.
Winter+Pond Co.
Juneau.

Other endorsements of the need and practicality of an all-Canadian route soon followed. In July the *Toronto World* argued that "there seems to be little doubt that such a route is not only possible, but not difficult of accomplishment, probably the route via Edmonton will be found as desirable and as convenient as any other." By August the Edmonton *Bulletin* had joined the campaign to ensure that Edmonton would receive a portion of the provisioning trade to be derived from the northern extension of the mining frontier. Mayor John A. McDougall called a public meeting for August 9 to discuss the question of a direct land road from Edmonton to the Yukon. Reportedly, F. Fraser Tims

made a vigorous speech on the possiblity and desirability of opening up a land route altogether through Canadian territory. He suggested that arrangements be made for a special edition of the Bulletin, *which would set forth the possibility and advantages of that route for the information of the government, municipal organizations,*

boards of trade and influential men generally with a view of inducing the government to open a wagon road and establish a telegraph line and mail service by this route.

These suggestions were endorsed by the other people at the meeting and steps were taken to carry them out. The first special Klondike edition of the Edmonton *Bulletin* appeared on August 12, 1897. Various Edmonton merchants prepared to meet the needs of Yukon-bound travellers. The stores of W.T. Henry & Company, Sigler & Cristall, and LaRue & Picard were only a few of the establishments that became Klondike outfitters. On August 25 at a second public meeting it was decided that the town of Edmonton should send an exploring party to the Pelly River overland. The exploring party returned with a favourable report in December 1897. But the most ambitious project was announced by William Pugsley of St. John, New Brunswick, who acquired the charter of the Edmonton District Railway with the intention of constructing a railway to the Yukon. The

Those would-be prospectors who went by boat from Seattle to Skagway were faced with scaling the Chilkoot Pass. Over 1,200 steps through the ice and snow were required to reach the top. Often a man would make two dozen trips just to get all of his gear to the summit. (COEA)

net result of these efforts was the creation of a new trail from Edmonton to the Peace River Country via the Swan Hills. The gold rush did not last long enough to allow for major improvements to the land-based communications system with the north.

Despite the relative lack of progress in improving the transportation links between Edmonton and the Yukon, an estimated 1,500 people used "the back door" route to the Yukon. The majority used the most appropriate means of transport. However, other more unusual means of travel did appear, such as a steam-powered sleigh and a wagon that used barrels for wheels.

fairgrounds like a dish rag.

In 1901 the Edmonton fair once again reappeared, now under the auspices of the Edmonton Industrial Exhibition Association Ltd., which had been created on August 21, 1899. The new site for the exhibition was on the Ross Flats. In September 1900 erection of buildings on the Exhibition Grounds began. The first annual fair of the Edmonton Industrial Exhibition Association took place on July 1-4, 1901. The change of date allowed for the traditional Dominion Day celebrations to be combined with the annual fall fair. The fair drew a large attendance from the surrounding country, including a band of Indians who camped near the entrance to the track. Colonel Dent, a special visitor to the exhibition, came to buy horses for the British army. Washouts on the railway prevented attendance by residents from Calgary. The program included the traditional displays of agricultural goods and handiwork, as well as a baseball game between Edmonton and Strathcona. "The game was a victory for Edmonton by the surprising score of 10 to 1. It was a first class exhibition of baseball in which the Strathcona team did not play its usual game and Edmonton never played better." The Edmonton victory was attributed to the pitching of Frank Ball, which "was most puzzling to the opposition batters."

The Minneapolis Attraction Company contributed various amusements to the fair, promising to show

Walter Scott Robertson, shown here circa 1900, initially came to Edmonton to speculate in real estate, which he did with some success. He made his real mark, however, as the first sheriff, and by opening the Edmonton Opera House, the first place in town built specifically for entertainment. (COEA)

1. *The Richards family, three in number, Aerial Artists, combining in their acts the Revolving Ladder and Japanese Perch Pole acts.*
2. *The De Vallas, three in number, Trick Cottage act, a very comic act introducing the Horizontal Bar act.*
3. *Prof. G. Bell, wonderful Slack Wire and Juggling act.*
4. *Prof. Nordquist, the World's famous High Diver.*
5. *Matthews and Newman Unicycle and Rolling Globe acts, a marvelous performance.*
6. *Prof. G. Richards, High Rope, doing all the latest tricks on the*

*high rope, standing on his head, walking in sacks, riding a
bicycle on his head, etc., and possibly Little Ray, the Boy High
Diver. He is only twelve and makes a dive of seventy-five feet.*

At the regular winter carnivals, the various participants
dressed up. In January 1895 the costumes, which were both
"artistic and amusing," included "South Edmonton News,"
"North West Mounted Police," "Sporting Lady," "Northwest
cowpuncher," and many other colourful characters.

Around the turn of the century, a number of new athletic
clubs were organized to enjoy various summer and winter

sports. The most successful winter sports included curling and
hockey. The senior hockey teams for Edmonton and South
Edmonton, the "Thistles" and "Shamrocks," were named after
the names of the rinks in which they practised. Cricket,
cycling, and golf were popular summer sports. The Edmonton
Golf Club was founded on April 4, 1896, with a membership of
"16 gentlemen and 9 ladies." The Hudson's Bay Company

*The 1909 Strathcona
women's team practices
face-off and stick-handling
skills. Despite their
unwieldy uniforms,
Edmonton's women
enjoyed hockey
competition. (COEA)*

THE CIRCUS COMES TO EDMONTON

Added to the excitement generated by the Klondike gold rush in Edmonton in the summer of 1898 was the performance of the Lemen Brothers' Circus. Advanced billing for the circus took the form of an advertisement and an article from the *Winnipeg Free Press*, both of which appeared in the Edmonton *Bulletin* and the South Edmonton *News*.

The circus, according to the advertisement, included a three-ring circus, five-continent menagerie of wild animals, trained exhibition, a real Roman hippodrome, and a free horse fair. The prize exhibit of the animal menagerie was the mighty Bovalapus, "the rarest, strongest, awfulest of all the mighty monsters of the great deep," and Rajah, "the biggest brute on earth, a towering giant. The very lord of beasts. Taller, longer, weighs more than any elephant ever captured. Bigger than the famous Jumbo." The human acts included Captain Santiago, high diver; Little Edna, "the girl wonder," the only lady to turn forward and backward somersaults on a bareback horse; and Kittie Krudger, the only lady four-and six-horse rider in the world.

The South Edmonton *News* was glad that the circus was coming since it was "another proof of the growing importance of our town and district." The paper noted that "all lines of business in this town will certainly reap large financial benefit on circus day." The paper also warned the citizens, however, about the potential evils that lurked in the circus:

It is one of the lamentable things about circuses in general that they have a following of gamblers, sharpers, pick pockets and thugs who are ever on the alert to catch the gullible and

unthinking. Every man, woman, and child who attends a circus should take all the wits they possess and as little money as possible. Enough cash to buy the ticket is sufficient. Then the pick- pockets will find poor picking and the man with a wheel-of-fortune, shell game or other delusions will have no charms.

As advertised, the circus arrived on Saturday morning, August 27, and it was in operation by 10 a.m. People from all over the district began to arrive by the "thousands" at an early

hour. The traditional street parade was cancelled because the management "judged aright that they would get the crowd anyway." The first item on the program was the high dive by Captain Santiago. This free exhibition was followed by the opening of the side show. The South Edmonton *News* described it as "largely a fake and indecent exhibition of dancing." It also noted that "obscene pictures were on sale for those who would buy." But the Edmonton *Bulletin* disclaimed any knowledge "as to the side shows and

skin games."

The main show, which began at 2 p.m., was attended by approximately 4,000 people. An evening show attracted an additional 1,000 patrons. Together these 5,000 patrons exceeded the total populations of both Edmonton and South Edmonton. The South Edmonton *News* reported that it was disappointed with the animal menagerie, which did not include the mighty Bovalapus. The reporter suggested that it may have been too dry in South Edmonton for it to appear. However, the circus performers, the reporter continued, were excellent. The *Bulletin*, on the other hand, was reasonably impressed with the entire performance. A large number of Mounted Police, which had a "salutary effect on both circus men and town rowdies," maintained public order. Despite its warnings, the South Edmonton *News* noted, "there were several fakes permitted that took many a hard earned dollar out of the pockets of gullible people." All told, however, just as the *News* had predicted, the circus made an

In the more than 100 years that circuses have been coming to Edmonton, amazingly little about them has changed. Even today no circus is complete without a juggler and either the largest or smallest man in the world. This circus has all the bases covered with a juggler and the "smallest giant" in the world. (COEA)

estimated $7,000 profit, and local businesses and saloons did a "roaring" business.

granted permission to the club for use of the flat ground at the foot of Ninth Street where the Legislative Building now stands. The company also donated a cup for competition. At the turn of the century, attempts to create baseball teams with regular practice schedules and competitions against other teams were more successful. In July 1895 the Edmonton team was beaten 45 to 10 by a team from Sturgeon, prompting the Edmonton *Bulletin* to observe that "the score looked as though the Edmonton men might be better at marbles than baseball."

The entertainments provided by the various churches and fraternal societies were supplemented by the establishment on November 2, 1893, of the Edmonton Philharmonic Society. The society, formed at a meeting held in Glover and Andrews music store, had 16 members: three first violinists, three second violinists, three flutists, one clarinetist, one first and one second cornet player, one slide trombonist, one euphonium player, one drummer, and one pianist. Its officers were President J.B. Spurr, Vice-President Dr. McInnis, Conductor George Purches, and Secretary-Treasurer and Librarian F.H. Andrews. Travelling shows, which could now come to Edmonton via the railway, offered additional amusement. The first to arrive was the Caroline Gage Company in May 1892. Their arrival was anticipated with great interest by the Edmonton *Bulletin:*

The Caroline Gage Theatrical troupe, which will visit Edmonton next week, is well spoken of by the press of every place they have visited in the Northwest, with the single exception of Moose Jaw, and even there the adverse critic admits the beauty and talent of

Left: *Wearing the traditional white uniforms of cricketers, the Edmonton Cricket Club, 1905 winners of the Ochsner Cup, pose for their official team photograph. (PAA, E. Brown Collection)*

Above: *Covering approximately 10 city blocks, from present-day 71st to 76th Avenue and from 106th to 108th Street, James McKernan's lake provides winter fun. While dozens of skaters promenade, more daring types try the toboggan slide. (PAA, E. Brown Collection)*

the leading lady. . . . The appearance of the first professional theatrical troupe marks an era in the progress of civilization here, and their enterprise should receive substantial recognition.

The group's first performance was well received by the audience, which "seemed likely to laugh themselves into hysterics at the comic passages of the play." The company's second performance, also before a packed house, was entitled "The Honeyman," apparently an adaptation of the "Taming of the Shrew." This performance was also well received; unfortunately, "the terrible downpour of rain which greeted the audience as they left the building skimmed the cream off most of the jokes." A variety of other groups followed the Caroline Gage Company, including the Fax Humorous Concert Company, the Sim Fax Concert Company, and the Big Bonanza Company. After 1894 the touring groups had the advantage of being able to use Robertson Hall. Also referred to as the Edmonton Opera House, this building was the first hall built specifically for entertainment. It was built by a local entrepreneur and sheriff, Walter Scott Robertson.

The presence of the Caroline Gage Company in Edmonton was an example of the city's widening horizons. In economic terms, the railway would be the means by which an ever-increasing number of settlers would arrive. It also provided a means for Edmonton's relatively isolated agricultural economy to gain access to national and international markets. The Calgary & Edmonton Railway, however, through its attempts to create a new townsite, also demonstrated its willingness to ignore the vested interests of Edmonton's original north-side residents. Edmontonians successfully responded to the challenge by waging an 11-year fight to bridge the North Saskatchewan River. This fight would ultimately involve the first non-resident entrepreneurs who demonstrated any sympathy for Edmonton's ambitions as a metropolitan centre. Out of this involvement with Donald Mann and William Mackenzie would come Edmonton's first sustained boom as a frontier community.

CHAPTER IV

THE BUILDING
OF A
"GREATER EDMONTON"
1903 - 1916

The completion of the Edmonton, Yukon & Pacific Railway in 1902 was the prelude to an era of unprecedented development in which the physical, economic, social, and cultural aspects of Edmonton would be radically transformed. This era was initiated in 1903 when the Town of Edmonton signed a terminal agreement with the Canadian Northern Railway Company to jointly purchase 68.88 acres of Hudson's Bay Company Reserve land for use as yards and station grounds. The Edmonton electorate endorsed the agreement with a favourable vote on By-law 237, which provided $30,000 to the civic administration for the purpose of acquiring all the property needed by the Canadian Northern for its right-of-way through town. The completion of the mainline to Edmonton on November 24, 1905, prompted a day of celebration:

In the presence of thousands of citizens of Edmonton and visitors from all parts of central Alberta, Hon. G.H.V. Bulyea first Lieutenant-Governor of the Province of Alberta, at 2:15 yesterday afternoon, drove home with unerring blow the silver spike which held in place the first rail of the Canadian Northern

Railway to reach the station in Edmonton.

The advent of a transcontinental railway to the city which is the distributing point for great stretches of land to the north, whose railway facilities have been limited, and whose people have waited long and patiently for a railway which would place them in direct and immediate connection with the commercial centres of the east: such a railway was certainly worthy [of the] most hearty and enthusiastic reception.

The Canadian Northern Railway right-of-way was located some distance to the north of all the existing buildings in town, except the recently completed Queen's Avenue School. This structure, described as a "Château in the Woods," was located adjacent to the tracks and therefore would ultimately be demolished.

In 1909 a second transcontinental line was built through Edmonton. The Grand Trunk Pacific was incorporated on October 24, 1903, to construct and operate a railway from Moncton in New Brunswick to the Pacific Coast via Quebec City, Winnipeg, Battleford, and Edmonton. Inducements provided by the Town of Edmonton to attract the Grand Trunk included a bonus of $100,000 payable in cash or municipal bonds and exemption from all municipal taxation for a term of 20 years after January 1909. The cash payment was intended to be used for the purchase of land, the value of which had skyrocketed since 1903. The company's obligations, as defined in the 1905 agreement, were of significant value to the city. These included the establishment and maintenance of Edmonton as its chief divisional point between Winnipeg and Prince Rupert on the Pacific Coast and obliged the company to "co-operate with the city in its endeavor to make the city a wholesale and distributing point." In addition to meeting these obligations, the Grand Trunk Pacific also built the Macdonald Hotel, which would dominate the Edmonton skyline to the 1970s. Construction on this $2.25-million structure began in September 1912 and was completed in July 1915. It was officially opened with a gala 420-person banquet attended by

The Honourable G.H.V. Bulyea, first lieutenant governor of Alberta, was a native of New Brunswick. A scholar by nature, he was recognized as an expert in mathematics and languages, especially French. He served as Minister of Agriculture and later as Minister of Public Works in the North West Territorial Government, prior to the creation of the Province of Alberta. (PAA, Public Affairs Collection)

Right: *A small boy balances on stilts with his friends nearby, in front of Queen's Avenue School. Constructed in 1902, the 10-room school was converted to Canadian National Railway's offices in 1927. The building was torn down in 1947 to make way for an extension to the CNR station. (PAA, E. Brown Collection)*

Below: *Spectators gather to view the last spike ceremony, and to see the first Canadian Northern Railway passenger train arrive in Edmonton, on a chilly November 24, 1905. (PAA, E. Brown Collection)*

Lieutenant-Governor Bulyea and Premier Sifton. The Château-style Macdonald became the established location for many of Edmonton's social functions.

The combined effect of the arrival of the Canadian Northern and Grand Trunk Pacific railways was the creation of two northern suburbs and the reemergence of Edmonton as a significant part of a transcontinental transportation system, as it had been prior to 1860. The village of West Edmonton, a residential subdivision better known as Calder, was developed around the Grand Trunk Pacific Railway terminal some distance to the northwest of the main town. The village of North Edmonton, an industrial subdivision, developed to the northeast of the old town at the junction of the Canadian Northern and Grand Trunk Pacific mainlines. Its most important industries were the meat-packing plants constructed by P. Burns & Company Ltd. and Swift Canadian Company Ltd.

The rapid progress on the north side induced by trans-continental railway construction prompted the Canadian

Left: *The gangway allowed workers ready access to the partially constructed piers of the bridge at Clover Bar in 1907. (PAA)*

Above: *The Patrick O. Dwyer Company's Swift Canadian plant, shown in 1912, employed 275 people. (PAA, E. Brown Collection)*

Right: *The P. Burns and Company plant, shown in 1912, was one of two major meat packing plants in North Edmonton. (PAA, E. Brown Collection)*

Pacific Railway to cross the river. This development began
with the CPR's outright purchase of the Calgary & Edmonton
Railway in 1903. Immediately after this purchase, the CPR
began surveys to determine where the bridge would be built.
The result was the High Level Bridge, which was completed in
1913. The CPR also built a new station and roundhouse in
Strathcona, which became a terminal. The CPR, after years of
neglect, was finally making an effort to "make Strathcona."
North-side construction activities included a station and an
office building on Jasper Avenue.

During this period Edmonton's transportation links with the
north were drastically improved by the construction of the
Edmonton, Dunvegan & British Columbia, the Alberta & Great
Waterways, the Central Canada, and the Edmonton & Slave
Lake railways. The Edmonton, Dunvegan & British Columbia
provided access to the agricultural land in the Peace River
district. Prior to the completion of this line to Grande Prairie
City in 1916, settlers going to the Peace River Country used the
Edson Trail. By 1916 the Alberta & Great Waterways had only
reached Lac La Biche, which was advertised as a good resort
for "jaded Edmontonians." There the company built a hotel
and instituted a passenger service using gas-operated Mckeen
cars.

Locally the Edmonton Street Railway, the Edmonton

Left: *In 1912, tremendous
supports allowed the
contractors to lay the lower
(foot and vehicle traffic)
portion of the High Level
Bridge. This, of course,
could only be done during
the winter while the river
was frozen. (PAA,
E. Brown Collection)*

Interurban Railway, and the Incline Railway met
Edmontonians' more immediate transportation needs. The
Edmonton Incline Railway was incorporated in 1907 by
Donald Ross, Joseph Hostyn, Pete Anderson, and Richard
Secord. Hostyn, the railway's manager, had travelled to New
York and Hamilton to investigate those cities' hoist systems.
Located along First Street, the Incline Railway was designed to
deal with Edmonton's age-old problem of transporting goods
and people to and from the flats in the river valley. As
industrial and recreational uses of the river flats developed,
solving this problem became particularly important. The

*Vacationers in 1910 dock
their sailboats after
travelling from the
mainland to Koney Island,
located in Cooking Lake.
This particular trip was so
popular a boathouse was
built on Koney Island.
(PAA, E. Brown Collection)*

industries located in the valley included the Edmonton
Brewing and Malting Company, the Dowling Grist Mill, John
Walter's north- and south-side lumber mills, and two ice
companies. Among the recreational facilities were the
Exhibition Grounds and Diamond Park.

The construction of the Incline Railway encountered
various problems, such as the procurement of an adequate
source of power. Attempts to utilize gas from a well drilled in
1897 were unsuccessful, and the city power plant could not
spare the electricity. Eventually a coal-powered engine with a
46-foot shaft was used to operate the hoist. On May 20, 1908,
the Incline Railway, described as a cross between an outdoor
escalator and a San Francisco cable car, went into operation.
A large pavilion atop the College Avenue hill provided shelter
for operator Frank Morris, a retired CNR engineer, the toll
office, and the steam plant. The hoist operated during the
summer months from 7 a.m. to 7 p.m., with extra runs for

Above: *The Anheuser-Busch Brewing Association of St. Louis, the makers of Budweiser Beer, received a permanent injunction in 1911 from Mr. Justice Stewart of the Alberta Supreme Court, stopping the Edmonton Brewing and Malting Company from using labels similar to those found on Budweiser bottles. As each of the bottles was returned, the company's employees placed new labels on their product. (PAA, E. Brown Collection)*

Left: *Spectators take a break from walking up the wooden steps leading to Macdonald Drive, to watch the labourers removing the rocks and dirt excavated to make room for the installation of the Incline Railway. (PAA, E. Brown Collection)*

Right: *Owners and employees of the Edmonton Incline Railway in 1908 stand beside the system of huge gears and pullies which provided the strength necessary to successfully operate the hoist. (COEA)*

Left, below: *Businessmen in a car and a teamster carrying a load of coal arrive at the top of the Incline Railway in 1909. The lift not only simplified the trip up to street level from the bottom of McDougall Hill, it also offered an excellent view of the river valley. (PAA, E. Brown Collection)*

baseball matches at a price of 5 cents per passenger and 15 cents per vehicle for a round trip. By June 16, 1910, a total of 144,760 foot passengers and 76,099 vehicles had been transported by the railway, which continued to operate until 1912.

In addition to Edmonton's development as a railway centre, the city gained new status as the capital of the newly created Province of Alberta. The Province of Alberta was proclaimed on September 1, 1905, by Sir Wilfred Laurier at a ceremony held in Rossdale. The legislation creating the province also designated Edmonton as its temporary capital, a decision that was confirmed by the Provincial Legislature in 1906. The new province constructed a residence for the Lieutenant-Governor in Glenora, one of Edmonton's new west-end subdivisions, and a Legislative Building designed by American-born architect Allan Merrick Jeffers that featured a dome and extensive use of marble in the interior. Meetings of the Legislative Assembly were held in Thistle Rink and McKay Avenue School until the completion of the building in 1912.

Another decision of the new provincial administration

resulted in the establishment of the University of Alberta. The legislation creating the institution was passed in 1906, and a site was purchased in Strathcona in 1907. Prior to the completion of Athabasca Hall in 1911, the university occupied various buildings in Strathcona. The Dominion Government also contributed to Edmonton's development by constructing buildings such as the federal prison, a new post office, immigration halls, and armouries on both sides of the river.

The most dramatic response to Edmonton's development as a transportation centre and political capital was a land boom on an unprecedented scale, the rapid extension of Edmonton's boundaries, and its acquisition of a city charter. Between 1903 and 1914 a total of 274 new subdivisions were created. This represented an 18-fold increase in the number of subdivisions on the north side alone compared with an 8-fold increase in

Members of Alberta's first Legislative Assembly stand on the steps of McKay Avenue School, in 1905. Front row, left to right: Lt. Gov. G.H.V. Bulyea, Premier A.C. Rutherford, and W.H. Cushing, the Minister of Public Works. (PAA, E. Brown Collection)

Above: *The Old Timers'
Association contributed
this log cabin to the 1905
Inauguration Day
celebrations. (PAA,
E. Brown Collection)*

Left: *The Immigration
Office was decorated with
fruits, vegetables, and
grains from Edmonton on
Inauguration Day, 1905.
(PAA, E. Brown Collection)*

Left: *Carpenters work on the frame of the Thistle Rink in 1901. Because it was the largest centre in 1905, it housed the first session of Alberta's Legislature. (PAA, E. Brown Collection)*

Below: *With the galleries packed with friends, family, and supporters, Alberta's first Legislature listened to Lt. Gov. G.H.V. Bulyea give the Speech from the Throne on March 15, 1906. (PAA, E. Brown Collection)*

the total population of Edmonton between 1904 and 1914. Subdivisions were located on both sides of the river with the largest concentration to the northeast of the central business district. The cumulative result was the creation of a blueprint for a "Greater Edmonton" that dazzled the imagination of Edmonton's boosters and strongly influenced many aspects of civic policy. This excess of new subdivisions came in the face of a severe housing shortage that forced many people to take up temporary residence in tents.

The vast majority of the land promoters, both individuals and companies, were interested in simply creating a subdivision for immediate sale without any interest in the actual development of the land. They were content to simply print advertisements stressing the beauty and investment potential of their respective subdivisions. Only a very small minority were prepared to go beyond the rhetoric of boosterism and make an effort to attract residential or industrial development to the area. Many of the promoters stressed the proximity of their subdivisions to the Grand Trunk Pacific Railway, the Legislative Building, or the Lieutenant-Governor's residence.

W.J. Magrath and Carruthers, Round & Company were among the subdivision promoters who tried to attract development. W.J. Magrath arrived in Edmonton in 1904 from Belleville, Ontario, where he had operated a cheese exporting business. Magrath entered the real-estate business soon after his arrival in Edmonton by creating Magrath, Hart & Company, which was subsequently reorganized in 1909 when B.A. Holgate bought out Hart's interest. Initially the company followed the traditional approach of simply creating subdivisions such as Bellevue in River Lot 28, Bellevue Addition in River Lot 30, and Victoria Place and City Park immediately to the north of the Bellevue Addition. The Highlands subdivision on River Lots 32 and 34 received much of the company's attention. The promotional campaign began in September 1910 when Magrath, Holgate & Company advertised that $50 in gold would be given to the person who provided the name for the new subdivision. In November 1911 Magrath-Holgate took out building permits for 28 private residences, including the homes of W.J. Magrath and Bidwell Holgate. In addition to their construction in the Highlands subdivision, Magrath-Holgate Ltd. also negotiated with the city to provide services for the district. In August 1911 the firm applied for extension of the street railway network to the Highlands. Magrath-Holgate agreed to bear the entire cost of the line from the East End City Park (Borden) provided that it was constructed during that fall and an hourly service was maintained. The company agreed to protect the Street Railway

Department against loss for a period of 18 months from date of commencement of operations. The company also negotiated an agreement for the paving of certain streets in the subdivision.

Carruthers, Round & Company, organized in 1905, was concerned with the creation of an exclusive district in the west end. The principal owner of the company, James Carruthers, was a Montreal-based grain merchant who had extensive real-estate investments in Western Canada. Henry B. Round, who functioned as the local agent for the company, was a former employee of the HBC who first came to Edmonton in 1884.

Left: *These bachelors made the best of a bad situation, circa 1907. With the addition of beds, a rug, and a wicker rocking chair their tent was reasonably comfortable. The frame of the tent conveniently became a good place to hang clothes. (COEA)*

Right: *The housing shortage of the early 1900s was hardest on the children. Families often had two tents: one for the adults, and one for the children. The problems of tent life were aggravated by a corresponding shortage of sanitation, recreation, and education facilities. (COEA)*

The development of the Glenora subdivision began in 1906 when Carruthers purchased River Lot 2 from Malcolm Groat. Initially he subdivided the northern portion of the lot into a standard grid pattern, but his greatest interest was in that portion of River Lot 2 located near the river valley. That portion was subdivided using curved streets to accommodate the ravine in one of the few departures from the grid system. The most significant and unique aspect of Carruthers' strategy in terms of Edmonton's history was the use of a restrictive covenant on all the Glenora property. One of the few documents respecting land-use control created during the early part of the century, this covenant, dated December 2,

William J. Magrath, co-owner of the Highlands subdivision, built and furnished this mansion at a cost exceeding $85,000 in 1912. The grounds cover 10 city lots. Magrath built the house at 6240 Ada Boulevard, naming the boulevard for his wife. (PAA, Edmonton Journal Collection)

1911, restricted the subdivision to single-family detached residences by prohibiting the construction of places of "public entertainment, amusement or resort." It also prohibited the use of the land for any trade or business purpose. An additional stipulation of the covenant prevented the construction of houses valued at less than a set amount, which ranged from $3,000 to $5,000, depending upon the location of the lot.

The high point of the land speculation mania was the Hudson's Bay Company land sale in May 1912. On April 24, 1912, the HBC announced that it would be offering "1300 business and residential lots centrally located in the City of Edmonton." These lots had been created in December 1911 when the HBC subdivided the remaining portion of its reserve. The plan of survey was a grid pattern modified by the addition of four parks and two diagonal streets named Kingsway and Portage avenues. A lottery was planned to determine the order by which individuals could purchase the land, and no more than four lots were to be sold to one person either directly or through the agency of a third party. In order to encourage sales, the company committed itself in advance to the paving of Portage Avenue and other improvements contingent on the City of Edmonton extending the street railway. In response to the Hudson's Bay Company advertisement, an estimated 1,500 people lined up on the morning of May 13 for an opportunity to purchase land. Many of the people in the line were representatives of other land companies, such as Magrath-

After entering the Magrath mansion through the leaded glass doors, visitors are struck by the glistening oak-panelled walls; this entrance leads to the bottom end of the main staircase. The hand-painted wallpaper adds to the elegance of the building. (PAA, Edmonton Journal *Collection)*

Holgate.

Edmonton responded enthusiastically to the pace being set by the land promoters with an ambitious annexation policy and the extension of urban services to the annexed areas. Edmonton made its first annexation bid in 1903 when a city charter was under discussion. Its primary objective was the industrial plants in Cloverdale at the north end of River Lots 17 and 19. But Strathcona annexed this territory before Edmonton could act, and Edmonton had to be content with 3.79 square miles of undeveloped land primarily to the north and east of the original townsite. In October 1911 Edmonton made its most ambitious and ultimately successful bid when it attempted to annex the villages of West and North Edmonton as well as the City of Strathcona. Strathcona's interest in amalgamation reflected the fact that it had largely been bypassed by the post-1903 economic growth. This was particularly evident during the winter of 1905-1906 when it failed in its attempt to change the route of the Grand Trunk Pacific Railway.

The provision of urban services to the new areas accompanied the process of political consolidation. The civic administration initiated a vast system of sewage, water, electric light, and streetcar extensions. As part of the expansion, the city decided in 1906 to purchase a site for the west-end park and a site for the Exhibition Grounds in the east end. Both sites were located beyond the existing boundaries of the city. Development of the new east-end Exhibition Grounds began in

THE PANTAGES THEATRE

The Pantages Theatre, constructed in 1913, was the crowning achievement of 20 years of theatre development in Edmonton, begun with the construction of Robertson Hall in 1892. The Pantages was built by Edmonton businessman George Brown, who envisaged the vaudeville theatre as part of a 10-story "Sky-scraper Block" to be located on the corner of Jasper Avenue and 102nd Street. Such an undertaking seemed possible given the frantic pace of Edmonton's economic development in 1912-1913 and the success of other Edmonton vaudeville theatres, such as the Empire and Lyceum.

The theatre component of Brown's development was supplied by Seattle-based vaudeville promoter Alexander Pantages. Pantages agreed to a partnership with Brown, but left him with the responsiblity of raising most of the money. A $50,000 loan from the City of Edmonton contributed considerably to Brown's fund-raising efforts. Brown's intention of constructing a skyscraper, however, was never realized. But the diminutive size of Brown's two-story building was compensated for by the interior of the theatre, which was designed by Benjamin Marcus Priteca, the principal architect for the Pantages network of theatres. Priteca's classically inspired interior, with its proscenium arch and Corinthian fluted columns, was unprecedented in the city's history.

The opening of the 1,600-seat theatre, which took place on May 12, 1913, in a gala ceremony attended by civic and provincial government officials, was described by the Edmonton *Journal* in detail:

The largest theatre in Edmonton, finished with the most modern kind of

The Pantages Theatre, referred to as "the most northerly high-class vaudeville playhouse in North America" by the Edmonton Journal, opened its doors to the public in 1913. The elaborate backdrops and live music provided the setting for such entertainers as Buster Keaton, the Marx Brothers, Stan Laurel, and Sophie Tucker. (COEA)

architecture, was opened in Edmonton last night. Yesterday the people waited anxiously for the advent of Alexander Pantages and his vaudeville into this city. Today they have it.

The opening was a well-managed affair. It was something unusual for this city, and will not soon be forgotten by the sixteen hundred souls who

attended . . .

A delay of about forty-five minutes was caused at the commencement, but this is explained by the fact that the workmen had not finished inside. However, when the doors were opened the public rushed in and soon were seated. The audience gazed around them and marveled at the splendor. The finish of the ceilings, the artistic way in which the boxes were laid out, and the cosy little loges in the balcony were something new to Edmonton.

And the *Journal* was not disappointed with the first performance:

There were live acts to the bill, and all

were good ones, considering the popular price charged. Two of these were exceptionally good and fully deserved the applause of the audience. The Alisky Hawaiians proved very entertaining with their singing and musical entertainments, while the beautiful scenery which the act carries with it is a feature in itself. Coogan and Cox . . . deserved special mention.

Following the official opening, the Pantages began a twice-daily schedule. Prices ranged from 15 cents to 25 cents for matinees, while prices for evening performances ranged from 25 cents to 75 cents. As indicated by the opening-night production, the Pantages Theatre stressed variety in its shows.

The variety in subsequent years was maintained by shows that included featured headline acts, displays of athletic skill, animal acts, playlets, patriotic acts, and comedians. By 1917 the Pantages Theatre also presented motion pictures, which featured romantic and adventure serials such as *A Romance of the Redwoods* with Mary Pickford, *Manhattan Madness* with Douglas Fairbanks, and various "Keystone Komedies." Demonstrations of athletic skills were provided by Lotti Mayer and her diving girls who "glitter, glide, sparkle and cavort in the limpid waters of a large glass tank, displaying all that is latest and graceful in the art of swimming and diving; the tango of the mermaids as it were."

Theatre-goers formed a block-long queue outside the Pantages Theatre. They were waiting to see the 1923 hit production "Canary Cottage," a musical comedy starring Jane Aubrey and James Coots. (COEA)

1910 when the City of Edmonton undertook the construction of new buildings. By 1914 a livestock pavilion had been added; it would eventually become the Edmonton Gardens.

The positive response of the civic administration was equalled by that of the Edmonton Public School Board, which adopted a policy of purchasing land in the new subdivisions in advance of settlement. This policy reflected, in part, the high cost of purchasing additional land to expand the size of the grounds of existing schools in the pre-1903 townsite. Between 1903 and 1914 the school board constructed a total of 26 new schools, ranging from a one-room cottage school to a 14-room high school.

The economic growth during this period resulted in a 700-800 percent increase in Edmonton's population. The increase,

Parasols and large hats protected these mothers from the sun while they kept an eye on their children, who found the wading pool at Borden Park to be the perfect place to cool off on a hot day in 1915. (PAA, A. Blyth Collection)

Expecting to get rich quickly, these Edmontonians lined up for the Hudson's Bay Company land sale in 1912. Many of them were buying their lots with only a small down payment, and with the hope that they could sell the lots at a profit. To their astonishment the bottom soon fell out of the land market. (PAA)

however, did not radically transform Edmonton's ethnic character. English, Scottish, and Irish ethnic groups continued to constitute the vast majority of Edmonton's citizens. Western European immigrants from France and Germany each represented less than 10 percent of the population. Eastern European immigrants from the various provinces of the Austro-Hungarian Empire represented less than five percent of the total. The small Jewish community created the Edmonton Hebrew Association in 1906, which counted Abraham Cristall, William Diamond, and Hyman Goldstick among its prominent members. Abraham Cristall and William Diamond were both clothing merchants, while Hyman Goldstick had come to Edmonton specifically to take on the formal teaching and religious leadership duties for the Edmonton Hebrew Association and the Hebrew Congregation of Beth Israel. Of the three, Cristall, who came to Edmonton in 1893, had resided in the city the longest.

Edmontonians substituted patriotism for boosterism with the declaration of World War I, which prompted what was described by the *Bulletin* as the "Wildest Night in Edmonton's History":

Not since the frenzied days of the South Africa campaign has such a patriotic demonstration been witnessed as that which took place in Edmonton last night under the auspices of the

THE FLOOD OF 1915

In the spring of 1915 Edmontonians were preoccupied with recruiting men for battle in Europe. However, on June 28, 1915, a more immediate security threat presented itself to the city. The Edmonton *Bulletin* reported that heavy rains had converted the North Saskatchewan River into a "swollen, raging torrent which rose 10 feet in as many hours." Although "John Walter said the river was gradually lessening and he expected it to cease within an hour or two," emergency measures were quickly taken. Bennett School on Gallagher Flats was designated as a relief centre, and on the morning of June 28, two hundred families moved their furniture into the building.

The river continued to rise until 7 a.m., June 29. At that point, the flood waters threatened every resident and structure in the valley. Tons of debris piled up against the Low Level Bridge, and the water began to erode its approaches. In an effort to save the bridge, the Canadian Northern Railway parked two trains of ballast on it with locomotives, steam up, attached to each end. The water also inundated the city power and water plants.

At 11:30 the pumping plant was still in operation. The pump house was flooded a foot over the floor and the great fly wheel of the pump was revolving in water sending a stream to the roof and deluging the engineers and helpers. The chief engineer in charge of this machinery worked for hours in water up to his armpits. The power plant officials determined early in the evening to concentrate on the pump house in order to keep the city's water supply intact as long as it was humanly possible to work. . .

Below: *A City of Edmonton police constable wades through the rising water to reach another home in his house-to-house search for stranded flood victims in Rossdale in 1915. (COEA)*

By 11:35, with the water rising inch by inch, the last of the city utilities had to be shut down. The city's firemen were ordered to leave any remaining fires.

Late in the afternoon of June 29 the water began to surround Bennett School, and "the refugees, becoming nervous, scattered into higher districts." Some were accommodated at St. Luke's Mission, the Presbyterian church at River Heights, and a number of private homes. One man with his supply of groceries and one family, however, remained in the building throughout the night. Elsewhere, at the other flats, the scenes were the same. On Rossdale, when the water continued to rise, a children's shelter became threatened. As a request, the children were

the memory of Edmontonians for tens of thousands watched anxiously last night from every point of vantage. On McDougall hill at the top of the flight of steps several thousand were gathered watching with absorbing interest the efforts that were being made to save that old landmark the low level bridge. The high level bridge was simply alive with pedestrians and automobiles and rigs of all descriptions.

It caused an estimated $750,000 in damages; and although no one was killed, 800 people were affected by the flood. Those affected were assisted by the Board of Public Welfare, which in 1915 was a fledgling organization. The efforts of the board were fueled by generous contributions of money and provisions from Edmonton citizens.

transferred to various houses around the city, and some were sent to the Edmonton Hotel. A woman and her four young children, living in a cottage on the flats at the front of 21st Street, were rescued at 7:20 p.m. by a constable who carried each member of the family to high ground. The shack had become surrounded by water and was in danger of floating away. Another resident, dog in tow, had become marooned on the city pound barn.

Efforts were made to secure the buildings to prevent them from floating away. The Alberta Motor Boat Company's premises, near the north end of the Low Level Bridge, were secured to the bank by means of ropes. A number of houses on the river bank near the old Edmonton brewery were barely visible above the water, and others, along with a number of barns, floated downstream and crashed against the Low Level Bridge.

The flood was a spectacle that attracted "tens of thousands."

It was a sight which will live long in

Residents of Rossdale escape the flood of 1915 by canoe while others patiently wait for their turn to leave. Citizens from all parts of the city helped in the rescue operation. (COEA)

All modes of transportation could be seen on Jasper Avenue and 101st Street in 1914. Pedestrians added to the near chaos caused by horse-drawn wagons, streetcars, and automobiles. A lone policeman, lower left, is trying to direct traffic. (COEA)

United Service club. Originally arranged to coincide with the date of departure of a number of Frenchmen for the front, the declaration of war between Germany and Great Britain coming, as it did, last night, fanned the flame of loyalty to furnace heat. Britishers, Frenchmen and Russians marched shoulder to shoulder in procession through the streets, alternately singing God Save the King, the Marseillaise, and God, the All Terrible, the Russian national anthem.

As the people of Edmonton prepared to enter the Great War, they were faced with a local calamity. The flood of June 1915, the highest in the city's history, caused an estimated $2 million in property damage. The height of the flood caught the city unprepared. The Bennett School in Cloverdale and the Donald Ross School in Rossdale, which were initially designated as emergency aid centres, had to be evacuated in the face of rising water. The Low Level Bridge survived because a train of boxcars filled with sand was parked on it. Two locomotives with steam up were attached to each end to pull the cars off if the bridge appeared to be going. Fortunately there was no loss of life.

But many Edmontonians would lose their lives or limbs in "the war to end all wars." With the coming of the First World War, Edmonton's existing military units were immediately put on active service, and new soldiers were recruited at the old Dominion land titles office on 100th Avenue (Victoria). After a decade of unprecedented economic and physical growth in which Edmonton became a vital centre of government, the city was ready to take an active part in a conflict of international import.

*The gold and green foliage and the crisp blue skies of autumn frame the Edmonton skyline.
Courtesy, Edmonton Economic Development Authority*

Throngs enjoy the music, food, crafts, and activities at the 1983 Klondike Days festivities. Courtesy, Chris Bruun, Masterfile

Above: *All of the night spots feature gold rush era entertainment during Klondike Days, and the entertainment would not be complete without dancing girls. These young women are performing the ever-popular "Can-Can." (COE)*

Left: *Dressed in period costumes, this couple greets visitors during the summer at Fort Edmonton Park, where craftspeople, farmers, and merchants bring the days of the pioneer to life. Courtesy, John de Visser, Masterfile*

Right: Alberta Crest, *on the north side of Alberta Place, was painted by Edmontonian Peter Field. Courtesy, Alan Duncan*

Below: *The Shaw Building on 105th Street and 102nd Avenue has been home to these advertisements for decades. (COEA, Hubert Hollingworth Collection)*

Right: *Located just east of 97th Street on 102nd Avenue, Rosemarie Baumgartner's colourful mural conjures up fantasies of a tropical paradise, which is the perfect thought on a sub-zero Edmonton winter's day. Courtesy, Alan Duncan*

The Alberta Legislature,
the seat of provincial
government, glows on a
winter night. Courtesy,
Chris Bruun, Masterfile

The city is alight at night. The Muttart Conservatory in the foreground, with the Château Lacombe perched on the hill, and modern Edmonton rising above it. Courtesy, Egon York, Canadian Government Office of Tourism

CHAPTER V

WORLD WAR I AND THE END OF THE BOOM

1916 - 1929

World War I brought an end to Edmonton's boom-town euphoria. It came at a very critical time in Edmonton's history, since the town was in the midst of a major period of expansion. The City of Edmonton had doubled its municipal debt in 1912 in order to pay for public works such as sewers and street railway systems. But the high levels of public and private investment that had fueled the boom were now being redirected toward the war effort. Northern railway expansion was also hampered by the difficulties encountered by J.D. McCarthur in selling the bonds for his railway. Immigration into the region for the purpose of agricultural settlement also reversed somewhat as many English settlers returned home to join the army.

Once war had been declared, the 101st Edmonton Fusiliers were mobilized immediately and sent overseas. The *Bulletin* reported:

Until Saturday afternoon, a great war in Europe meant little more to Edmonton than eager perusal of the newspapers, a quickening of the pulse, high thoughts of patriotism. Saturday a

World War I commander James K. Cornwall, better known as "Peace River Jim," meditated on the shores of the Athabasca River prior to trading the serenity of the North Country for the brutality of the battlefields of Europe. He commanded the 218th Canadian Battalion. (PAA)

brief glimpse of the reverse side of the picture was shown — the farewells, the heart-aches, the breaking of home ties.

As the soldiers marched from the Fourth street armories along Jasper avenue to the station, scores of women were in the lines. These were mothers and wives and sisters and sweethearts. They all were smiling bravely . . .

By the end of the First World War, Edmonton had contributed to 14 units of the Canadian army. These units included Princess Patricia's Canadian Light Infantry, the 101st Edmonton Fusiliers, the Special Service Squadron of the 19th Alberta Dragoons, and the Third Squadron Canadian Mounted Rifles, as well as a series of numbered infantry battalions specially raised for the war. The majority of these units were recruited between January 1915 and April 1916. Among their commanding officers were such notable citizens of Edmonton and Northern Alberta as William A. Griesbach, who organized the 49th Battalion, and James K. Cornwall, who commanded the 218th Battalion. The soldiers trained at Sarcee Camp in South Alberta, and some stopped back in Edmonton before leaving for the front.

Most of the numbered battalions recruited in Edmonton were used primarily to provide reinforcements for various active service units. The only infantry battalion from Edmonton that saw active service was the 49th, which fought at Ypres, the Somme, Vimy Ridge, St. Eloi, Passchendale, and Mons. Individual members of the unit who distinguished themselves during the war included Private John Chipman Kerr and Cecil John Kinross. Kerr, a Peace River homesteader, won his Victoria Cross during the Battle of the Somme in 1915 when his attack on an enemy trench led to the capture of 62 prisoners. Kinross, who had come to Lougheed from England prior to World War I, earned his Victoria Cross in October 1916 when he single-handedly knocked out a machine gun. Regimental historian George R. Stevens described him as "strictly a frontline soldier who gloried in being there but who loathed parades." A third military hero, Danish-born Pete Anderson, had come to Canada in 1888 and arrived three years later in Edmonton where he established a brickyard. In 1914 he joined the 101st Battalion Edmonton Fusiliers and went overseas with the first Canadian contingent. He won prominence in the organization of a Canadian sniping corps that operated up and down the front lines in France. He was captured during a German offensive in 1915, but after five months' imprisonment, he escaped to his native Denmark and made his way to England. In 1918 Anderson was sent to Russia to aid the White Russian forces during the civil war. He received the Distinguished Service Order and was promoted to the rank of colonel for his exploits in France and Russia.

The most decorated member of the 49th Battalion was its commanding officer, William A. Griesbach, who rose to the rank of brigadier general by the end of the war. The son of A.H. Griesbach, who commanded "G" division of the Royal

JOHN "MIKE" MICHAELS AND THE NEWSBOY'S BAND

The Newsboy's Band personified the business career, interests, and personality of John "Mike" Michaels. Mike was a New York City newsboy. At the age of 10 he started selling newspapers under the statue of Horace Greeley at the corner of 33rd Street and 6th Avenue with his partner Red O'Leary. O'Leary developed lung trouble and decided to travel north to Edmonton to cure his condition. It was O'Leary's letters to Mike that eventually brought the two of them together again, this time in Edmonton, in 1912.

They quickly got to work setting up a newsstand business on a busy street corner. Mike wanted to have the best newsstand in all of Canada. And he did. He and O'Leary carried local, national, and international papers— they had 17 foreign-language papers. But O'Leary's condition didn't improve; he died shortly after the newsstand became successful. Mike then moved the business to 101st Street and Jasper Avenue, where he eventually created the Provincial News Company, which handled the wholesale distribution of newspapers and magazines throughout Western Canada, the Northwest Territories, and the Yukon.

During his days with the news company, Mike got together with the Edmonton *Journal* editor and managing director and in 1913 established the Edmonton Journal Newsboy's Band. The idea for the band evolved from Mike's goal to help curb juvenile delinquency among the newspaper boys. No previous musical experience was required to be a member of the band, and from many Edmonton street corners came curious newspaper boys.

In order to buy the instruments and uniforms, funds were originally raised

The Edmonton Newsboy's Band entertained thousands of visitors at the Imperial Exposition at Wembly, England, in 1924. The band attended the exposition at the invitation of His Royal Highness, the Prince of Wales. (COEA)

via flower and newspaper sales, which the boys themselves conducted. Later funds were raised by public subscription. R.A. Bullock, a 13-year veteran of the English Cavalry Band and the original musical director of the Edmonton Orchestral Society, also took an active part in the organization of the band. Ruth Michaels would later serve as associate band master and "fairy godmother of the band."

The band's first public performance was on June 13, 1914, when it provided the musical accompaniment for the departure of the Edmonton Industrial Exhibition Association delegates to Toronto. From Alex Taylor School the band paraded down Jasper Avenue to the strains of the Eureka March. Near 101st Street, the boys met the industrial association delegates and led them as far as the depot. On August 24, 1914, the band and Mike began their long association with the armed services of Edmonton and the north. On this day the band played for the departure of a 900-man contingent of the 101st Regiment Edmonton Fusiliers. It later provided the musical accompaniment for events associated with the 49th, 51st, 63rd, 138th, and 194th battalions. These units reciprocated by making donations to cover the expenses of

the band.

The newsboys' first out-of-town trip was to Buffalo, New York, to accompany a group of Edmonton and Calgary Shriners to a convention in that city in July 1916. The Al Azhar's Alberta-to-Buffalo special train, provided by the Grand Trunk Pacific Railway, left Edmonton for Buffalo on July 5 via Winnipeg, Minneapolis, St. Paul, Chicago, and Detroit. On the train with the 40-member Newsboy's Band and more than 300 Edmonton and Calgary Shriners was "Little Allie Zar," a young buffalo from Wainwright Park, and two bear cubs.

In most of the cities the band visited, it would "serenade" the mayor and the leading newspaper offices. In Buffalo, however, the newsboy musicians added an extra to their city-to-city serenade. After marching in a parade with 58,000 Shriners and 3,000 uniformed musicians, the band presented Little Allie Zar to Buffalo's mayor and then serenaded the editors

and management of the *Buffalo Daily Transcript*.

The highlight of the band's career came in 1924 when it attended the British Imperial Exposition in Wembley, England, as ambassadors of Edmonton. Funds to finance the trip were partially provided by public subscription and by Mike himself. The trip included a command performance and a concert before 35,000 people at Edmonton, England.

The band continued to perform for mayors, newspaper offices, and crowds in many cities until 1926 when Mike announced that the Newsboy's Band would no longer operate. Many of its members had joined professional orchestras in Canada and the United States, and jazz, a new type of music, was becoming popular. But Mike was not to sit still for long. Less than one week later, he created a new organization, and a total of 381 boys applied for membership. In 1927 a complete set of 101 instruments costing $7,000 was purchased through public subscription. This group, however, was disbanded in 1929 because of the

With their successful concerts at Wembly and Edmonton, England, behind them, the Edmonton Newsboy's Band boarded a ship to return home. They are seen here aboard ship, clad in their informal uniform of knit sweaters and newsboy caps. (COEA)

Depression. (The instruments were eventually used by the Edmonton School Boy's Band, which was organized in 1936.) A total of 1,800 boys had been associated with Mike's band between 1914 and 1929.

United Coal Co., Limited
Phone [illegible] 916 or 2222
"[illegible] COAL"
Uptown Office:
Ground Floor McLeod Building

The Morning Bulletin

20,776
Was the average combined circulation of The Bulletin (Daily and Semi-Weekly Editions) for the week ending Nov. 9, 1918. Get our attractive combined advertising rate.

Vol. IX, No. 169 FOURTEEN PAGES EDMONTON, ALBERTA. MONDAY, NOVEMBER 11, 1918 CITY EDITION PRICE FIVE CENTS

GERMANY ACCEPTS TERMS

THEY PRESERVE CIVILIZATION

GENERAL FOCH AND GENERAL HAIG

Tow leaders of the Allied armies.

British Cross Franco-Belgian Border--Are Almost Within Gun Range of Brussels

LONDON, Nov. 10.—The British have crossed the Franco-Belgian frontier south of the Sambre river, Field Marshal Haig reports from headquarters tonight. They have advanced four miles east of Renaix, bringing them almost within gunfire of Brussels.

WITH THE AMERICAN FORCES ON THE MEUSE FRONT, Nov. 10.—(6 p.m.)—General Pershing's troops this afternoon captured Stenay, on the east bank of the Meuse, notwithstanding terrific opposition.

French General in Sedan

WITH THE FRENCH ARMY IN FRANCE, Nov. 10.—The French General Gouraud made his official entry into Sedan at two o'clock this afternoon.

Saturday Proves a Record Day for Canvassers of Victory Loan in City--$136,107 Secured

HOW THE TEAMS STOOD AT WEEK-END

		Saturday's Report.	Total for Week.
Team No. 1.	O. R. Cameron, captain	$5,850.00	$33,150.00
Team No. 2.	A. Rodenberg, captain	6,700.00	43,600.00
Team No. 3.	Lieut.-Colonel Arnett, captain	2,550.00	22,850.00
Team No. 4.	Chas. McManus, captain	23,250.00	61,700.00
Team No. 5.	H. L. Humphries, captain	6,850.00	28,450.00
Team No. 6.	Frank Dallison, captain	3,150.00	50,605.00
Team No. 7.	W. W. Hutton, captain	7,257.00	30,407.00
Team No. 8.	Dan McDougall, captain	8,950.00	27,000.00
Team No. 9.	Fred Watson, captain	3,700.00	18,100.00
Team No. 10.	L. L. Pearce, captain	15,350.00	48,350.00
Totals for team canvassers		$83,607.00	$335,057.00
Other subscriptions not enumerated above		52,500.00	155,450.00
Totals for work of canvassers		$136,107.00	$490,507.00
Sales reported by banks		10,250.00	
Total sales in city		$146,357.00	

Last week closed in a blaze of glory for the city Victory Loan organization, the canvassers coming in with a record day's sales of $136,107, which, with $10,250 from the banks, made a grand total for the day of $146,357.

Not a small share of credit for this splendid day's work must be given to the kindly efforts of the theatre-folk from the Pantages theatre, who are laid up in the city waiting for the lifting of the ban on the theatres because of the "flu" epidemic. About twenty of the members of this organization turned out on Saturday afternoon and between entertainment and exhortation were responsible for at least $12,000 worth of bond sales during the afternoon and a proportionate amount during the evening. On a motor truck which moved from one corner to another so that there was no great crowd at any one point for any length of time, these clever and enthusiastic entertainers interested more people than have been seen on the streets since the "flu" started [illegible] produced the psychological condition which canvassers took advantage of to write applications for Victory bonds in goodly numbers and for satisfactory amounts.

Keen Race by Teams

There has been a merry race on during the past week among the different city teams for a special distinction which is to be shown the team bringing in the largest amount of applications. Teams two, four, six and ten all had apparently an even chance of winning out on the closing day Charlie McManus' team came through with a record of $23,250, and this put them well in the lead, but Frank Dallison and L. L. Pearce, who were runners-up, declare that there will be a different story on the closing day of the campaign.

Figures for Province

The province had gone close to the ten million dollar mark on Friday night, the last day for which complete figures were available, the total on that day being $9,603,850, of which the southern portion was responsible for $7,321,450, and Northern Alberta for $2,282,400. With Saturday's work it is certain that Alberta will have gone well over $10,000,000.

Reports from Country

The work in the country districts is being carried on under extreme difficulties in [illegible], the epidemic of [illegible] greatly with the [illegible]. In many districts there is a strict quarantine in force and Victory Loan workers are unable even to interview prospective buyers, while in other cases the workers then[illegible] are either victims of the disease or are working to alleviate the sufferings of others. These conditions are responsible for the failure of several of the districts to raise as much as they otherwise would have done.

Great World War Is Brought to End

Washington, Nov. 11—The world war will end this morning at 6 o'clock, Washington time, 11 o'clock, Paris time. The armistice was signed by the German representatives at midnight.

Terms of Armistice Forecast

WASHINGTON, Nov. 11.—The terms of the armtistice, it was announced, will not be made public until later. Military men here, however, regard it as certain that they include:

Immediate retirement of the German military forces from France, Belgium and Alsace-Lorraine.

Disarming and demobilization of the German armies.

Occupation by the Allied and American forces of such strategic points in Germany as will make impossible a renewal of hostilities.

Delivery of the German high seas fleet and a certain number of submarines to the Allied and American naval forces.

Disarmament of all other German warships under supervision of the Allied and American navies which will guard them.

Occupation of the principal German naval bases by sea forces of the victorious nations.

Release of Allied and American soldiers, sailors and civilians held prisoners in Germany without such reciprocal action by the associated governments.

Revolution Reaches Berlin

German Capital the Scene of Fighting on Saturday---Red Forces in Control and Order is Restored---Many Are Killed In Street Fighting.

WASHINGTON, Nov. 10.—William Hohenzollern arrived in Holland on Sunday morning and is proceeding to the town of Deistig, near Utrecht, according to a dispatch received by the American general staff Sunday from The Hague.

Copenhagen, Nov. 10—Berlin was occupied by forces of the soldiers' and workmen's council on Saturday afternoon according to a Wolf bureau report received here.

London, Nov. 10.—Severe fighting took place in Berlin between six and eight o'clock last night and a violent cannonade was heard from the heart of the city. The revolution is in full swing in Berlin and the Red forces occupy the greater part of the German capital, according to a Copenhagen dispatch to the Exchange Telegraph quoting Berlin advices sent from there at three o'clock this morning.

When revolutionary soldiers attempted to enter a building in which they supposed a number of officers were concealed shots were fired from the windows. The Reds then began shelling the building.

Many persons were killed and wounded before the officers surrendered. The Red forces are in control and have restored order. Strong guards are marching through the streets.

When the cannonade began the people thought the Reichsbank was being bombarded and thousands rushed to the square in front of the Crown Prince's palace. It was later determined that other buildings were under fire.

SEIZE CROWN PRINCE'S PALACE

London, Nov. 10—(10:14 a.m.)—The Crown Prince's palace has been seized by the revolutionists. The people are shouting "Long live the Republic!" and are singing the Marseillaise.

THE REVOLUTION SPREADS

London, Nov. 10.—Leipsic, the largest city in Saxony; Stuttgart, the capital of Wurttemburg, and Cologne and Frankfort have joined the revolution, according to reports from the Danish frontier telegraphed here by the Copenhagen correspondent of the Exchange Telegraph company. The soldiers' council at Stuggart, Cologne and Frankfort have decided to proclaim a republic.

THE STRIKE ORDER

In an extra edition of the Vorwaerts the following call for a general strike was published:

"The workmen's and soldiers' council of Berlin has decided upon a general strike. All the factories are at a standstill.

"The necessary administration of the people will be maintained. A large part of the garrison has been closed and bodies of troops and machine guns have been placed at the disposal of the workmen's and soldiers' council.

"The movement will be guided in common by the Social-Democratic party of Germany and the Independent Social-Democratic party of Germany. The workmen's and soldiers' council will take charge of the maintenance of quiet and order. Long live the Social republic!"

From all parts of the German empire news has been received regarding similar revolutions which almost everywhere remain within the bounds of economic order.

Additional news of Revolution on next page.

Announcement That Armistice Had Been Signed Was Made at Washington 2:45 This Morning

WASHINGTON, Nov. 11.—Armistice terms have been signed by Germany, the state department announced at 2:45 o'clock this morning. There was no announcement as to whether hostilities had ceased or the hour at which they would cease.

The department's announcement simply said:

"The armistice has been signed."

Made Verbally

WASHINGTON, Nov. 11.—The announcement was made verbally by an official of the state department in this form:

"The armistice has been signed. It was signed at five o'clock a.m. Paris time, and hostilities will cease at 11 o'clock this morning, Paris time."

Instructed by Wireless

WASHINGTON, Nov. 11.—There was no information as to the circumstances under which the armistice was signed, but since the German courier did not reach German military headquarters until ten o'clock yesterday morning, French time, it was generally assumed here that the German envoys within the French lines had been instructed by wireless to sign the terms.

Forty-seven hours had been required for the courier to reach German headquarters and unquestionably several hours were necessary for the examination of the terms and a decision. It was regarded as possible, however, that the decision may have been made at Berlin and instructions transmitted from there by the new German government.

War Ends at Time Foch Set

WASHINGTON, Nov. 11.—Germany had been given until 11 o'clock this morning, French time, 6 o'clock Washington time, to accept. Hostilities will end at the hour set by Marshal Foch for a decision by Germany for peace or for continuation of the war.

The momentous news that the armistice had been signed was telephoned to the White House for transmission to the President a few minutes before it was given to the newspaper correspondents. Later it was said that there would be no statement from the White House at this time.

Edmonton Celebrates Peace News With Impromptu Demonstration

Did Edmonton celebrate the news of peace?

Well, rather!

As soon as the first "flash" came into The Bulletin office over the wires, "Armistice Signed," the mayor and commissioners were notified, the men in the C. P. R. and C. N. R. shops, the Great West Flour Mills, the P. Burns Co., and others, and in a few minutes a shrieking chorus of whistles was proclaiming the glad tidings far and wide.

Bells joined in, the sirens of the fire department added to the racket, and soon, although it was 2 o'clock in the morning, a gigantic jollification was in progress. Crowds gathered as if by magic. The fact that there had been a snow storm "cut no ice" whatever. Automobiles grew up out of the ground and impromptu parades with horns blaring, bugles calling and joyous people shouting and whooping, marched up and down the streets.

Buildings were lighted, firecrackers were set off and a big bonfire at the corner of 101st St. and Jasper painted the sky red.

Telephone calls by the thousand inundated The Bulletin office and many a heartfelt "Thank God" answered the confirmatory reply. Most of them knew what the racket was for, but they wanted to be assured.

The news came through on the Canadian Press wires from Washington in just three minutes.

Quick work, eh!

A little later The Bulletin was on the streets. The papers sold like the proverbial hot cakes, people literally tearing them from the hands of the newsboys in their anxiety to get the news.

It was a memorable night in Edmonton's history.

Some enthusiast rang in a fire alarm and the rush and shriek of the apparatus added the finishing touches to the pandemonium.

Kaiser Thought Accompanied by Von Hindenburg and Crown Prince in Flight to Holland

LONDON, Nov. 11.—12:32 a. m.)—The former German Emperor's party, which is believed to include Field Marshal von Hindenburg, arrived at Eysden, on the Dutch frontier, at 7:30 o'clock Sunday morning, according to Daily Mail advices.

Practically the whole German staff accompanied the former Emperor, and ten automobiles carried the party. The automobiles were bristling with rifles and all the fugitives were armed.

The ex-Kaiser was in uniform. He alighted at the Eysden station and paced the platform, smoking a cigarette. Eysden lies about midway between Liege and Maastricht, on the Dutch border.

Crown Prince There, Too

LONDON, Nov. 10.—Both the former Emperor and his eldest son, Frederick William, crossed the Dutch frontier Sunday morning, according to advices from The Hague.

Abdication Delights Rome

ROME, Nov. 9.—News of the German Emperor's abdication was received here with great satisfaction, it being accepted as an indication that Germany will sign the armistice conditions imposed by the Allies, which, it is contended, could not have been done so long as the Emperor remained in power.

Kaiser's Flight Confirmed

LONDON, Nov. 11.—The flight of Emperor William to Holland is confirmed from several sources, but there is a divergence in reports relative to the identity of a number of his companions. A Copenhagen dispatch to Reuter's says it is semi-officially reported in Berlin that the Emperor, accompanied by ten men, has arrived at Arnheim and occupied Count von Bentinck's chateau.

Thirteen Deaths Occur in City From the Flu Sunday--Epidemic Decreasing--Only 30 New Cases

Although there were 13 deaths in Edmonton on Sunday as a result of the influenza epidemic, making a total of 25 for the 48 hours elapsing since the noon report Saturday, the situation is distinctly better and the disease is evidently decreasing.

Only 30 new cases were reported Sunday, which is a falling off of fully 50 per cent. from previous days, and the cases as a rule are of a much milder type.

Dr. Whitelaw, city medical health officer, who is himself just recovering from a seige of illness, told The Bulletin over the 'phone last night that it appeared as though about all the inhabitants of Edmonton who were susceptible to the disease had had it. A steady improvement all round was to be looked for henceforth. The peak has been passed.

It is hardly fair to charge all the dead on Sunday's and Saturday's list of fatalities to Edmonton. A number were those of patients brought in from out of town and were already in a desperate condition. One girl, for example, from Morinville, died half an hour after being brought into the city and placed in a local hospital.

The twelve deaths reported Sunday, which brings the total up to 263, were as follows:

By Connelly & McKinley:

MIRKOVITCH, MRS. ANNIE, 19, of Edmonton, died at General hospital.

ARSENEAULT, ALPHONSE, 24, of Edmonton, died at General hospital.

LAROQUE, ALPHONSE, 20, of 71st street, died at General hospital.

BRANDER, PTE. GERARD, of Wallaceburg, Ont., died at military isolation hospital.

MYSCHYNUK, MIKE, 30, of Edmonton, died at Pembina Hall hospital.

SABOURIN, MISS, 17, of Morinville. (This patient died at the General hospital 30 minutes after being admitted. She is the last of a whole family who have died of influenza and complications, except the father, who is critically ill at the same hospital.)

The body of another woman concerning whom there are no particulars available was brought to Connelly & McKinley's Sunday night.

McCoppen reports:

OBERG, CARL, died at Pembina Hall; no particulars.

GILLHOOLY, BABY, Clover Bar Road; no particulars.

NEAL, MRS., of 68th avenue, died at Pembina Hall; no further particulars.

Andrews Bros.:

STEWART, WM., returned soldier, [illegible] 11209 [illegible]th street; particulars [illegible] where in The Bulletin.

Wainwright & Jackson:

One death reported at General hospital; no particulars.

The death is also reported [illegible] General hospital on Sunday [illegible] from influenza, of:

GIHN, MRS. ADOLUNE, aged [illegible] years.

Canadian Mounted Police at Fort Saskatchewan, William had served as an alderman in Edmonton in 1906 and as its youngest mayor in 1907. He became an officer in the 19th Alberta Dragoons in 1906, rose to the rank of major, and accompanied the unit to Europe in 1914. He received the Companion of the Order of the Bath, the Companion of the Order of St. Michael and St. George, Distinguished Service Order, and the Bar of Distinguished Service Order.

Edmontonians such as Jimmy Bell, Wilfred "Wop" May, and Roy Brown also made significant contributions to the Royal Flying Corp. In his first combat action on the western front, Wop May had been pursued by the Great Red Knight Baron Richtofen. Wop's squadron leader and former school-mate, Roy Brown, had come to his assistance and shot Richtofen down. By war's end, May had 13 enemy aircraft to his credit and had been awarded the Distinguished Flying Cross.

On the home front the war effort was supported with fund-raising drives for such organizations as the Canadian Patriotic Fund and the Edmonton Board of Public Welfare. The Canadian Patriotic Fund drive was launched on September 24, 1914. The money raised was to be used "for the relief of those families in the Dominion which have been temporarily rendered fatherless by the War and also for the alleviation of the suffering that will be in evidence in the city during the winter." Public appeals were made throughout the war to replenish the fund administered by the Daughters of the Empire. Edmonton also participated in the Red Triangle Campaign, launched in May 1918 to raise funds for the YMCA's work with soldiers at the front.

With the end of the war in November 1918, Edmonton enthusiastically welcomed the soldiers home with a number of private and public receptions. One such reception was a businessmen's "at home," which was given to the returned soldiers in honour of Private Kinross at the Prince of Wales Armoury in February 1919. At this event the Edmonton business community entertained 500 soldiers. G.A. Carnes, manager of the Hudson's Bay Company stores, declared:

The boys have gallantly fought and conquered on our behalf; we at home have carried on the civilian life as citizens under conditions most trying at times, and now that the boys are returning to civilian life it is the desire of the businessmen of Edmonton to meet you, not only at the railway station, in church halls or on the street to salute and cheer you, but to get together for a quiet evening's chat that we might understand each other a little better.

This "quiet evening's chat" included four boxing matches, the presentation of a purse of gold to Private Kinross, piano selections by Leslie Grossmith, and the singing of "The Waggle of the Kilts" by Mr. Muir and of "Rule Britannia" and "Annie Laurie" by the Edmonton Male Chorus. Providing the highlight of the musical portion of the evening, Mayor Clarke whistled a solo. Refreshments consisted of sandwiches, crackers, cheese, and a foamy two-percent mixture. The Edmonton *Bulletin* reporter indicated that "it was brought in jugs and then in wash tubs but disappeared almost as fast as it could be produced. It had a very pleasant 'kick' and proved to be a most popular beverage."

This event was followed by the return home on March 22, 1919, of the entire 49th Battalion. Plans for the reception began in February 1919 with the news that the Third Division, which included the fighting 49th, had arrived in England. On February 13 a general citizens' meeting was held in the council chambers to arrange for the reception. Manager Stock of the Exhibition Board was given general charge of the arrangements. Mayor Clarke read a letter inviting every organization that could to participate in the celebration. The letter conveyed the enthusiasm and scope of the planned reception:

Edmonton's own battalion — the 49th — is expected to return to the city in a body early in March. It is the intention of the city,

district and province to give them a welcome that has never before been equalled for enthusiasm, gaity and heartfelt thanks for their safe return. Every organization in the city—fraternal, commercial, national—is asked to join in organizing a demonstration that will be remembered so long as the war is talked of.

By March 22 all was ready for the reception. The first train was expected to arrive at three o'clock in the afternoon at the

CPR station on the north side. The second train was to arrive 10 minutes later. The return of the 49th had special significance since it was the first Western Canadian battalion to return home as a unit. Consequently, Winnipeg had also planned to welcome the battalion home. The troops were supposed to reach there at noon for a big reception, but the two troop trains carrying the battalion passed through the city at about five o'clock in the morning.

But the train stopped in Edmonton on schedule. The sound of the whistle:

ran electrically through the crowded thousands from mouth to mouth down the avenue and communicated with the throng way downtown to whom the whistle was inaudible.

The school boys massed on Jasper west of the subway started cheering and it was immediately taken up as the long line of coaches upon each of which was chalked in bold letters the crest of the 49th, and the names of the battles in which the battalion had fought, Ypres, St. Eloi, The Somme, Bourlon, Passchendale, Cambrai, Mons; the whole glorious list of them rolled in. "Hail, Hail the Gang's all Here" played the news boys band.

From every window helmeted heads were thrust and clustered like bees on the platforms between the cars. Admission to the station premises had been by special ticket to the next-of-kin and to the representatives of the province and of the city and before the train had stopped there was a rush to the cars, frantic handshaking throught the windows, joyful greetings, blown kisses.

"There's Harry! Oh Hare. e-e-e-e!"

"Hullo, Daddy, here we are! Look there's Daddy!"

"Oh, Boy ain't it great to be back!"

"Hi, Bill old scout how are you?"

"Put 'er there, old fell!"

"My boy, my boy, oh thank God."

It was an undescribable frenzy of emotions, of sobs, of shouts, of yells, of cheers, of excitement.

Eighteen years after the last shot of World War I was fired the money was found to erect the cenotaph in 1936. Originally located behind the Edmonton Journal *building between 101st and 102nd streets on 100th Avenue, it was moved in 1978 to a more prominent site directly in front of city hall. (PAA, A. Blyth Collection)*

Officers sprang out, slim-legged, helmeted, business looking. Real soldiers just like the pictures. There were more hand-shaking, more greetings.

After the arrival of the trains, a triumphant parade travelled through the principal streets of the city, ending up at the Legislature where the provincial authorities planned to hold their reception. The evening celebrations included a banquet and smoker and general reception at the armouries with the 49ers and their dependents as the guests of the city.

Memorial Hall was constructed in 1920 with funds provided by the public and the provincial government as a permanent monument to the efforts of the soldiers. Prominent Edmonton businessman H.M.E. Evans played an important role in

W.F. "DEACON" WHITE

Deacon White arrived in Edmonton in August 1906 as the playing manager of a touring baseball team from Anacortes, Washington. Shortly after he arrived, White wrote a letter to the sports editor of the *Winnipeg Free Press*. In it he explained how he happened to travel to Edmonton and why he chose to stay.

I took the Fargo team through to the coast last fall on the Northern Pacific, remained in Seattle over winter, played with Spokane in the Northwestern League for two months until I received a "charley horse," went from there to Anacortes, Washington, managed the ball team there, and just recently took them on a long trip to Calgary and Edmonton, over one thousand miles. The country and climate about Edmonton has pleased me so much that I have cast my fortunes with Edmonton for the rest of the season and will locate here permanently.

But it wasn't just the "country and climate about Edmonton" that attracted White. He was also attracted by the various professional players on the Edmonton baseball team, particularly Wild Bill Setley. He indicated to the *Winnipeg Free Press* that "the climate has put new life into the old timer Setley and his great speed on his feet has come back so that it is nothing unusual to see him take a long sprint and make one of his famous catches behind his back."

With the conclusion of the 1906 baseball season, Deacon played a major role in the formation of the Western Canada Baseball League. He was subsequently hired to coach the Edmonton team, which he did until 1914 when the league disbanded because of the war.

White's sports interests during these pre-World War I years also included football. In 1911 he became the coach of the Edmonton Eskimos Rugby Club. This club participated in the Big Four Rugby Association, which also included a team from the University of Alberta and the Tigers and Roughriders from Calgary. The 1913 season culminated in a final game between the Eskimos and the Tigers on October 20.

This afternoon at three o'clock the championship game in the Big Four Rugby league series will be played at Diamond Park. The game is an annual affair but this is the first time that the deciding game has been played in Edmonton. This year also the Edmonton team is stronger than in any previous season and is opposed by a team that is correspondingly stronger than last year. The battle should be a red hot one.

The players are ready for the battle. If they win it means a playoff at Red Deer and ultimately a game or two for the championship of Western Canada and possibly a chance against the eastern teams for the Dominion title.

The Eskimos won 13 to 12. The victory took the team to Red Deer, where in an equally hard-fought game the Eskimos also won by one point.

White's interest in challenging an Eastern team for a national championship was deferred, however, to the 1921 season, which began with a 72-2 victory for the Eskimos over the Calgary Tigers. Joe Price, the coach of the Tigers, reportedly

Deacon White, back row, second from left, is seen here with the 1922 Edmonton Eskimos. They were the Western Canadian Champions that year. The uniforms, especially the amount of protective gear, have changed considerably since these early days. (COEA)

conceded, "The Eskimos are the best team I have ever seen in Western Canada." A Calgary sports columnist, also impressed by Deacon's team, described it as the "greatest galaxy of rip roaring, bronco-busting, line plungers the west ever had the pleasure of witnessing." The Eskimos completed the season undefeated, scoring a record 143 points, with only 5 going to their opponents combined.

On November 14, "Deacon White and his Tribe of Igloo Dwellers" arrived in Winnipeg to play the Victorias for the Western championship. The report in the *Bulletin* indicated that the Eskimos were impressive during the practice before the final game.

After seeing the Eskimos in a workout on Saturday evening, Winnipeg team admits that they are a formidable aggregation and that possibly the Victorias may have to extend themselves to win. Even such an admission from Winnipeg is something.

The practice was conducted on a snow-covered field where "they produced their ghost ball and considerably amazed the Winnipegers by going through a snappy workout in darkness and did it without a fumble or miscue." Deacon's preparations led them to victory over Winnipeg the following day by a score of 16 to 6.

Upon the team's return to Edmonton, plans were immediately started for a trip east. On November 18, 1921, it became official. The Eskimos were going to play the undefeated Eastern team, the Toronto Argonauts. The Eskimos travelled east that December, met the Toronto Argonauts, and lost miserably. The Eskimos lost to the Argonauts again the next season. As a result, White took his team back home, and the Eskimos did not play again in the national East-meets-West finals for 30 years.

organizing the fund-raising campaign for the hall, which was built for the use of the Edmonton branch of the Great War Veterans Association. In 1929 the site for the construction of a cenotaph to commemorate Edmonton's slain servicemen was acquired, but the monument was not constructed until 1936 because of lack of funds. Originally located on the north bank of the Saskatchewan River near the Journal Building, the cenotaph commemorating Edmonton's 3,000 war dead was unveiled on August 13, 1936, by His Excellency Lord Tweedsmuir, Governor-General of Canada. It was constructed with 65 tons of grey granite from British Columbia. A highly decorated sarcophagus at the front of the cenotaph symbolizes the Tomb of the Unknown Soldier and is supported by three lions emblematic of the Empire. In 1978 the cenotaph was moved to a more prominent location in front of the city hall, and a reference to the Korean War was added to it in 1983.

In 1918 Edmonton's joy at the return of its soldiers from overseas was dampened by the outbreak of an influenza epidemic. Influenza was first reported in Edmonton about October 11 of that year. In an effort to prevent the rapid spread of the disease, on October 18 the City Board of Health ordered the closing of all schools, churches, theatres, picture shows, and public meetings. On October 25 the Provincial Board of Health passed a resolution ordering every person in the Province of Alberta to wear a mask outside his or her home and to only partially remove the mask for the purpose of eating. This mandatory requirement remained in force until November 23 when it was made optional, after which practically no masks were worn except in hospitals. The city police were also ordered to strictly enforce the no-spitting ordinance.

By October 19 forty-one cases of influenza had been reported, and incidence of the disease was rising rapidly. On October 21 an additional 100 cases were reported. Edmonton's regular hospitals were soon overcrowded, and other buildings, such as Athabasca Hall at the University of Alberta, were used. On October 26 the Board of Health adopted an emergency plan to divide the city into districts, with a graduate nurse assigned to each district to supervise volunteer workers. By the end of November 1918 the crisis had passed; there had been a total of 456 influenza-related deaths in Edmonton in a two-month period.

The influenza epidemic was, however, only one indication that postwar Edmonton would not immediately return to pre-1914 normality. World War I had brought success to the proponents of Prohibition. They had campaigned for the imposition of Prohibition since the 1890s but had only met with success when it was imposed as a war measure in 1916, supposedly to improve the efficiency of the war effort. With the end of the war, the original justification for Prohibition disappeared, and anti-Prohibition forces began to call for its repeal. Efforts to maintain Prohibition after the war fell to such organizations as the Alberta Social Service League and the Women's Christian Temperance Union. In January 1919 the meeting of the general executive of the Edmonton branch of the WCTU requested that the local chief of police be replaced and the whole police force be reorganized for the purpose of better enforcing the liquor regulations. These regulations permitted the distribution of liquor only by a drugstore, and then only to fill a prescription from a doctor. In March 1919 the Edmonton *Bulletin* reported that a record total of 214,999 ounces had been sold by Edmonton drugstores in the previous month. This statistic led the paper to conclude that "a great number of doctors in the city and immediate district prescribed with considerable regularity." One doctor in St. Albert wrote 212 prescriptions for one drugstore alone. The most popular liquor for medicinal purposes was whisky, the total quantity prescribed reaching 103,719 ounces. Brandy was a far second at 10,351 ounces.

The effort to extend Prohibition ultimately proved futile. In November 1923 the Alberta Liquor Control Act was passed, ending Prohibition. During the referendum campaign the Edmonton Prohibition Publicity Committee argued that maintaining Prohibition would lead to "a still further

The Women's Christian Temperance Union was the prime mover behind the Prohibition movement of the teens and 1920s. Its successful campaigns led to a win for the "Drys" in 1915 and again in 1920. In 1915 the WCTU led a parade of 12,000 people, the largest demonstration of any kind in Edmonton to that date. (COEA)

reduction in crime, more money available for the necessaries of life, happier homes, better opportunities for the children and a higher standard in public life." The anti-Prohibition forces, led by the Edmonton branch of the Moderation League, included such prominent citizens as W.A. and Janet Griesbach, Senator J.L. Cote, and former mayors William Short and Joe Clarke. This group exhorted the people to vote down Prohibition and "Make Alberta Safe for Democracy and a Good Place to Live."

Post-World War I reform movements in Edmonton attracted many women, among them Emily Murphy. She was in a particularly good position to address the need for reform by virtue of her post as a police magistrate. She had arrived in Edmonton in 1907 with her husband, the Reverend Arthur Murphy, an Anglican minister. In 1910 she inaugurated the establishment of the Victorian Order of Nurses in Edmonton, and from 1919 to 1921 she served as the first president of the Federated Women's Institute of Canada. From 1916 to 1931 Emily Murphy was a police magistrate for the Province of Alberta, the first woman in the British Empire to hold that position. She was also active in the National Council of

On November 5, 1923, Albertans voted to resume the legal sale of alcohol. The ballot presented voters with four choices: "A" Prohibition, "B" Licensed sale of beer, "C" Government-only sale of beer, or "D" Government sale of all liquors plus licensed sale of beer. The majority overwhelmingly voted for "D." (COEA)

Women, the Social Service Council of Canada, the Canadian Association of Child Protection Officers, and the Canadian Council of Child Welfare. In addition to her political activities, she was also a noted author. Books published under her pen name, Janey Canuck, included *Janey Canuck in the West, Open Trails, Seeds of Pine,* and *The Black Candle,* which deals with the drug problem in Canada and the United States.

Emily Murphy bravely challenged the discriminatory provisions with respect to women of the BNA Act. In 1922 she was nominated by the Montreal Women's Press Club for the Canadian Senate. The Senate, however, refused the application on the grounds that under the BNA Act women were not persons for "rights and privileges," but only for "pains and penalties." Through her efforts and the help of four other Alberta women, the Privy Council in London ruled that women were persons in Canada and could hold a seat in the Senate. Long-term effects of her activism involved passage of the Dower Act of 1911, which provided that a wife was

entitled to a third of her husband's estate during his lifetime and after his death, even if he left no will. She also undertook a pioneering study of drug addiction that lead to the passage of the Patent Medicine Act of 1919, which banned the use of opium and its derivatives from being used in patent medicines.

While the debate over social issues raged, economic problems developed, such as the collapse of the real-estate boom, the relatively slow recovery in the construction industry, and unemployment. As W.A. Griesbach wrote to Prime Minister Robert Borden:

I am inclined to think that the Government should begin to consider very seriously the situation which will prevail during the coming winter. A great many men will be out of employment, particularly returned soldiers. It is desirable that this element shall not be in a state of discontent beyond reasonable limits as this element constitutes at the moment a very loyal and vociferous block in the public opinion of this country.

Newspaper announcements advertising new subdivisions as guaranteed investments were replaced by notices of land tax sales by the City of Edmonton. The largest of these sales took place in 1917 when the city sold 44,348 lots. The real-estate collapse meant the financial ruin of Edmonton businessmen like W.J. Magrath, who had promoted the development of the Highlands subdivision before the war. In the majority of cases, the subdivisions were totally cancelled or were used for gardening. On May 10, 1919, the Edmonton *Bulletin* reported, "The Edmonton Horticultural and Vacant Lot Garden Association are doing their best again this year." In 1918 the association allocated 3,000 lots to about 4,000 individuals.

The abrupt decline in land speculation was matched by the more positive influence of the Edmonton Federation of Community Leagues. Individual community leagues had been established as early as 1917 when the 142nd Street District

Prior to the demonstration, organizers direct their allies into formation, passing out signs proclaiming "Our Aim A Clean City" and "Vote Yes" for Prohibition. Despite their splendid organizational skills, their cause would eventually be lost in the third and last vote taken on Prohibition in 1923. (COEA)

Community League was organized. This league succeeded in having a somewhat poorly built school razed to the ground and a new school built in its place. By November 1920 a total of eight community leagues had been created. This situation prompted A.E. Ottewell, director of the Department of Extension at the University of Alberta, to suggest that a central organization be created. This suggestion led to a meeting on January 24, 1921, when the Edmonton Federation of Community Leagues was established. This development was endorsed by Mayor Duggan, who felt that the organization could voice opinions on general matters such as taxation.

Efforts to solve the economic problems brought a new emphasis on the development of Northern Alberta. The war had interrupted the development of transportation systems into the region. The Edmonton, Dunvegan & British Columbia Railway, which had been completed to Grande Prairie in 1916, was inoperative by the spring of 1920. The railway was in such poor condition that it was difficult if not impossible for settlers to travel into the Peace River Country or for established farmers to ship grain out. The Province of Alberta acquired the railway in 1920 and began a program to rehabilitate this crucial link to the north. The rehabilitation and extension of the railway network in Northern Alberta brought in new settlers and opened up new land for agricultural use. Between 1920 and 1930 the Peace River Country emerged as Alberta's last agricultural frontier. The Soldier Settlement Board provided soldiers with relatively cheap land and cattle and thus promoted the agricultural development of the region.

Northern development after World War I had the advantage of a new technology — air transportation, which assisted northern mineral exploration. Edmonton's association with airplanes had begun as early as Labour Day, 1909, when Reginald Hunt flew the first plane in Western Canada. Reginal Hunt was a carpenter by trade who had worked on his "gasoline bird" for three years prior to this flight. During those years he concentrated on the design of a proper wing, motor, and propeller. On the morning of the flight, finishing touches were made. According to an Edmonton *Journal* reporter, the propeller "was a fan-like affair similar to those used to keep flies from sleeping in restaurants."

In the afternoon about two o'clock Hunt . . . seated himself in the machine and set the motor in motion. The propellers commenced to rotate, at first slowly, and then at terrific speed. Hunt's heart stood still. Would it fly?

The exciting moments of suspense were not long. The machine rose slowly at first, barely cleared a few buildings, then gaining momentum soared high.

After remaining in the air for about 35 minutes during which time he flew over the neighbourhood at a height ranging from 35 to 50 feet above the housetops, the investor descended to earth triumphant conqueror of the air.

Hunt continued to pursue his interest in flying until 1910 when he crashed while attempting a turning manoeuvre. Hunt walked away from the wrecked plane and left Edmonton for Athabasca Landing soon after.

Edmonton got its first good look at an airplane in April 1911 when Hugh Robinson and Bob St. Henry "went aloft in one of the $5,000 high speed atmospheric boats." The demon-

Radio came to Edmonton on May 1, 1922, when Mayor D.M. Duggan, M.L.A., spoke the first words officially broadcasted by CJCA. The station, owned and operated by Dr. G.R.A. (Dick) Rice, was located in the Edmonton Journal *Building. Hubert and Lillian Hollingworth listened to CJCA on a battery-operated tube radio. Most Edmontonians listened on a three-dollar crystal set, which they assembled themselves. (COEA, Hubert Hollingworth Collection)*

stration of powered flight took place at the Exhibition Grounds as thousands of people watched. Mayor Armstrong declined the opportunity to take a ride in the airship, and an anonymous letter to St. Henry asked the aviator to "bring down the members of the Council who were somewhere up in the air." Katherine Stinson, who performed at the 1916, 1917, and 1918 exhibitions, maintained the barnstorming tradition. During her last appearance, on July 10, 1918, she carried the first air mail from Calgary to Edmonton.

The development of commercial aviation awaited the end of the war and the return of Wop May and Jimmy Bell. Their arrival in Edmonton coincided with the arrival of a Curtiss JN 4 or "Jenny," which Montreal real-estate promoter James Carruthers gave to the city. With this plane, Wop May began Edmonton's first commercial airplane company. On May 17, 1919, the Edmonton *Bulletin* announced the creation of May Airplanes Limited. One of its first jobs was the delivery of the noon edition of the Edmonton *Journal* to Wetaskiwin. Lack of business, however, forced May into the barnstorming business. After a lull in the early 1920s, "airmindedness" returned to Edmonton with the creation of Canada's first municipal air harbour, Blatchford Field, out of a portion of the HBC Reserve and the formation of the Edmonton and Northern Alberta Aero Club in October 1927. The decade ended with Wop May's famous mercy flight to Fort Vermilion with diptheria vaccine, which prevented an epidemic.

During the period from 1910 to 1929 Edmonton was concerned with dealing with the social and economic problems that had been created by the previous boom. It had taken its first tentative steps toward the creation of a public welfare system through the Board of Public Welfare. The Federation of Community Leagues had replaced the subdivision promoter as an influence on civic policy. The portents of economic disaster evident during the war and the early 1920s had been swept away in the face of a revitalized agriculture. The recovery in the late 1920s, however, was only a temporary return to the boom-town conditions of the prewar era.

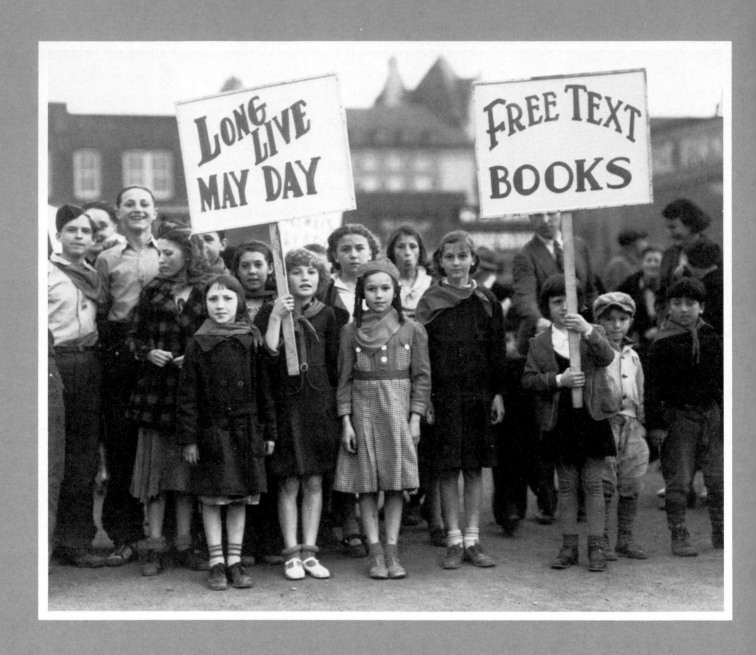

CHAPTER VI

DEPRESSION
AND
PROTEST
1930 - 1939

Signs of prosperity blunted the immediate impact of the October 1929 New York Stock Exchange crash. A Canadian Press story carried in the Edmonton *Bulletin* on November 19, 1929, described how "bull forces which had controlled the wheat market for several days took a strong grip today as they hoisted values 1¾¢ to 2¼¢ higher than yesterday's close." The newspapers also announced that "Oil prices zoom as crowds throng brokerage houses." Land filings at the Dominion Land Office during 1929 reached a new high, demonstrating the continued expansion of Edmonton's northern agricultural frontier. The Edmonton real-estate market also appeared to be recovering after 15 years of relative inactivity. On January 18, 1930, "the first big real estate deal in Edmonton city property this year and the first for some time was consummated Friday afternoon" when the Fairbairn Apartments were purchased for $60,000. The collection of a record amount of taxes in Edmonton boosted the relatively healthy financial position of the city, and the city-operated power plant made a profit of $295,333 during 1929 despite a drop from eight cents to five cents in the unit rate per kilowatt hour. The Province of

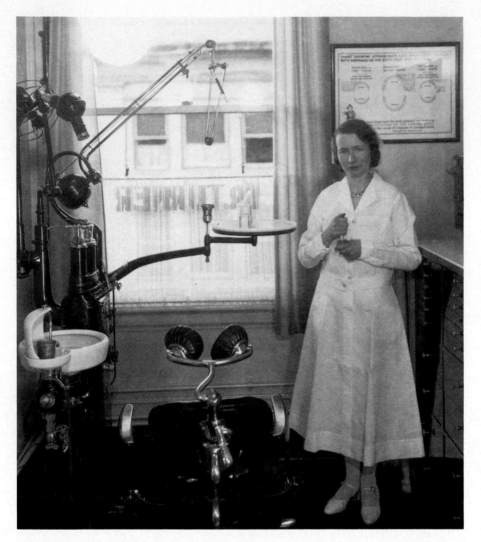

Left: *Dr. W.J. Turner's office was furnished with the latest dental equipment in 1932. The pain involved in a visit to the dentist in the 1930s was reduced by the use of nitrous oxide, or as it was commonly known, laughing gas. Edna Pollard (née Wilson) was his assistant. (COEA, Hubert Hollingworth Collection)*

Alberta anticipated that good economic times would result from the transfer of the natural resources from the federal government to the province. The Edmonton construction firm of H.G. Macdonald was awarded the contract for the construction of the new provincial Natural Resources Building. The provincial railway policy also seemed to be bearing fruit: the government-operated Edmonton, Dunvegan & British Columbia Railway showed a profit of $185,984.

But with the dawning of the new decade came ominous signs of depression. In January 1930 a Winnipeg paper reported a drastic drop in the wheat price:

The wheat market today stumbled over a swelling pile of unloading orders, righted itself momentarily and then plunged to

The drought and falling crop prices combined to defeat many farmers at the start of the Depression. (PAA)

the depths in the most surprising show of weakness since the new year. Values were down 3½¢ to 2½¢ a bushel at the close, and it was all attributed to a statement by Governor McKelvie of the United States Farm Board to farmers of Kansas State.

McKelvie warned farmers that crop prospects were good for 1930 and that, although the Board had fixed a price of $1.35 a bushel for Minneapolis wheat, it applied only to the present crop and the price to be paid on the new crop could not be fixed until the crop was made. As Chicago reacted bearishly to the McKelvie statement, Winnipeg followed suit. Prices sagged about 1½¢ in the early part of the session and slumped the rest of the way as support failed to materialize near the finish.

The Edmonton price for Number 1 Northern Wheat fell from 111 cents in January 1930 to 34 cents in January 1931. Other grains fell in a similar dramatic fashion, with oats and barley going to 13 and 11 cents respectively. By December 20, 1932, Number 1 Northern Wheat sold for 23.5 cents a bushel, oats for 10 cents, and barley 12.5 cents. Edmonton grain prices would not regain their 1930 levels until 1937.

The effects of the price collapse were registered in the farming area around Edmonton. In May 1931 a slight

In 1935 this farmer surveyed his drought- and wind-ravaged crops. Edmonton farmers would not begin to recover until 1937. (PAA)

reduction in grain acreage throughout the northern part of the province was reported, with many farmers going more extensively into mixed farming. Also, throughout Northern Alberta farmers were reportedly dispensing with extra help and doing the spring work themselves. The most telling sign of the state of the agricultural economy was the increased sale of horse harness. In May 1931 the Edmonton *Bulletin* reported:

There is evidence that farm operators are dispensing with tractors and all power plowing and breaking in favor of horse power again. S.D. Johnston, manager of the Great West Saddlery company, states that "More cash orders have been received from farmers for harness this year than any year since the fad for power farming hit the country. This year has seen an increase of harness orders of over 60 per cent on last year which is a very satisfactory condition when you consider how hard the farmers have been hit by the price of wheat."

Building activity in Edmonton followed the declining trend of grain prices in the early 1930s. The total value of building permits fell from a high of $5.67 million in 1929 to $4.3 million in 1930 and then to a low of $428,000 in 1933. From 1933 to 1937 the figure rose slowly to $865,000, and in 1938 it increased to $2.8 million. The only major construction projects undertaken between the completion of the Birks

In 1929 the City of Edmonton incorporated the idea of working for relief during the Depression. Unemployed people could do necessary city work in return for a cash relief payment or for the reduction of taxes owed on property located in the city limits. (COEA, Hubert Hollingworth Collection)

Building and the new Natural Resources Building in 1930 and the construction of a new plant by Canada Packers in 1936 was the new Masonic Hall, which opened officially in June 1931.

The declining economy and rise in unemployment sparked demonstrations throughout the country. On New Year's Eve 1929, about 100 single men staged the first march of unemployed in Edmonton. They marched to the city hall and demanded to work New Year's Day in order to earn a dollar for food. City officials readily agreed, and the men were all at work on Wednesday clearing brush out of the various city parks and ravines. On January 2, 1930, seven hundred and fifty unemployed men were registered at the special office

1937 May Day parade participants get ready to display their support of Dr. Norman Bethune, a Canadian medical doctor who left Canada to work for the democratic forces in the Spanish Civil War. In 1939 Dr. Bethune died in China while assisting the army of Mao Tse-tung. (COEA, Hubert Hollingworth Collection)

opened by the provincial government for work clearing brush. On January 9 the federal government announced that it would contribute to the make-work projects by permitting the razing of the buildings on the old penitentiary site. This was expected to "prove of great benefit towards ameliorating the acute unemployment situation which exists in the city at the present time as upwards of 200 men can be employed on the job for a couple of weeks." However, the federal government was unable to evict the tenant of the building, the Big Four Moving Company, and the project failed to materialize.

The precipitous rise in unemployment and the social dislocation caused by the Depression placed an enormous financial burden on the city, which felt the initial impact of unemployment to a greater degree than either the provincial or federal governments. Initially the City Council faced these burdens with a united front. As Mayor Douglas explained at its

January 13, 1930, meeting:

We are spending more money on relief than ever before in the city's history. If we take on these additional 100 men, we would have to pay out $600 a day. . . . We are endeavoring to prevent starvation and privation. We must continue to give relief and we must afford it. We cannot allow our people to starve, even if it means an increase in the tax rate.

As world tensions mounted, Canadian political parties adopted peace planks as part of their official platforms. The youth wing of the Co-operative Commonwealth Federation, forerunner of the New Democratic Party, gathered in 1937 around a decorated truck expressing the goals of their party. (COEA, Hubert Hollingworth Collection)

This approach brought praise from a number of community groups, including the Edmonton Trades and Labour Council.

The city's relief program, in addition to costing the city money, was also holding up a number of public works projects, such as the bridge replacement at Connors Road. As Assistant City Engineer R.J. Gibb explained:

Regular employees of the City who might be engaged on such work are compelled to act as straw bosses in charge of brushing gangs. Gangs number about 35 or 40 men each at present and with some 800 men employed it can be seen that a large number

of bosses and straw bosses are required to supervise operations.

Despite various conferences, the unemployment problem grew. By January 1931 City Relief Officer Thomas Magee reported that a total of 5,171 men were registered as unemployed in the city. This represented an increase of 361 over the previous week and 544 over the week before that.

The size of the problem and the lack of assistance from the federal government made the municipal and provincial authorities increasingly nervous. In January 1932 Mayor Douglas prohibited the unemployed from demonstrating in parades. When presented with a petition condemning this action and when accused by Alderman C.L. Gibbs of discriminating against the unemployed, the mayor indicated that he had been requested to do so by "Premier Brownlee, the Superintendent of the Provincial Police and others."

The debate on the parade issue broke the City Council's unanimity as its members argued about the importance or relevance of "communist" influence in the unrest. The provincial government's preoccupation with communists dated as far back as May 1924 when an undercover agent, Detective Lesley of the Alberta Provincial Police, attended a meeting organized by the Communist Party of Canada at the Rialto Theatre. The concerns of the Alberta Provincial Police increased in 1925 when an estimated 1,000 people took part in Edmonton's May Day parade. On the advice of Commissioner Bryon, the Department of National Defence increased its military guard around the armouries in Edmonton on the day of the parade.

By May 1931 delegations of the unemployed were bringing the problems of the Depression directly to the City Council. At the May 5 meeting, the delegation met Mayor Douglas on his arrival at the city hall entrance and, after hearing their arguments, he allowed the men a few minutes to present their case to the council. The city hall was closely guarded during council meeting, and uniformed police escorted the delegation to the council chamber. This delegation precipitated a debate

Below: During the Depression The Daily Clarion, *a labour-oriented paper, presented what it thought was a more accurate interpretation of news events and analysis of the country's economic troubles than was available in the traditional press. (COEA, Hubert Hollingworth Collection)*

Above: *Thousands of militant labourites parade up 101st Street and turn west onto Jasper Avenue in support of unionized workers, peace, freedom, and democracy. This orderly demonstration, unlike those of the early 1930s, was free of violence and confrontation. (COEA, Hubert Hollingworth Collection)*

between Alderman C.L. Gibbs and J.T.J. Collisson over the "question whether men of the type of the unemployed had contributed anything to the up building of the community." Answering in the affirmative, one member of the delegation said he had been in Canada since 1904. The council indicated that many of the demands were beyond the power of the municipal government but did indicate that "something might be done to supplement the meals of porridge."

Other delegations followed. On May 27 two delegations of unemployed came before the council to ask for better housing and feeding.

Council was told of dozens of young men sleeping at night on the cold floor of the lavatory in the immigration hall for want of something better. Every night now witnesses holes in the river bank peopled by these homeless men who creep into anything that promises any sort of shelter from the weather. By day they are staving off the pangs of hunger with bowls of porridge and seeking a little variation by begging from house to house.

The unemployed involved a number of organizations in their parades and delegations to the municipal and provincial governments, including the United Empire Loyalists, the Unemployed Ex-Servicemen's Association, and the Communist Party. Parades began to increase in frequency in the spring of 1931. A crowd of approximately 1,500 gathered in the market square at around 6:15 p.m. for the May Day parade and, after a preliminary series of speeches, formed a column of fours and marched through the centre of the city "flaunting red banners bearing radical slogans." The Edmonton *Bulletin* also observed that "some 60 women and children well dressed were in the parade and many of the marchers wore red rosettes peddled by hawkers." The May Day parade was followed by a parade on May 20 organized by the Unemployed Ex-Servicemen's Association. Members of the association formed up at market square at two o'clock and then marched to the Legislature to present a letter setting forth

Elected M.L.A. in 1921 on the United Farmers of Alberta ticket, John E. Brownlee was appointed Attorney General in the same year. He became Premier of Alberta in 1925, and in 1929 he managed the transfer of ownership of Alberta's natural resources from Ottawa to Alberta. He was forced to resign as Premier in 1934 amidst personal scandal; a government typist won a civil suit charging him with seduction. The scandal and his perceived inability to respond positively to the worsening economy aided the Social Credit movement sweep of 1935. (PAA)

their situation to the Honourable J.E. Brownlee and members of the cabinet.

In May 1931 the city opened a porridge kitchen for single unemployed men. The kitchen was located in the old immigration hall and was to serve as a substitute for meal and bed tickets. The porridge was provided in unlimited quantities, and an average of 2,500 bowls were served daily. This kitchen remained operative until 1938.

But porridge kitchens and similar kinds of short-term relief were only stop-gap measures that could not hold off the developing crisis. On June 11, 1931, the Edmonton *Bulletin* announced that "workless men were invading the city." An estimated 1,000 unemployed drifters had "blown" into the city in the past week, the majority via freight train. The machinery set up by the city to deal with the distribution of relief could not handle the volume of requests, and the registration of those requesting relief could not be processed fast enough by the officials at the relief centre in the Canada Dry Building. On the afternoon of June 10, an estimated 800 unemployed "stormed" city hall in search of immediate assistance. They were persuaded to leave by Mayor Douglas who said that their request would receive attention from the council's unemployment and relief committee, which he had created to advise the council and to deal with the increasing number of delegations. After the demonstrators' departure a squad of city police guarded the entrance to the Civic Block with a fire hose at the ready. The committee decided to issue food and bed tickets immediately and waive the registration procedure in order to defuse the situation.

The events of June 10 and 11 resulted in a meeting of Premier J.E. Brownlee, Mayor Douglas, Commissioner Mitchell, Alderman Collisson, and City Relief Officer Thomas Magee to discuss the situation. In the view of Premier Brownlee and Mayor Douglas, "certain unemployed under the leadership of Communist leaders are getting out of hand." Immediately following this meeting, Premier Brownlee requested military assistance. The press coverage of the arrival of the troops reflected the "Red Scare" created by Brownlee.

Helmeted horsemen made ready to cope with the rising tide of red in Edmonton as khaki clad cavalry, four officers and 59 men of the Strathcona horse de-trained from a special train from Calgary at the CPR station at 6 a.m. on Saturday and rode through the city to quarters at the Prince of Wales armouries.

A less panicky response to the situation was made by the Edmonton Trades and Labour Council, which organized a coalition of community groups to deal with the problem. The coalition had representatives from the local Council of Women, Women's Labour Council, Public School Board, Canadian Legion, Civil Servants Association, Red Cross, Edmonton Diocese of the Roman Catholic Church, Ministerial Association, Chamber of Commerce, Hope Mission, Federation of Community Leagues, and the Alberta Federation of Labour. On June 26, 1931, the coalition elected an executive committee to ensure a greater degree of cooperation between the city and private relief agencies.

Following the crisis of June 1931, the protest movement was more specifically directed toward the provincial government. Edmonton thus became the scene for a protest movement organized on a province-wide basis. One such protest was the hunger march of December 1932 organized by the Farmers Unity League. Following the format of other similar events, the marchers were to gather in market square and then proceed from there to the Legislative Building where a delegation would be sent to meet with Premier Brownlee. Since farmers and unemployed workers were expected from all over the province, the League made arrangements in advance for their billeting and feeding. People from the surrounding rural area provided the marchers with beef, turkeys, potatoes, turnips, flour, milk, cream, and butter in large quantities.

The protest, however, ran into problems almost immediately when Premier Brownlee, after meeting with Chief

After the election of Social Credit in 1935, the government issued scrip which became known as "funny money." Many merchants refused to accept the scrip, but the Army & Navy stores posted signs to welcome customers wanting to spend Social Credit currency. (COEA)

Constable Shute and Mayor Knott, turned down the application for a parade permit. Despite efforts by the Royal Canadian Mounted Police to stop people from coming to Edmonton, delegations of farmers arrived from the agricultural districts to the north, miners came from Drumheller and the Coal Branch, and unemployed workers came from Calgary and Lethbridge. By 2:30 p.m. on December 20, 1932, an estimated crowd of 13,000 people had gathered at the market square. They were opposed by the city police and the RCMP, which had been reinforced by 150 constables from Regina. Thirty policemen were stationed inside the market square, machine guns were placed on the top of the post office, and merchants along the route were ordered to clear their displays from their windows. As soon as the march began, it was broken up, and 30 members of the League were later arrested for being members of an unlawful assembly. Several were sentenced to terms of six months and three months, but the cases against the majority were dismissed. Six delegates were later able to meet Brownlee.

The protest movement of the early 1930s culminated with the defeat of the Brownlee government by William Aberhart and the Social Credit movement in the 1935 provincial election. Edmonton's enthusiasm for the new administration was somewhat dampened by its new Press Bill, which was attacked in a Pulitzer Prize-winning editorial by the Edmonton *Journal.* Edmonton was one of the few places in Alberta that initially resisted the Social Credit landslide. In the 1935 election only two out of a possible six Social Credit members of the Legislative Assembly were elected in Edmonton.

Adding to the strain of unemployment, the city's finances suffered other setbacks during the Depression. The value of tax arrears increased from $465,113 in 1929 to $1,225,215 in 1934, forcing the city to pay a portion of its employees' wages in civic bonds. The overall response of the city was one of retrenchment. This mood was set as early as January 1931 when "Thrift Day" was declared for January 21. On this day the Edmonton *Bulletin* urged every firm and resident

to observe the fundamental principles of thrift, the sensible expenditure of cash. Business distress at this time makes Thrift Day singularly appropriate and many business and financial houses in the city are entering the campaign with thrift as their watchword for the day.

Thrift Day coincided with Life Insurance Day with the result that the various insurance companies also promoted the idea of systematic savings. The tactic of retrenchment also affected the Edmonton Public School Board. In June 1913 ratepayers defeated the school board's proposal to build four new schools at an estimated cost of $783,000. With the defeat of the new school-building program, the chairman of the school board indicated that the board was faced with adopting one of three options—operate a double shift system, exclude all nonresident pupils, or exclude all students over 16 from attending grade 12 in the high schools.

The worst years of the Depression in Edmonton occurred between 1930 and 1937. The modest recovery underway by 1938 was reflected in Edmonton's shanty town, which was finally "hit by depression." Edmonton's shanty town consisted of 65 inhabitants who lived at the foot of the Grierson Hill dump. By February 1938 its inhabitants were finding it increasingly difficult to market the odds and ends they manufactured or recovered from the dump. As one-eyed Tim Lane, an Irish-born veteran of the town, indicated to an Edmonton *Bulletin* reporter:

Things aren't what they used to be around here, now that those up-town can afford to buy more expensive parts for their autos and things. . . . Two or three years ago, we used to earn a fair decent living selling handicraft and odd parts we could salvage from the dump. You'd be surprised at the class of people who used to drive down in their big cars to see if they couldn't pick up a fourth-hand part cheap. . . . But now that they're better off, it's us fellows that are taking the beating.

By the late 1930s Edmonton was returning to some degree of normality as indicated by the closure of the soup kitchens and the return of professional football. As in the 1920s, this improvement was overshadowed by events taking place outside the city.

Facing page: *Shanty town, located within a stone's throw of the elegant Macdonald Hotel, became home for the most destitute Edmontonians during the Depression. Some of the shacks were located at the entrance of abandoned coal mine shafts. The people of shanty town eked out a living by turning refuse into useable items. Cleaned paint cans became storage containers for nails and screws, broken coloured glass was pressed into newly molded clay pots, and auto parts were repaired and sold to those fortunate enough to own a car. (COEA, Hubert Hollingworth Collection)*

THE EDMONTON GRADS

What began as an Edmonton women's high school basketball team in the fall of 1914 was later to become the most successful basketball team in Canadian sports history. The story of the Edmonton Grads, so called for their shared status as graduates from various Edmonton high schools, was launched from McDougall Commercial High School.

McDougall Commercial High School entered a team in a high school basketball league. The team was made up of students from two commercial classes in the school. John Percy Page became the team's

Above: *The Grads and Coach Page, right, circa 1921, have their picture taken beside a donated vehicle used by the team for travel. As amateurs, the team had to count on ticket sales, donations, and their own financial resources to keep them afloat. (COEA)*

Above: *The 1923 Edmonton Commercial Grads march along Jasper Avenue as part of the Exhibition parade. That year they won the prestigious Underwood Trophy for the first time. They won this trophy every year until 1939 when the trophy was retired. (COEA, Hubert Hollingworth Collection)*

coach. He not only taught the two classes at McDougall Commercial, but he also directed the physical education program, into which he had incorporated basketball. The first year the team captured the league championship and trophy. In 1915 the same team participated in the Intercollegiate Basketball League, which consisted of teams from two other city high schools as well as a team from the University of Alberta and a team that represented the city teachers. After this second successful year for the McDougall team Page sought further competition beyond the boundaries of Edmonton. On March 27, 1915, the McDougall Commercial High School team beat the Normal School in Camrose to win its first provincial women's basketball title. The following year the women, though graduating, wanted to remain a team. Convincing Page to continue coaching them, the members formed the Commercial Athletic Society. Membership in the society was granted to graduates of McDougall High School as well as graduates of any other business school. The members became known as the Commercial or Edmonton Grads. The Grads continued to play in the Edmonton high school and intercollegiate leagues until December of 1920 when they went to Saskatoon to play the Saskatoon YWCA and the University of Saskatchewan. The victory over the university team gave the Grads their first Western Canadian Championship.

After 1922 the team concentrated on Western Canadian, Canadian, international, and world championships. The team's accomplishments in these competition fields brought widespread recognition, which was reflected in the large numbers of spectators attracted to their games, both home and away. The Grads won their first Canadian title in 1923 when the team challenged the London Shamrocks to a two-game series. On their return home the Grads were greeted as conquering heroines and given the first of many civic receptions:

Students of the local high schools and public schools turned out en masse this morning and together with Mayor Douglas, aldermen, members of the school board and other prominent citizens rendered an enthusiastic welcome to the members of the Commercial Graduates Ladies' basketball team on their return from eastern Canada where they annexed the dominion title after a hard played series with the London Shamrocks.

Hearty cheers and school yells

Fifty years after the 1915 formation of the Commercial Grads, the players and Coach Page, front centre, gather for their Golden Anniversary reunion. (COEA)

greeted the girls as they stepped from the train and were congratulated by their friends. Miss Winnie Martin, captain of the team, was carried shoulder high by her girl friends to the waiting automobile led by the newsboy's band. The parade left the depot at 109th Street and headed uptown along Jasper Avenue. The members of the team rode in automobiles while the large number of students kept pace to the music and cheered the ensemblage. Upon reaching McDougall Avenue, the parade turned south and stopped in front of the MacDonald hotel where a civic reception and breakfast was tendered the members of the team.

International competition began in June 1923. The Cleveland Favourite Knits team, holders of three consecutive United States championships, was the first to play the Grads for this title. Eleven thousand fans watched the two games, and the Grads won both encounters (played according to men's rules), taking the series and the international title by a 53-to-33 aggregate score.

On June 19, 1924, the team left on its first European tour. During this trip the Grads trounced three teams from Paris and one each from Roubaix, Lille, and Strasbourg. Most

of the games were played on outdoor courts where the Grads could use their short passing game to advantage. The team won the world title from the Women's International Sports Federation for its European victories. The peak years for the team occurred between 1925 and 1983, during which time it undertook extended exhibition tours and participated in North American Championships beginning in 1933. In 1936 the team went to the Berlin Olympics where it played a series of games arranged by the Women's International Sports Federation. While basketball was not an official Olympic sport, the team did march in the opening parade as part of the Canadian delegation of athletes.

Throughout the team's 25-year history, every member of every team, with the exception of two women, was either a student or a graduate of McDougall Commercial High School. The club, which was never sponsored by private organizations, was supported year to year by gate receipts. But the individual players did not receive any money for their services. Over the 25 years the Grads played 522 official games in Canada, the United States, and Europe, winning 502 for an average of 96.2 percent.

GRANT McCONACHIE: BUSH PILOT AND AIRLINE PRESIDENT

Grant McConachie grew up in the railroad suburb of Calder, located to the north of Edmonton's municipal airport. McConachie pursued his education in the Edmonton public school system and later at the University of Alberta. While still in school he spent considerable time at the airport where he met Edmonton's first bush pilots, Wop May and Punch Dickins. On October 21, 1929, at the age of 20, he received his first flying lesson. His instructor, Maurice Burbidge, was also closely associated

with Edmonton aviation.

The following spring McConachie soloed in a DeHavilland Moth after seven hours and 20 minutes of instruction, thereby completing and receiving his private pilot's license. And on November 10, 1931, he obtained his commercial license. With this license McConachie planned to go to China, where he hoped to fly for a Chinese company. His uncle, however, convinced him to remain in Canada to serve as the president and general manager of a new company

known as Independent Airways. The company was incorporated that next summer, and Princess L. Galitzine, McConachie, and McConachie's uncle were the shareholders.

The company started with two standard Fokker Trimotor Universal aircraft and a Puss Moth. McConachie began his first commercial flights by flying fish from lakes in Northern Alberta and Saskatchewan. On October 29, 1932, McConachie and the company's chief mechanic carried out a mercy flight to the Pelican

Grant McConachie, far left, poses with a group of bush pilots and airport officials in a hangar at Blatchford Field. Originally named for Edmonton Mayor Kenneth Blatchford, the airport was renamed Edmonton Muncipal Airport. (COEA)

fast. There was a tearing sound and I thought the undercarriage was gone. But it was a stake to hold a trap that we had hit and it ripped the fabric right down the centre. Green sewed it up as best he could with a needle made out of wire.

McConachie continued his commercial flying, and in 1933 he formed a new company known as United Air Transport. This company pioneered many northern routes. On December 15, 1936, it started a regular run from Edmonton to Peace River and Grande Prairie, leaving Edmonton on Saturdays and returning on Mondays. It carried mail, passengers, and freight. Three years later the company was renamed Yukon Southern Air Transport and had offices in Edmonton and Vancouver.

Still ambitious, Grant McConachie sold his Yukon Southern Air Transport to the Canadian Pacific Railway Company on November 28, 1941, and thus Canadian Pacific Airlines was formed. He became president of the airline five years later, and during his career with Canadian Pacific, McConachie helped the airline chart the Polar Route. In recognition of his contributions to northern aviation, the Department of National Defence presented McConachie with the Trans Canada Trophy in 1946.

Rapids telegraph station. They had volunteered to pick up two people who had been injured in a gas explosion. The SOS had been flashed to the Dominion Government telegraphs at Edmonton, and from there arrangements were made to secure a rescue plane.

Independent Airways had a plane at South Cooking Lake, but ice prevented it from taking off. McConachie himself, with his wheel-equipped plane, volunteered to make the flight. In the meantime the injured men were moved to a nearby lake and a signal fire was started in anticipation of McConachie's arrival. When McConachie returned he confessed to the press that "it was a ticklish job landing on the narrow beach."

We had a width of about 10 feet to land on. . . . The fire was a big one and right at the end of the runway that we wanted to land on. We couldn't see the landing through the smoke so I circled and came in downwind. We hit pretty

CHAPTER VII

WAR
ABROAD AND
AT
HOME
1939 - 1945

Facing page: *Many women ably assumed traditionally male jobs during the war. These women, members of the Air Commonwealth Training Program, service an Avro Anson airplane at the Edmonton Municipal Airport. (COEA)*

On September 1, 1939, Edmontonians awoke to the cry of "Extra" shouted by newsboys through the main streets, side streets, and back alleys of the city. "War" in red type, the largest ever used in the *Bulletin's* history, announced that the long-expected European conflict had broken out. Barefoot men and women clad in nightgowns and pyjamas appeared at doors, gates, and windows, eager to purchase the morning paper.

With the announcement of hostilities, Edmontonians rushed to grocery stores. The *Bulletin* reported that:

Edmonton housewives have apparently decided to prepare for the worst by stocking up on staples such as flour and sugar. So heavy has been the demand for these two commodities this week and especially since hostilities were announced early Friday that by noon Friday grocery departments of city department stores, chain groceries and other grocery stores found their stocks on hand practically used up.

Despite a 10-day delay in Canada's declaration of war on

THE WEATHER

GOVERNMENT WEATHER FORECAST

If You Don't Get The Bulletin, You Don't Get All the News, Nor the Pictures

Edmonton Bulletin
— AN INDEPENDENT ┃┃┃ NEWSPAPER IN ┃┃┃ PUBLIC SERVICE —

WHEAT CLOSE

WINNIPEG CLOSING — Oct., 66 5/8c.

FIFTY-NINTH YEAR, NO. 224, No. 224   EDMONTON, ALBERTA—FRIDAY, SEPTEMBER 1, 1939   Single Copy, Five Cents

WAR

SEA POWER.—Great Britain's navy greater than potential menacing fleets combined

POLAND IS INVADED BY NAZI ARMS

Amid shattering blasts of heavy artillery and the crash of aerial bombardments, war broke out along the Polish-German frontier at about 9:55 p.m. Thursday night. German troops crossed into Polish territory at a dozen different border points, and today fierce battles are raging all along the far-flung frontiers. Germans in Danzig have announced their allegiance to the Reich and hoisted the Swastika, and fierce fighting in the streets of that city is reported.

German planes penetrated far into Poland and bombed Warsaw, Krakow, Katowice, Tczew, Czestochowa and other Polish towns and cities, and a heavy fire was directed on Gdynia, new Polish port on the Baltic. Dispatches from Gleiwitz on the Polish-Silesian border say that heavy fighting is going on in that region, and German wounded are pouring back into Germany.

The fighting, which broke out while Adolf Hitler was addressing a meeting of the Reichstag, took Europe by surprise. Earlier in the day the German leader had sent a sixteen-point proposal to Poland, and it was thought that there would be some negotiations over this last proposal before any fighting took place. However, German residents of Danzig precipitated action by announcing their allegiance to the Reich and the Fuehrer immediately responded by ordering that a law effecting the reunion be enacted immediately.

Cheering Reichstag Carries Out Order

A cheering Reichstag carried out the order as inflamed by their leader's declaration that Germany would "meet bomb with bomb," and that "nothing will stop me for one second from fulfilling my duty" they hastened to pass the necessary legislation.

Great Britain and France are not yet involved directly, but in view of the British announcement that fighting is actually in progress it is expected that the next diplomatic step will be a diplomatic note to Great Britain and France invoking military aid under the alliances which provide that if Poland considers her independence is menaced and resists the German advance the two countries will come to her aid.

Chamberlain of Great Britain and Premier Daladier of France have already announced that if the test came they would meet force by force and would assist Poland even to the extent of taking the field against Germany, and now that the crisis has arrived it is expected that they will be drawn into the conflict.

King George Summons Privy Council

In London King George summoned the Privy Council as the reports of the German offensive in Poland were received and the British parliament has been called to meet this afternoon to consider the grave situation which has arisen.

Premier Daladier has also convoked a council of ministers, supreme authority in France, to meet this morning.

Meantime both Great Britain and France are preparing for military action. In France general mobilization was ordered early this morning and it is expected that Great Britain, already in a general state of preparedness, would also place its army, navy and air force on a full war footing.

In every capital in Europe foreign office officials kept vigil all night and in London, Berlin, Paris and Rome air defence steps were being taken.

In the British capital all air-raid precautions were taken and the evacuation of school children and others was begun immediately.

Although no mention has been made of a formal war declaration on Poland the German chancellor published a proclamation to the armed forces of the Reich in which he asserted that Poland was no longer willing to respect Germany's frontiers, which he said had been regarded

(Continued on Page 2, Col. 3 and 3)

NO BOMBING OF CIVILIANS, PLEADS F.D.R.

Roosevelt Addresses His Plea to All Powers Likely to War

WASHINGTON, Sept. 1 — President Roosevelt today asked all powers participating in a European war to pledge themselves against bombarding unfortified cities from the air.

Mr. Roosevelt's appeal was sent at 4:50 a.m. E.D.T. to the governments of Great Britain, France, Italy, Germany and Poland. He is urging "in humanitarian terms."

Earlier, with mounting reports from Europe to Paris and Warsaw, Mr. Roosevelt was called from bed at 2:50 a.m. and told that Germany and Poland were at war.

"The ruthless bombing from the air of civilians in unfortified centres of population during the course of the hostilities which have raged in various quarters of the earth during the past few years, and which have resulted in the maiming and in the death of thousands of defenceless men, women and children, has sickened the hearts of every civilized man and woman, and has profoundly shocked the conscience of humanity."

"If resort is had to this form of inhuman barbarism during the period of the tragic conflagration with which the world is now confronted, hundreds of thousands of innocent human beings who have no responsibility for, and who are not even remotely participating in, the hostilities which have now broken out, will lose their lives.

I am therefore addressing this urgent appeal to every government which may be engaged in hostilities publicly to affirm its determination that its armed forces shall in no event, and under no circumstances, undertake the bombardment from the air of civilian populations or of unfortified cities, upon the understanding that these same rules of warfare will be scrupulously observed by all of their opponents.

Canadian Crisis Briefs

BOMBERS BASE ON HALIFAX

MONCTON, N.B., Aug. 31.—Ten Royal Canadian Air Force bombers landed here tonight and will take off for Halifax in the morning. While over Quebec they picked over the others, also en route to Halifax, which landed at Millicoshel, Me.

ONTARIO WOMEN ORGNIZE

TORONTO, Aug. 31.—Due to the seriousness of the international situation, the executive of the voluntary organization of Canadian women last night was called to speed up organization plans. The meeting was attended by 200 women.

BAN COMMUNIST MEETINGS

TORONTO, Aug. 31.—Meeting in private, the Toronto board of police decided today to ban Communist meetings from Toronto parks during the international crisis.

Polish Embassy Avers Germany Violates Frontier

PARIS, Sept. 1.—The Polish embassy here announced today that "Germany violated the Polish frontier at four points.

"German reports of pretended violations of German territory by Poland are pure inventions, as is the fable of 'attack' by Polish insurgents at Gleiwitz," the embassy announcement said.

Earlier it was disclosed that official French dispatches from Germany indicated that "the Reich began hostilities against Poland this morning."

The report caught Paris by surprise in a quiet morning when newspapers were producing that "French and British troops can still save peace."

Hitler Air Defence League Mobilized

BERLIN, Sept. 1.—Germany's air defence league was mobilized early today. Men and women wearing coveralls and steel helmets and with rifles making their way through streets and squares to protective posts. Emergency fire squads in private apartment houses also were mobilized.

NAZI WARPLANES BOMB WARSAW

WARSAW, Sept. 1.—German planes bombed Warsaw this morning, causing some damage to railways and other property.

Krakow, Katowice, Tczew and Czestochowa were also bombed by German airplanes early this morning, but full extent of the damage is not yet known.

— Paris —

PARIS, Sept. 1.—The Havas News Agency said today that official French dispatches from Germany indicated that "the reich began hostilities on Poland this morning."

Premier Edouard Daladier, informed that German troops crossed the Polish frontier today, summoned an urgent meeting of his cabinet for 10:30 a.m. (5:30 a.m. Edmonton time).

— Gleiwitz —

GLEIWITZ, Germany, Sept. 1.—An army ambulance carrying wounded soldiers arrived at the emergency hospital here today at 9:10 a.m. (1:10 a.m. Edmonton time).

The men, carried in a wagon, were on stretchers. One had on a first aid field bandage. It could not be ascertained where the ambulance came from.

At about 9:10 a half-mile-long truck train manned by the engineering corps drove through the heart of the city with pontoon bridge building material. In the train were caterpillar tread 20-passenger motor vans.

Obviously the train had been on the road for a considerable time. All equipment was thickly covered with gray mud.

A scouting plane of the air force was patrolling an area over Gleiwitz.

Early today Gleiwitz residents reported artillery fire was heard "in the distance" a few miles from the Polish-Silesian border.

— Warsaw —

WARSAW, Sept. 1.—The foreign office said today that German planes had bombed Krakow and Katowice, in southwestern Poland.

German planes also bombed Czestochowa, Tczew and Grudiadz early this morning, the foreign office said.

It was reported officially that German troops had attacked Polish defences near Mlawa, bordering the southern part of East Prussia.

There was no announcement of the damage resulting from the bombings.

The foreign office also confirmed that fighting has

(Continued on Page 3, Col. 3 and 4)

DANZIG IS IN HANDS OF HITLER

WARSAW, Sept. 1.—Poland, it was stated here last night, will insist on full restitution of her rights in Danzig.

BERLIN, Sept. 1.—Fuehrer Hitler today accepted the free city of Danzig into the reich. The fuehrer acted after Albert Forster, Nazi chief of state of the free city and Nazi district leader there, had proclaimed the reunion of the Baltic city with Hitler's Germany, and begged the Fuehrer to accept it.

BERLIN, Sept. 1.—The German official news agency, D.N.B., announced today that Albert Forster, Nazi chief of state in Danzig, had proclaimed the reunion of the free city with the reich.

Forster notified Fuehrer Hitler of Germany, of his action, by telegram, D.N.B. said.

"Mein Fuehrer," Mr. Forster, replying pledge to you imperishable thankfulness and eternal loyalty. Heil my Fuehrer.

"Signed, ALBERT FORSTER, Gauleiter."

Forster followed the act with a proclamation to Danzigers that "the hour for which you have longed for for 20 years has come.

"Effective today, Danzig has returned to the great German Reich. Our Fuehrer, Adolf Hitler, has freed you."

"The Swastika flag, the flag of the German Reich, waves for the first time today as the public buildings in Danzig. It waves, however, also from former Polish buildings and everywhere in the harbor.

"Church bells peal forth and now thank the Lord for our liberation and also the Fuehrer who has given us the opportunity to get rid of the evils of the Versailles treaty.

"Long live a free Danzig, now returned home, and long live our great fatherland."

Hitler Orders Battle

BERLIN, Sept. 1.—The German army was ordered to "meet force with force" and Poland was declared dangerous territory for foreigners by Fuehrer Hitler at 5:30 a.m. (9:30 p.m. Thursday, M.S.T.).

At the same time a naval blockade of the Polish harbor of Gdynia was announced. The fuehrer proclaimed his action was because of alleged Polish violations of the German frontier. Neutral ships in the Baltic were warned they entered Danzig harbor or nearby harbors at their own peril.

The announcement said military operations progressed three measures. Hitler gave his orders in his army at 5:30 a.m. (11:30 p.m. M.S.T., Thursday) to meet "force against force." The command also issued to the order of the day to the army against any Polish frontiers from the Baltic to the high Tatra mountains, and in East Prussia.

LONDON SAYS WILL FULFILL OBLIGATIONS

German Story of Course of Negotiations Is Said Misleading

LONDON, Sept. 1.—(Passed by British Censor)—Text of an authoritative statement:

It is pointed out in official circles that if the proclamation to the German people by Herr Hitler which has already been announced should mean as it would seem to mean that Germany has declared war on Poland, it can be stated on the highest authority that Great Britain and France are infinitely determined to fulfill to the uttermost their obligations to the Polish government.

The German account of the course of the negotiations is of course wholly misleading.

On Aug. 27th the German chancellor informed the British ambassador that he expected a Polish plenipotentiary to appear in Berlin by the following day with full powers to negotiate a settlement.

He added that in the meantime he hoped to elaborate the proposals, in clearer words the Polish government were expected to submit to the government of Chancellor Hitler even so desperate and summary as Berlin was to appear.

The Polish state has rejected any effort to reach negotiation which would implied that intolerable summary demands to the Polish government.

There was no formal violation of a Polish frontier, as was said, but German troops crossed the frontier at four points.

A series of border violations were reportedly for a great matters were reported to Berlin.

INSANE IMITATIONS

"Do not ask me if these terms of resurrected German history are true or not, but bear them with a look of ..."

(text obscured)

FIRST EXTRAS

The first extra edition of a Berlin newspaper to reach the streets after Hitler's proclamation bore the head:

"Force Against Force"

There was no suggestion yet other than an official of any other treaty of a declaration of war.

Toward the end of the day the ...

Swiss Mobilize

BERNE, Sept. 1.—The Swiss general staff today ordered general mobilization. Martial law was proclaimed in Paris.

Germany, recruiting for Edmonton army units began immediately. On September 1 Lieutenant Colonel E. Brown, officer commanding the Edmonton garrison, announced that recruiting to full war strength would begin immediately by the Edmonton Regiment; the 61st and 92nd batteries, Royal Canadian Artillery; the wireless telegraphers' section; the 9th Army Transport Company, Royal Canadian Engineers; "E" Troop Royal Canadian Signals; the 4th Casualty Clearing Station, Royal Canadian Army Medical Corps; and the 13th Field Hygiene Section, Royal Canadian Army Medical Corps. Recruiting officers from these units and medical boards began evaluating the recruits and processing applications on Monday, September 4, at the Prince of Wales Armoury. Enlistment regulations required that the recruits be between 18 and 41 years of age, be physically fit, and have no more than three dependents. Veterans of World War I were generally deemed either too old or not fit enough to participate. One of the many veterans of World War I who offered his services was Jack Brinker, who appeared downtown on September 1 with his kit-bag packed. He indicated to a reporter that "I am ready to go if they'll take me; I served for three years with the 28th Battalion Signallers in the Great War and I'm 58 years old now, but I'm still in pretty good shape."

Major F. Armoor Ford and Major Leslie Suness commanded the 61st and 92nd batteries, which were limited to 209 men of all ranks. Lieutenant Colonel Philip Debney, former commander of the Edmonton Regiment, commanded the company of engineers. He hoped that 300 tradesmen, such as carpenters, electricians, plumbers, and machinists, would enlist at the Victoria Armoury recruiting center. Captain J.T. Freeman's signal corps recruited 40 men; Lieutenant Colonel R.T. Washburn, M.D., commander of the 4th Casualty Clearing Station, enlisted those interested in hospital and medical work; and Lieutenant G.M. Little, Edmonton's medical health officer, recruited for the 13th Field Hygiene Section of the medical corps. Thus, though Edmonton had provided mainly infantrymen for service in World War I, the city's residents contributed to many facets of the army in World War II.

The largest unit recruited was the Edmonton Regiment, which had been created in 1920. Commanded by Lieutenant Colonel W.G. Stillman, a career provincial civil servant, the 850-man unit was designated the Loyal Edmonton Regiment on July 7, 1943. The 1st Battalion of the regiment perpetuated the memory of one of Edmonton's oldest units, the 49th Battalion of the Canadian Expeditionary Force, by flying its colours. In fact, Major General W.A. Griesbach, former commander of the 49th Battalion, assisted in the recruiting effort. The Edmonton Regiment drew 450 of its 850 men from Edmonton, and Colonel Stillman sent medical and recruiting officers to draw 100 each from Peace River, Vegreville, Wetaskiwin, and Wainwright. The presence of a large number of Northern Albertans in the Edmonton Regiment perpetuated another military tradition: in the original Edmonton Regiment, the 49th Battalion C.E.F., an entire company, "Steady D," had been recruited from the Peace River territory.

Throughout Edmonton posters encouraged young men to enlist. At a downtown recruiting depot at Mike's News Stand, a sound truck equipped with loudspeakers gave out messages urging men to join the colours. It sent out slogans such as "Your King and Country Need You," and "You said you would serve when you are needed, you are needed now." Behind the sound truck a transfer truck with seats waited to take recruits to the Prince of Wales Armoury for enlistment. On September 16, 1939, the Edmonton Regiment's regimental band played an hour of martial music, wartime marches, and songs in front of Mike's News Stand to aid the recruiting effort. The band was made up of former members of the Edmonton Symphony, the Newsboy's Band, town bands from the coal branch, and various dance bands. The same day the Edmonton Regiment's pipe band went to Fort Saskatchewan along with a "flotilla of cars and trucks," which were used to bring back recruits reportedly "drawn . . . by the irresistible skirling of the pipes."

The recruiting efforts proved successful. On September 30 Colonel Stillman announced that the Edmonton Regiment was up to full strength and, along with the 92nd Field Battery, would be sent overseas as part of the First Canadian Division. The regiment would participate in the Italian and Northwest European campaigns.

Reminiscent of World War I, Edmontonians donated a variety of gifts to the unit, including instruments for the regimental band. The funds for the instruments were raised through a campaign organized by John Michaels, who had begun the Edmonton Newsboy's Band. The presentation of the instruments to the regiment took place in a ceremony held in market square on December 18, 1939. As a final musical

Numerous prisoner of war camps were built across Canada to hold captured Germans. These prisoners at Wainwright, near Edmonton, set up a camp library to help relieve the endless hours of boredom while in captivity. (PAA, A. Blyth Collection)

donation, Darrell B. Robertson, president of the All-Canadian Musicians Union Edmonton Branch and a former member of the Edmonton Fusiliers' band, composed a song specially dedicated to the regiment. One verse of his song went:

We're feeling happy, we're off to war
With Adolf Hitler, we'll wipe the floor
And we hope we'll get to the front in time
To blast our way through the Siegfried Line
Then march back home once more
We'll keep on marching along to war
To Germany we've been before
Sure our air force, army, navy,
Will drive poor old Hitler crazy
Come along we're off to war.

Edmonton's contributions to the war effort, however, extended beyond the army. On September 10, 1939, the "H.M.C.S. Nonsuch" went on active service. This naval unit had originally been formed in April 1923 and had adopted its unusual name in 1939 after the Department of National Defence purchased the HBC horse barn to convert into a naval training facility. The *Nonsuch*, the first ship owned by the Hudson's Bay Company, arrived in Canada in September 1668. The ship returned to London in October 1669 with such a large and valuable cargo of furs that the king granted the charter for the company to carry the trade into Hudson Bay and Canada.

Edmonton also contributed to the Royal Canadian Air Force in World War II. The air force recruiting centre was opened on 101st Avenue on October 5, 1939, and Ernest James Allen was its first recruit. In 1944 the City of Edmonton adopted a squadron at the suggestion of Gordon Williamson, a former Edmontonian and a public relations officer with the RCAF. The Edmonton City Council endorsed the suggestion in February 1944. The City of Edmonton Squadron No. 418, which included many Edmontonians, flew mosquito bombers.

The squadron celebrated its adoption by dropping copies of the Edmonton *Journal* wrapped around bricks during one of its raids. G.N. ("Lefty") Miller, a former *Journal* newsboy, participated in the raid.

During World War II Edmonton built upon its interwar development as a centre for northern aviation. It operated facilities at the municipal airport for the Air Commonwealth Training Program, a cooperative air training plan for the United Kingdom, Canada, Australia, and New Zealand based

Conditions in the prisoner of war camps were spartan, but provided for all the basic necessities of life. Many Germans were so impressed by the fairness of their treatment in Canadian camps that after returning home to Germany, they applied to immigrate back to Canada. (PAA, A. Blyth Collection)

on an agreement reached in the fall of 1939. The program involved the training in Canada of pilots, observers, gunners, and navigators from the member countries. The Edmonton facilities for the program included the Number Two Air Observer School, established on August 5, 1940, and the Number 16 Elementary Flying School, established on November 11, 1940, and operated by the Edmonton Flying Club. A third facility, the Number Three RCAF Manning Depot, was established at the Exhibition Grounds in August

W. LEIGH BRINTNELL'S AIRCRAFT REPAIR LTD.

World War II, unlike World War I, generated economic development in Edmonton. Aircraft Repair Ltd., which went into operation in April 1941, was one of Edmonton's major war industries. The driving force behind the company was W. Leigh Brintnell. Brintnell began his flying career as a flight instructor for the Royal Canadian Air Force during World War I. From 1924 to 1927 he flew for the Ontario Provincial Air Service. In January 1927 he joined Winnipeg-based Western Canada Airways, Canada's first commercial airline, and one year later became its general manager. He later branched out on his own and in 1932 created Edmonton-based MacKenzie Air Services. Brintnell, along with Grant McConachie, played a major role in making Edmonton a centre for northern aviation during the 1930s. In an article in the staff newspaper, *The Planesman*, Brintnell recalled the services provided by commercial airlines.

During the period of 1933 to 1939 many unusual air freighting operations were carried out. Numerous trips were made by aircraft to isolated areas with medicine, food and clothing for small bands of Indians who were being decimated by an influenza epidemic. Aircraft would land on skis in out-of-the-way places where no aircraft had ever landed before. This humanitarian aspect of air freighting has saved the lives of countless hundreds in Northern Canada.

In the same article he noted the crucial role of planes in the development of Canada's northern mining frontier.

In April 1935, after the radium company commenced operation of its mill at Great Bear Lake, the flying company was requested to bring radium concentrates out to the railhead. This was the first time that this precious metal had been transported by air in Canada. The round trip was 1,800 miles and the aircraft carried 3,500 pounds of concentrates.

Aircraft Repair Ltd. was cramped and crowded. Housing and industrial space was at a premium during the war years, so planes were kept close together to conserve space. (COEA)

As one shift leaves, another arrives at Aircraft Repair Ltd., where men and women worked side by side. Employees not only worked hard but were also well-known for buying lots of Victory Bonds. (COEA)

After six years Brintnell expanded the operations of MacKenzie Air Services to include the maintenance of planes owned by other companies such as United Air Transport. With the expansion came the creation of a new company: Aircraft Repair Ltd. It attracted much of the staff of the MacKenzie Air Services and became known for the motto "To keep 'em flying," which summarized the activities of the plant. When it opened in April 1941, its main function was to assemble and repair Avro Anson and Harvard planes. By the end of the war, the plant handled everything from service checks to major crack-ups on 25 to 30 different types of planes and performed routine overhaul on both airframes and engines. This included advanced trainers from the British Common-wealth Air Training Program schools in Alberta and Saskatchewan, as well as engines crated and flown in for overhaul. The engine shop could handle, if necessary, up to 10 or 12 engines a day. American P-40s were also repaired at the plant.

The company began with 25 employees in April 1941 and by 1943 had expanded to 2,500. These included young men recruited from the Dominion Provincial Youth Training School as well as those who were already employed as garage mechanics, carpenters, cabinetmakers, and metalworkers. Some of these new recruits were as young as 15 years old. Women comprised 40 percent of the company's workers by October 1943 and were an essential part of the labour force at the plant.

But the company was not strictly work-oriented. Its recreation council organized sports and social events, such as regular Saturday night dances in the plant's cafeteria. The music for these weekly events was provided by a dance band made up of company employees.

1941. There new recruits received their uniforms, were inoculated for diphtheria, scarlet fever, and typhoid, and received six weeks of training consisting largely of drill, physical exercise, and some study of aeronautical subjects. From the Manning Depot the recruits went to training centres for specialized instruction on air crew work, wireless, mechanic, and other branches of the service.

A World War I flying instructor for the Royal Flying Corps, W. Leigh Brintnell, began operations at Aircraft Repair Ltd. in April 1941. Between the wars Brintnell had worked for Western Canada Airways Ltd., and in 1931 he organized his own airline, MacKenzie Air Services Limited and later United Air Services Limited, which were sold to Canadian Pacific Airlines in 1941. When Aircraft Repair Ltd. began operations in April of that year, it employed 25 workers to repair airframes and engines of planes used by the Air Commonwealth Training Program. By October 1943 the company had more than 2,400 employees, an estimated 40 percent of them women.

Edmonton's population organized around the war effort in such civilian involvements as the Spitfire Campaign. The Spitfire Campaign was inaugurated in September 1940 when

Above: *The Edmonton Industrial Airport became essential to the Allied war effort as a pilot training centre for the Air Commonwealth Training Program, and as a stopover point for planes being sent to Russia. These views from the air and the ground are circa 1943. (COEA)*

Right: *The Edmonton Public Library's streetcar library was the first of its kind in Canada. The blue and cream 1909 converted streetcar could hold 1,500 books, and complete reference services were provided. Library employee Nick Alexeeff, right, is prepared to assist patrons in boarding the car in 1941. (COEA)*

Mayor Fry received an appeal made by Edmonton, England, to Edmonton, Alberta, to assist in the purchase of a Spitfire fighter for approximately $25,000. Mayor Fry established a committee to conduct the campaign. Over the next three months, a number of organizations raised funds from a variety of groups. Shortly after the campaign was announced, Mayor Fry gave a talk to representatives of more than 30 women's organizations, which resulted in many offers of assistance. Members of the Women's Liberal Club planned to hold a tea in Campbell's Furniture Store at which a regimental band would provide martial music and jellies and jams would be sold. One Edmontonian contributed a diamond ring and a wedding band to be raffled in aid of the Spitfire fund. A military whist party providing accommodation for 400 persons and bridge parties were also organized in support of the fund. By October 22 Mayor Fry was able to announce that Edmonton had not only reached but had surpassed the amount required.

Public involvement in the war was spurred through displays of British "blitz" conditions in market square in aid of the Queen's Fund. In February 1942 Edmonton also had an air raid drill, during which the city was blacked out for five minutes. Mayor Fry, among others, monitored the success of the exercise in an airplane provided by Yukon Southern

EDMONTON PREPARES FOR WAR

As a city, Edmonton had a particular interest in the bombing of English cities during World War II. In an effort to raise money for the Queen's Fund for the relief of bomb victims, Edmonton citizens took part in a mock blitz at the Civic Block on October 21, 1941. The preliminary events began when the band of the 2nd Battalion Edmonton Regiment marched to the market square and played several lively marches while a special squad of garrison troops prepared the area in front of the Civic Block for display. Then, after ample warning, the area was blacked out and the "raid" was under way. Together, firemen, citizens, and soldiers became critical play actors in a simulated wartime bombing.

With sirens wailing mournfully, four pieces of fire department equipment manned by 25 firemen under the direction of Acting Chief Ferguson rolled into the raid area.

Simultaneously C.S.M. Clucas and C.S.M. Gray, of the Edmonton Garrison, lighted a number of smoke candles. The smoke rolled upward nearly concealing the west side of the Civic block.

The effect became really weird when the soldiers lighted a number of red fuses. The red glow on the pillar of black smoke made the west wall of the building appear to be afire. Then came three or four ear-splitting detonations, caused by setting off of "thunder flashes" by the troops.

The climax to the "show" came a few seconds later when the fire department power driven extension ladder was raised to [a] sixth floor window of the Civic block and a "casualty" lowered successfully to the street by means of ropes. The "casualty," a victim of smoke, was rushed to "hospital" in a waiting R.C.A.F. ambulance. A Jack Hays ambulance took other blitz victims to "hospital" after they had been given first aid by nursing sisters with the St. John Ambulance Brigade.

This display was followed four

CITIZENS of EDMONTON

We have gone over our quota in every campaign so far, BUT always at the ELEVENTH hour.

Each One of Us Can Gauge Our Capacity NOW!

LET US LOAN FOR VICTORY EARLY!

Then...Friend and Enemy Will Know We Are on the Job!

BLACKOUT
Sunday, February 15th, 9:30 to 9:35 p.m. Full instructions appear elsewhere in this paper, please co-operate.

LADIES' DAY
Monday, February 16th, 9:00 a.m. to 9:00 p.m.

$500.00 IN BONDS FREE!
500 members of the Army, Navy and Air Force will be on duty on the downtown streets during the above hours to escort ladies to headquarters to buy bonds. LADIES! Come down and get your man. Both you and he can get a bond free.

GRAND VICTORY LOAN RALLY
Tuesday, February 17th, to be held at the Arena (by permission of Wing Commander J. C. Malone) 8:30 sharp.

Program
Local Stars
Air Cadets—N.C.O. Class
R.C.A.F. Band, No. 4 I.T.S. (by permission Wing Commander J. A. Hutchinson)
The Band of the 2nd Battalion Edmonton Regiment (R), CA by kind permission of Lt. Col. R. Walter Hale, M.C., officer commanding.
The noted British actor from Hollywood, MR. IAN HUNTER.

VICTORY BONDS
Buy Your Share of Freedom!

Come on Canada

Strike a Deadly Blow at Hitler

DAY AFTER TOMORROW, Canada launches a new VICTORY Loan.

To every red-blooded man and woman the call to action is irresistible . . . lend your dollars to Canada. Let your money make our fighting forces the best equipped the World has ever seen.

The small investor can help tip the scale for victory. You may have done much already to help in the war . . . you can do more. The call is to every Canadian.

North Alberta and City of Edmonton
Victory Loan Headquarters
Bank Canadienne Nationale Building,
Edmonton, Alberta. Phone 24243.

BUY the new VICTORY BONDS

Facing page: *Prior to the air raid drill of February 15, 1942, the Victory Loan Committee, initiators of the drill, reminded Edmontonians of the blackout in this Victory Bond advertisement. Note the Morse code, triple-dot dash (SOS) surrounding the "V for victory" symbol. (COEA)*

months later by a city-wide air raid drill. The idea of conducting an air raid drill originated with the publicity committee of the 1942 Victory Loan Campaign. Mayor John Fry felt that it was a good chance for the city administration to get involved. In a public statement Mayor Fry indicated that:

since the war has taken such a serious turn and since city council has deemed it wise to set up an Air Raid Precautions organization, that committee feels that it should seize the opportunity of the blackout to test the efficiency and to learn where the weak spots may be. It is therefore hoped and expected that all our citizens will take this matter seriously and co-operate by following the instructions in the daily press and on the radio. Let us not have the "it cannot happen here attitude."

Various military units were also involved. Major A.P. Chattell, commanding officer of the Edmonton Battalion of the Veterans Volunteer Reserve, provided 350 volunteers who were to act as air wardens throughout the city. Acting garrison commandant Lieutenant Colonel Alan H. Elliott arranged to have 20 flash bombs explode in different sections of the city at the start of the blackout. The "bombing" of the city was to continue for 30 seconds. The flash bombs were designed to make the exercise as realistic as possible. Realism was also

to be introduced by the use of sirens provided by the Canadian National Railway, gas company, and the fire department, as well as the firing of rifles. During the blackout airplanes would drone overhead. In addition, these planes would observe the effectiveness of the exercise. Mayor Fry was a passenger in one of the planes.

Edmonton citizens at home or at their place of employment were advised to "stay put." Those people driving cars were requested to pull into the curb in order to keep the streets clear for the movement of emergency vehicles. All vehicles entering the city were to be stopped at the city limits. All lights were to be shut off. This included store lights, matches, and cigarettes. The citizens were also requested not to use the telephone in order to prevent interference with emergency communication.

The exercise was declared to be a

This advertisement placed in the Edmonton Bulletin by the Victory Loan Committee is typical of the ads which appeared in all newspapers and magazines as well as on posters and billboards during the war. Edmontonians never failed to surpass their quota for each Victory Loan drive. (COEA)

success. Coverage of the event by the *Bulletin* indicated that Edmontonians responded to the air raid with a variety of feelings.

Young people of both sexes, who braved a biting wind to take in Edmonton's first blackout Sunday night on the city's busiest corner at Jasper Avenue and 101st Street, indulged in a lot of good-humored wise cracks. Oldsters were for the most part silent. It seemed that older men and women were thinking of the practice "blackouts" that were staged in so many other cities of the world before the real thing became general.

Airlines.

The war in the Pacific spurred a number of building programs such as the Northwest Staging Route, the Alaska Highway, and the Canol project. The Northwest Staging Route, a series of runways between Edmonton and Alaska, was built to facilitate the movement of aircraft and supplies from Alberta to Alaska. In early 1941 bases were constructed in Grande Prairie, Alberta; Ft. Nelson, British Columbia; and Watson Lake and Whitehorse, Yukon Territory. This air route followed the one pioneered by Grant McConachie and his Yukon Southern Air Transport in the 1930s.

The construction of the Alaska Highway, which began on February 14, 1942, also brought a number of pre-World War II plans to fruition. In 1898 the Public Works Department of the Canadian government evaluated the feasibility of building a road from Edmonton to the Yukon goldfields in order to ensure the maximum benefit to Canada of the rush to Dawson. In February 1898 the Town of Edmonton hired W.P. Taylor to explore the route from Edmonton to the Pelly River, which would be used for Yukon-bound travellers. American interest in the inland route also dated from the turn of the century when American railroad

Left: *The "Milk for Britain" drive was led by the Kinsmen Club and was supported by Edmonton's children. (PAA)*

Above: *Parts of the Alaska Highway were barely passable during construction, as shown in this 1943 view. (PAA, H. Pollard Collection)*

Above, right: *Despite the hardships of isolation and harsh weather, the men who built the Alaska Highway maintained their sense of humour. They painted this sign to greet the drivers who were about to descend "Suicide Hill." (PAA, H. Pollard Collection)*

Right: *These 1943 soldiers pose for a souvenir picture at the Alaska Highway. (PAA, A. Blyth Collection)*

builder F.H. Harriman proposed a Canada-Alaska railroad linked with a Russian railroad by bridging or tunnelling the Bering Straits. However, after defeating Russia in the Russo-Japanese War of 1904, Japan pressured Russia into abandoning the idea. In 1905 the Dominion Government ordered Major Constantine of the North West Mounted Police to blaze an overland trail to the Klondike goldfields. He was able to build 375 miles of road before the project was halted. In 1928 Donald MacDonald, a United States government engineer, proposed an overland road from Alaska to Panama. In 1933 the United States Congress authorized President Roosevelt to set up a joint commission with Canada to study a proposed road to Alaska. But once the members had been appointed, no action was taken. The Canadian-American Permanent Joint Board of Defence took over the Alaska Highway Project in August 1940.

Initially the board considered three routes. The first and second routes began in the interior of British Columbia. A third route favoured by the United States Army Corps of Engineers began at Edmonton and ran to Fairbanks, Alaska, via Dawson Creek, Fort St. John, Fort Nelson, Watson Lake, and Whitehorse. This prairie route had the advantage of being far enough inland to avoid attack by enemy planes from the sea, and it also connected the vital air bases of the Northwest Staging Route. It traversed level terrain without any pass over 4,250 feet high. There was also a railroad at Dawson Creek and a winter road from Dawson Creek to Fort Nelson, which facilitated the movement of men and equipment to the construction site. On February 2, 1942, the third route was chosen. On February 14 work began, and the Alaska Highway was finally completed on November 20.

The Canol (short for "Canadian oil") pipeline project was developed to provide fuel for the vehicles and airplanes operating over the Alaska Highway and the Northwest Staging Route. The possible closure by the Japanese of the shipping lane to Alaska and the need for tankers in other theatres of war made the procurement of local sources of fuel necessary.

These sources of oil were available at Norman Wells, 75 miles south of the Arctic Circle on the Mackenzie River. The Norman Wells oil sources had been discovered in 1919-1920 but had remained unused until 1939 when a small refinery was installed to meet local demand. On the recommendation of a U.S. Special Cabinet Committee, the decision to construct a pipeline from Norman Wells to a new refinery in Whitehorse was made in April 1942. On May 27 and 28 the advance guard of the Canol project reached Edmonton, which was to be headquarters for the architect-engineer, the officer in charge for the Army Corps of Engineers, and officials of the civilian contractors and of the United States Engineers Department. Twenty-five hundred engineer troops, along with hundreds of tons of equipment, came pouring through Edmonton. Men and supplies travelled over the Northern Alberta Railways to Waterways where they began a 1,100-mile trip down the Athabasca, Slave, and Mackenzie rivers to Norman Wells. On February 16, 1944, the final well was made. Two months later crude oil from Normal Wells flowed into Whitehorse.

The rapid increase in the number of American, Canadian, and Commonwealth military and civilian personnel in Edmonton and the city's role as a staging route for the north led to a demand for space and facilities. Military personnel occupied many of Edmonton's existing buildings, and a military building program was launched on September 4, 1939, with the construction of huts at the Prince of Wales Armoury. In October additional space for the rapidly expanding Edmonton garrison was found in the Fane Building, which had served as a soup kitchen for single unemployed men during the Depression. The air force occupied the Exhibition Grounds from 1942 to 1945, and in 1943 and 1944, for the first time since 1901, the Edmonton Exhibition did not take place. Units of the Canadian air force and army also occupied buildings at the University of Alberta, and American personnel occupied the Jesuit College in northwest Edmonton.

Major construction took place at Edmonton's municipal

airport, including runway extensions and hangar construction, and work on the Namao airport, a new facility north of the city, was begun in June 1943 and completed in September 1944. The City of Edmonton built a $60,000 administration building that provided office space for the various private companies and military organizations operating out of the municipal airport, waiting room space, and an air traffic control tower. These facilities were required to accommodate the increasing number of airplanes that utilized the Northwest Staging Route. By 1943 the flow of airplanes also included planes being shipped to Russia under the terms of a lend-lease program. "On September 29, 1943," recalled Captain Bell about the municipal airport, "we had 860 planes in one day."

In addition to the military construction activity, a record number of houses were built to accommodate the expanding population. Edmonton's population increased from 90,000 in 1939 to 113,116 in 1946. A good portion of this increase was made up of military personnel from the Commonwealth countries, such as Britain and New Zealand, as well as from the United States and the Soviet Union. The combined effects of military and civilian construction brought the total volume of building activity from $1,661,109 in 1939 to $7,988,348 in 1945. The construction took place on the old subdivisions that had been created before World War I. The Hudson's Bay Company Reserve north of the airport was a major area for wartime housing.

Increased construction activity was but one of the signs of the economic recovery brought to Edmonton by the war. The army and military activity offered jobs for the unemployed, as did the construction industry. The cost to the city for unemployment relief took a dramatic drop from $225,082 in 1940 to $89,606 in 1941. In 1942 direct cash payments to the unemployed were discontinued entirely. That year the City Land Department sold a record $1,103,014 worth of land that had reverted to the city because of the nonpayment of taxes. The sales resulted in the reinstatement of lands and improvements to the active tax rolls. All this restored civic

confidence and renewed Edmontonians' interest in town
planning and city beautification programs.

The Loyal Edmonton Regiment returned home on
October 6, 1945.

*The Loyal Edmonton Regiment is home. It arrived in the rain at
the CNR station at 6:35 p.m. Saturday with a strength of
580 men, most of whom had fought with the unit through
Sicily, Italy and Northwestern Europe. An all-day rain neither
dampened nor dimmed the enthusiasm of the reception which
will rank with the all-time great occasions of the city's history. A
crowd estimated to run as high as 50,000 greeted the regiment.*

*Tumultuous cheers greeted the regiment as the train drew to
a halt in the station and enthusiasm mounted as the troops
paraded through city streets to receive official and impromptu
welcomes.*

Unlike World War I the troops did not arrive in a city that
had been ravaged by depression and influenza. Edmonton was
a prosperous city on the verge of even greater economic growth.

*Built in the U.S., these Bell
P-39s known as Aircobras
are on their way to Russia
to join the fight against
Germany on the eastern
front. Equipped with an
1,100 horsepower Allison
engine, the Aircobra was
particularly popular with
the Russians for attacking
tanks from the air. (COEA)*

Left: The Allied military leader in the Pacific, Gen. Douglas MacArthur was honoured by being placed squarely in the middle of a huge red "V" on the front page of the August 15, 1945, Edmonton Bulletin. *(COEA)*

Facing page: These Johnstone Walker window displays expressed gratitude to those who served, and the genuine hope at the end of World War II for a lasting peace. The Allied leaders soon found that their postwar differences outweighed their wartime agreements. (PAA, A. Blyth Collection)

Crowds gathered along Jasper Avenue to cheer a parade of men in uniform on V-J Day. Though enthusiastic and joyous in their celebration the massive crowds gave the police no difficulty, save a few people who over-indulged in their favourite spirits. (PAA, A. Blyth Collection)

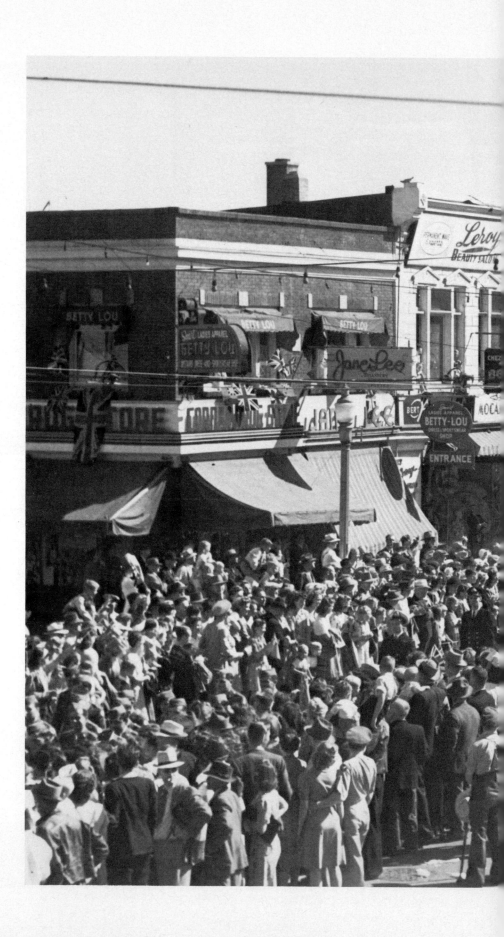

Facing page: *Many children joined in the festivities of V-J Day by waving flags, scrambling aboard slowly moving cars, or riding their bicycles in the impromptu parade. Others climbed to the top of stationary streetcars to watch the masses below. (PAA, A. Blyth Collection)*

Right: *The Edmonton Bulletin of May 8, 1945, announced the end of the war in Europe with this bold one-word headline over a picture of Sir Winston Churchill. Although a joyous day in Edmonton and throughout the Allied countries, Edmontonians saved their most exuberant celebrations for V-J Day. (COEA)*

Above: *This mother's prayers were soon answered, as she waited with other families and friends of the Loyal Edmonton Regiment for loved ones about to arrive at the train station from their long journey overseas. (PAA, A. Blyth Collection)*

Right: *Major Gilchrist's family greets him on his arrival in Edmonton after serving overseas in 1945. (PAA, A. Blyth Collection)*

Soldiers of the Loyal Edmonton Regiment pose for one last group photo before going their separate ways. This sergeant has brought home a special souvenir, a puppy, for his family. (PAA, A. Blyth Collection)

CHAPTER VIII

EDMONTON

AND THE

OIL BOOM

1946 - 1984

The economic growth boosted by the Second World War made a significant contribution to restoring Edmonton's self-confidence, which had been seriously undermined by the Depression. New investment was required, however, to sustain Edmonton's economic development. It came in February 1947 when Leduc Oil Well No. 1, located 13 miles southwest of Edmonton, gushed oil. This event marked a turning point for the economic, physical, and social transformation of the city.

On November 20, 1946, Imperial Oil Ltd. began drilling the well as part of an exploration program on a 500,000-acre parcel of land southwest of Edmonton leased from the provincial government earlier in the year. On February 5, 1947, the Edmonton *Bulletin* reported that "Drillers Hit Oil Gusher In Vicinity of Leduc." The newspaper's source was Mike Turta, owner of the quarter section on which the well was located, who said the gusher shot into the air about 90 feet, covering the inside of the 156-foot derrick. Head driller Charles Visser of Calgary and Vernon Hunter of Edmonton, who were in charge of the drilling operation, would not confirm or deny the report. Imperial Oil production manager Walker Taylor, other company officials, and provincial government officials also would not officially confirm the occurrence of an oil strike. On February 6 the local press provided further information "based on a highly reliable authority." The source indicated that high gravity light oil, the equal of Turner Valley limestone crude, had been struck. The company, however, continued to be cautious in its public statements about its future plans for the well. The *Bulletin* reported:

After obtaining encouraging oil and gas showings in several drill stem tests at its Leduc No. 1 well, Imperial Oil is running seven inch casing in preparation for a test of the productive possibilities of this well presently in the Devonian limestone at 5,066 feet. When definite production data is available, the information will be officially released.

In anticipation of the production test, which was planned for Thursday, February 13, fifteen flatcars loaded with tubing, separation tanks, and other necessary equipment arrived in Leduc over the weekend. The production test involved dropping sleeve-type tubing down the well and then removing the concrete plug holding the gusher. With the plug gone and with air going down through the outer sleeve, oil could rise in the inner section of the tubing and then flow into tanks. The first liquid to come through the tubing would be in the form of an emulsion consisting of gas and oil, which would need separating. Once separated, analysis would determine the type of oil that had been found. All of the equipment had to be in place before the plug could be removed.

In addition to preparing for the production test, Imperial Oil also obtained blocks of property under reservation leases comprising approximately 635,000 acres immediately north and northwest of Edmonton. It also made preparations for drilling a second well south of Leduc No. 1. By Wednesday, February 12, a 100-foot derrick had been raised for the second well.

Harry Ainlay, mayor of Edmonton from 1946 to 1949, ensured that the oil boom would be as advantageous to Edmonton as possible. His policies on housing, recreation, industrial development, and education laid a sound economic and social foundation upon which future mayors could build. (COEA)

Ross Flats was the scene of natural gas exploration just after the turn of the century. Unfortunately for investors, the well did not produce commercial quantities. (PAA, E. Brown Collection)

By Thursday all was in readiness for the production test. The events of the day began with a morning conference at the Macdonald Hotel attended by the Honourable N.E. Tanner, minister of lands and mines; Mayor Ainlay; Dr. John A. Allan, head of the Department of Geology at the University of Alberta; L.E. Drummond, secretary-manager of the Alberta and Northwest Chamber of Mines; S.R. Stevens, manager of the Edmonton division of Imperial Oil Ltd.; T.A. Lawrence of Toronto, representative of the public relations branch of Imperial Oil; City Commissioner D.B. Menzies; and City Engineer A.W. Haddow. At the meeting, Frank Roberts, head

Employees of the Geological Survey of Canada discuss their work beneath their drilling rig. They were searching for oil at Victoria, which today is known as Pakan, Alberta. The Geological Survey of Canada, an arm of the federal government, was one of the first organizations to look for oil in Alberta. This well was capped in 1899 when natural gas was found. (PAA)

of one of the geophysical seismic parties that had been working for several months in the Edmonton area, explained the work undertaken by the company. Samples of cores from the Leduc well were also displayed.

Following the meeting a convoy of cars containing the various provincial, civic, and company officials moved to the drilling site. The group first visited the second well where drilling operations were underway. When the delegation arrived at Leduc No. 1, they found the crew busy swabbing the well, thereby clearing out mud and water in preparation for the 1 p.m. test. Mechanical problems, however, delayed the

time of the test. But the delay failed to discourage the estimated 500 people who joined the various officials to witness the event. The crowd included hundreds of Edmontonians and residents of the Leduc and Calmar districts, including real-estate agents, lawyers, truckers, farmers, and businessmen. The majority were not properly dressed for a wait in the 14 degrees Fahrenheit temperature, but coffee, sandwiches, pickles, cake, and doughnuts were served by Pauline McLean of the Cottage Tea Room in Edmonton on instructions from the oil company.

Edmonton businessmen in 1910 examine the oil-laden earth near Fort McMurray. Each one knows he is standing on a black gold fortune. Sadly for them, the technology required to profitably remove the oil would not be finally developed until the 1950s. (PAA, E. Brown Collection)

By 2 p.m. the test had finally begun. At 2:10 the excitement mounted as water, mud, gas, and oil spurted about 60 feet high as the workers pulled the swab from the hole. When the gas and oil were lit, a perfect ring of smoke about 20 feet in diameter rose about 200 feet in the sky before breaking up. The production test that followed indicated that the well would produce 500 barrels a day, at an estimated worth of $2 per barrel.

This success followed many years of relative failure to locate and exploit the petroleum resources of the Edmonton area and Northern Alberta. The petroleum resources of Northern Alberta had been noted as early as 1788 when Peter Pond reported the seepage of oil from the sands along the Athabasca River in the Fort McMurray area 300 miles northeast of Edmonton. The next year Pond's observations were confirmed by Alexander Mackenzie. The scientific investigation of the area began with John Macoun's 1875 trip through Northern Alberta with a party from the Geological Survey of Canada. Macoun travelled from Peace River Landing to Fort Chipewyan via the Peace River and then to Prince Albert, Saskatchewan, via the Athabasca River and the Methy Portage. On his trip up the Athabasca, he made the first scientific observations of the tar sands. His observations would

Left: *Even in 1914, geologists knew there was oil near Edmonton; the problem then, as it is now, was knowing the exact location. The American-Canadian Oil Company's exploration in the Morinville area proved fruitless. Years later, Imperial Oil would strike it big at nearby Redwater. (PAA, E. Brown Collection)*

Since the first decade of this century Redwater, located 36 miles northeast of Edmonton, has been a village which serves as a centre for the farmers of the area. Within two years of the discovery of oil and gas there in 1948, over 890 oil wells were put into operation. Redwater has grown to town status, and continues to enjoy an agricultural and petroleum economic base. (PAA, H. Pollard Collection)

result in further investigations by other members of Canada's Geological Survey. The first large-scale drilling operations were undertaken by the Geological Survey between 1893 and 1899. Technical difficulties plagued these early ventures as well as later attempts to develop the tar sands during the 1920s and 1930s. In December 1904 the Edmonton *Bulletin* described the drilling of a gas well in Edmonton by the North West Gas and Oil Company in Rossdale. The *Bulletin* reported that "none are more enthusiastic than Mr. Dingman, manager of the company. The prospects were good from the start but the success which has already attended their enterprise is abundant proof that a very great pressure of gas will be stuck as the well is sunk deeper." Despite these optimistic predictions, the well was never developed for commercial use.

The only success achieved with respect to oil development in Northern Alberta was the discovery and development of the reserves at Norman Wells. Other oil fields discovered at Wainwright and Vermilion were too remote from Edmonton to create a local boom. A gas field near Viking was developed, and gas was piped to Edmonton in 1923. Edmonton, however, continued to be dependent on agriculture for its economic base and on coal as a fuel for domestic use.

With the success of Leduc No. 1, Imperial Oil accelerated its work on a number of step-out wells to determine the extent of the field. Imperial Leduc No. 2, located 1.5 miles south of Leduc No. 1, reached oil at a depth of 5,370 feet. The well was completed on May 10 and came in as a producer on May 21. A

The Great Canadian Oil Sands operation, on the shores of the Athabasca River at Fort McMurray, was built at a cost of $235 million. When it opened in 1967 it was the largest single capital venture in Alberta's history. GCOS was the first company to commercially separate oil from the oil sands of the region. (PAA, Edmonton Journal *Collection)*

second step-out well, located three-quarters of a mile northeast of Leduc No. 1, came in as a producer on the same day. By the end of 1947, Imperial Oil drilling crews had completed 23 producing wells.

In addition to drilling step-out wells close to the first discovery, Imperial Oil drilled a series of outpost wells miles away in several directions to determine the extent of the pool. One of Imperial's outpost wells, north of the North Saskatchewan River in the Woodbend area, was started on October 14, 1947, and completed successfully on January 18 to a depth of 5,340 feet. The Canadian Atlantic Oil Company also found success in the Leduc-Woodbend field. In 1951 alone more than 300 wells were completed in the Leduc-Woodbend field, and by 1954 it contained 1,278 wells capable of producing oil. It would continue producing black gold until 1983.

The discovery and initial development of the Leduc field was followed almost 20 months later by the discovery of the Redwater field northeast of Edmonton by Imperial Oil. It was to become an even greater field than Leduc-Woodbend. The Redwater discoveries confirmed that the Edmonton area was a major oil-producing region with original recoverable reserves exceeding one billion barrels. By 1953 a further 21 oil fields confirmed this fact. The largest of these discoveries was the Pembina field 85 miles southwest of Edmonton, which by August 1956 had become Canada's leading producer with an output of more than 100,000 barrels per day. It was followed by the discovery of additional oil and gas fields. More than 80 percent of the oil wells eventually developed in Alberta were in the Edmonton market area.

The discovery and development of the conventional reserves of oil in the 1950s were complemented by the first successful attempt to exploit the tar sands, which cover an area of 29,800 square miles in Northern Alberta. Great Canadian Oil Sands Ltd., a company organized in 1953, constructed a large-scale pilot plant, an operational plant, and a pipeline to Edmonton. The initial design work for the plant

Left: *Ernest C. Manning, Premier of Alberta from 1943 to 1968, turns the valve that starts the oil flowing through the Edmonton-Regina section of the Interprovincial Pipeline. The $93 million project replaced over 800 railway tank cars which had been used previously to move the oil to eastern markets. (PAA, Public Affairs Collection)*

The Sherritt Gordon plant, located at Fort Saskatchewan, was built at a cost exceeding $60 million. It presently employs over 1,000 people. The plant produces ammonium phosphate fertilizers, extracts nickel and copper from ore concentrates, and makes blank coins which are later stamped for denomination by the ordering country. (PAA, Edmonton Journal Collection)

was begun in 1962 by Canadian Bechtel Limited, a subsidiary of the Bechtel Corporation of San Francisco, which had also completed the Canol project during World War II. The plant officially opened on September 25, 1967, and other plants followed by Syncrude and Suncor.

The discovery of oil reserves led to the development of a pipeline system, which began when in 1947 Imperial Oil constructed an eight-inch pipeline from the Leduc field to the railway eight miles away. Pipe was very difficult to obtain, but enough pipe was eventually found in the United States where a pipeline between Greensboro, North Carolina, and Richmond, Virginia, was being disinterred. Prior to its use in North Carolina, the pipe had been used in a West Texas field. The Leduc line began operations on November 3, 1947, when G.M. Blackstock, chairman of the Board of Public Utilities Commissioners of Alberta, filled the first tank car. A tank

Facing page: *Despite its
significant size for its day
the 1950s plant, as seen
here, was expanded during
the 1960s. Celanese
Canada produces
chemicals essential for the
manufacture of plastics,
man-made fibres such as
polyester and nylon, and
alcohols and glycols
necessary for the
manufacture of varnishes
and lacquers. (PAA, Public
Affairs Collection)*

farm, consisting of three tanks with a combined capacity of
20,000 barrels, was also constructed during the year.

The first pipeline system to reach markets beyond Alberta
was developed in 1949 with the incorporation of the Interprovincial Pipe Line Company. Completed in December 1950,
the line ran from Edmonton via Winnipeg to markets in the
eastern United States over a total distance of 1,129 miles. With
its incorporation on March 21, 1951, the Trans Mountain Oil
Pipe Line Company began construction of a second pipeline,
which would provide a connection between Edmonton and the
West Coast. The 718-mile, 24-inch line built between February
1952 and September 1953 ran along the CNR line from
Edmonton to Jasper National Park, crossed the Yellowhead
Pass, and then followed river valleys into Burnaby, a
Vancouver suburb. An Edmonton pipeline terminal, consisting
of eight 150,000-barrel and four 80,000-barrel steel tanks and
a pumping station, was also constructed as part of this system.

These trunk lines were supplemented by the construction of
various feeder lines. By the end of 1954, the Imperial Pipeline
Company's 219 miles were serving the Leduc-Woodbend,
Redwater, and Excelsior fields. The British American Alberta
Pipeline Company laid 21 miles to deliver Redwater oil to the
Interprovincial Pipeline. The Canadian Gulf Pipe Line
Company constructed a system 200 miles long to serve the
Duhamel, Malmo, New Norway, Stettler, Fern-Big Valley, and
West Drumheller fields. The Edmonton Pipe Line Company
laid almost 100 miles to deliver oil to the city from wells in the
Joarcom field. The Texaco Exploration Company built 135
miles of line to deliver crude from Wizard Lake, Bonnie Glen,
Glen Park, and Westerose field to Edmonton, primarily to the
McCall-Frontenac refinery. The Pembina Pipe Line, which
extended just over 72 miles from the Pembina oil field to
Edmonton, was built in 1954 and 1955.

The oil development of the post-World War II era added
another important sector to Edmonton's economy. By 1972
industrial development in Edmonton included petrochemical
and synthetic textile industries. These new industries

One of the first chemical plants to set up operations in Edmonton was Celanese Canada. The plant in the east end required three years to build, at an initial cost of $40 million. Construction of the plant was finished by the mid-1950s. (PAA, Public Affairs Collection)

complemented Edmonton's traditional industries, such as food processing, and its traditional role as a transportation centre. Edmonton's petrochemical industry was officially inaugurated on July 17, 1948, when Imperial Oil opened Edmonton's first refinery. Originally constructed in Whitehorse as part of the Canol project, the plant was disassembled and reconstructed in Edmonton. British American, McCall-Frontenac, and Celanese Canada all built local petrochemical plants shortly thereafter. In the 1950s other plants were built in the Edmonton area by Canadian Industries Limited to produce polyethylene, by Sherritt Gordon Mines Ltd. to produce nitrogen fertilizer, and by Borden Chemicals to produce urea formaldehyde and phenol formaldehyde resins. In the 1960s local plants were also built to produce chlor-alkali, glycol, ethanolamines,

The oil companies located on Edmonton's east side, known as refinery row, not only make a significant economic contribution to the city, but provide a unique nighttime beauty. (PAA, Public Affairs Collection)

fertilizers, and carbon disulfide.

As with the boom induced by railway construction prior to World War I, the oil boom resulted in dramatic changes in all aspects of life in Edmonton. It served as a catalyst for increased investment in other aspects of the local economy, such as the construction industry. As the city's traditional employers, among them the provincial government and the University of Alberta, increased in size, they made demands for new construction. As jobs opened up through the growth of business, industry, and government, population increased dramatically from 113,166 in 1946 to 551,314 in 1982, with the majority of the new Edmontonians coming from Eastern Canada. Throughout the interwar years Edmonton's physical appearance had remained relatively unchanged, but by the

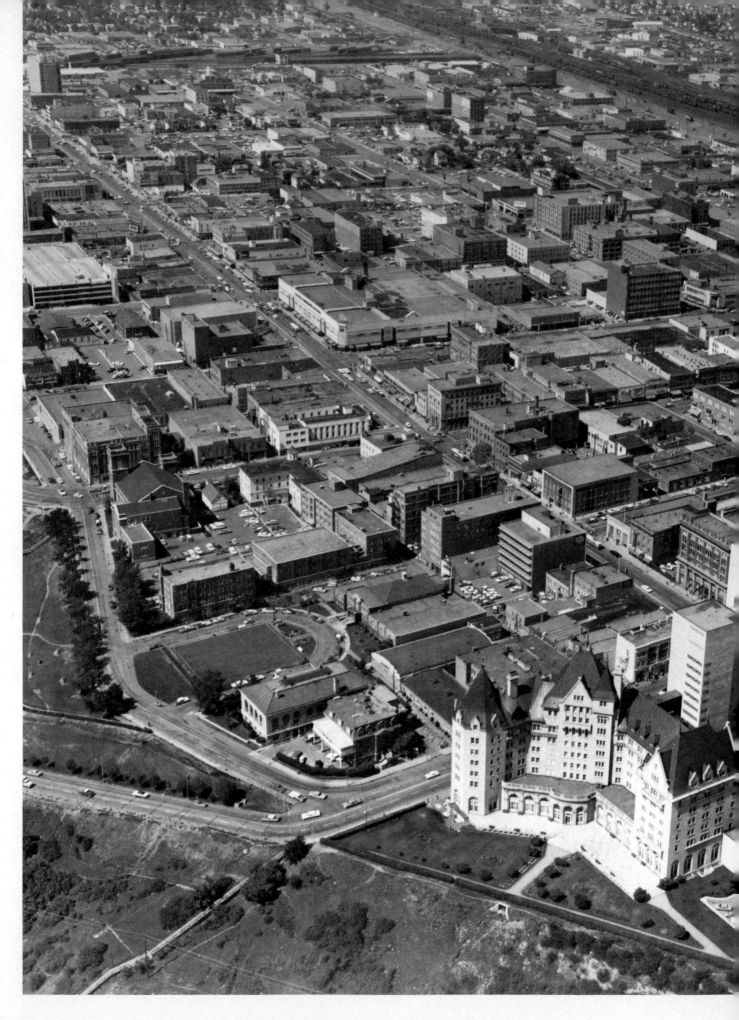

In this 1961 aerial view of Edmonton the Macdonald Hotel still captivated the skyline. Within 20 years the city's downtown would be virtually unrecognizable with the addition of dozens of new buildings. (PAA, Public Affairs Collection)

Designed by architect Maxwell Dewar, Edmonton's city hall has 130,000 square feet of floor space. The cornerstone, laid by Mayor William Hawrelak, holds silver coins, a one-dollar bill, a copy of the Edmonton Journal, *and microfilm of City Council minutes dealing with the planning and construction of the building. (PAA, Wells Studio Collection)*

early 1960s the process of rebuilding a city based on oil had begun. The value of building permits increased from $15 million in 1946 to $1.5 billion in 1981. Change was particularly evident in the central core, and the demolition of the civic market symbolized the change.

The City Market, originally built in 1912, operated for only two years before closing when a new market building was erected on 101st Street and 107th Avenue. The new location, however, did not emerge as the new centre of Edmonton, and

the city turned the building over to the Edmonton Public School Board for use as a technical school and returned to the original market location. In 1932 the market was expanded to accommodate 141 small stalls and 72 large greenhouse stalls. Stalls rented by the day at 50 cents per three-foot stall. Greenhouse rental was $1.00 on weekdays and from $1.75 to $2.50 on Saturday. In addition to its association with Edmonton's position as an agricultural market centre, the square, located to the east of the building, had been the scene of military parades and Depression protests. Commenting to a reporter in 1962 on the market's role as a social centre, 88-year-old stall operator Anna Triska from the Belvedere Poultry Farm, who had been selling eggs and poultry at the market since 1916, said she liked spending Saturdays there because she "sees all her boy friends." Norman Peck, a poultry and dairyman from Leduc, took care of the market stall his father opened in 1913. Many of his customers had bought eggs from the Peck farm for nearly 50 years. Norman Peck kept his father's stall until the market building was demolished in 1962 to make way for the new municipal library.

The City of Edmonton had already abandoned the old Civic Block constructed adjacent to market square in 1912 in favour of a new city hall built in 1956. The new city hall, located a block north and west of the old Civic Block, was the first building in a new civic centre plan. The new building featured a fountain designed by Lionel Thomas that was meant to suggest a flight of Canada geese but has been referred to as "the spaghetti tree." Other new downtown additions included the Alberta Government Telephone Building and the recently completed Manulife Centre office tower.

The rebuilding of the city did not mean the removal of all the monuments to Edmonton's earlier period of growth. Both the McLeod Building and the Macdonald Hotel will be renovated in such a way as to preserve their historical character. The major effort toward the preservation of the earlier chapter of Edmonton's history has taken place in Old Strathcona, primarily around the intersection of 104th Street

Bottom: *The first shopping centre in Edmonton, known originally as Westmount Shoppers Park, began operating on August 17, 1955. With the over 40 stores, and parking spots for 3,000 vehicles, Westmount covers a space exceeding 30 acres. (PAA, A. Blyth Collection)*

and Whyte Avenue. With the cooperation of the city, a community group has launched efforts to save such buildings as the Canadian Pacific station, post office, armoury, and former Presbyterian church. These buildings all date back to the pre-amalgamation era when Strathcona was a separate city.

Changes to the central core were matched by the rapidly expanding suburban areas. The pre-World War I subdivisions that had remained only partially occupied throughout the 1920s and 1930s began to fill up immediately after World

The Queen Elizabeth Planetarium, built by the people of Edmonton to commemorate the visit of Queen Elizabeth II and Prince Philip to the city in 1959, first opened its doors to the public in 1960. It was the first municipally operated planetarium in Canada. (PAA, Public Affairs Collection)

War II. By 1949 Edmonton had liquidated the substantial land holdings it had accumulated during the interwar years. Between 1947 and 1983 the city also resumed annexing outlying areas, including the existing municipalities of Beverly and Jasper Place. The rash of subdivisions created during the pre-World War I boom, with relatively few exceptions, utilized the grid pattern. The subdivision process after World War II was subject to greater design control. Edmonton hired its first town planner, Noel Dant, to oversee this process. In the new subdivisions efforts were made to create self-contained neighbourhoods with a minimum amount of through traffic. Crescents were used to implement this approach, which was first applied in North Glenora. Suburban shopping centres also began to develop, starting with Westmount in 1955 and ending with the recently completed West Edmonton Mall.

A significant aspect of the physical evolution of the city was the development of existing park sites through the addition of such facilities as the Queen Elizabeth Planetarium and the expansion of the park system, primarily in the river valley. Prior to World War I, both the City of Edmonton and the City of Strathcona councils ignored recommendations to preserve the valley for park and recreational use. As a result much of

THE EDMONTON ART GALLERY

The Edmonton Art Gallery, constructed in 1967, climaxed a 54-year tradition in the display and creation of art in Edmonton. The first art exhibit took place in the summer of 1913 and was organized by Professor Adam of the University of Alberta. The exhibit included pictures from the Ontario Society of Artists, a group of water colours loaned by Canon Boyd, and a collection of lithographs by Ethel Gabain.

The Edmonton Art Institute was founded in November 1914 by Mr. Hedley. Seventy Edmonton public schoolteachers and other art enthusiasts who wanted to study art had enrolled in Institute courses of instruction given in the Alex Taylor School. In November 1915 the Edmonton Art Institute, with the cooperation of the Edmonton Public School Board, organized its first show at the McKay Avenue School. Other exhibitions followed in 1916, 1918, and 1921. In all of these exhibitions, a broad range of art was on display, collected from the public and separate school systems in Edmonton, local

artists, and other Canadian or American art institutions.

In 1921 the development of art in Edmonton took another step foward with the creation of the Edmonton Art Club. This organization has survived to become the oldest club of its type in Alberta. The club included Edmonton's first resident professional artist, William Johnstone, an Edinburgh man who opened a studio in the Tegler Building in 1912, and under whose leadership and promotion art students met for discussion. Club activities included organizing art displays and presenting lectures on art appreciation. This latter responsibility was assumed by the Edmonton Museum of Art, created in August 1923. Many of the same

---

The Edmonton Art Gallery attracts thousands of visitors each year. The gallery strives to bring Edmontonians a wide variety of local, Albertan, Canadian, and international art. The Edmonton Art Gallery also offers films, lectures, art courses, art rentals, and art sales. Courtesy, Edmonton Art Gallery, Eleanor Lazare

people who helped create the Edmonton Art Club were involved with the museum. The first president of the organization was Maude Bowman who as director was a tower of strength for the organization for 20 years.

The first gallery of the Edmonton Museum of Art was opened in the public library, but it was moved to the Civic Block in 1927 where it remained until 1944. Soon after the creation of the Edmonton Museum of Art, efforts were underway to find it a permanent home. As early as 1928 a resolution had been passed by the City Council that approved the setting aside of a site for an art museum building in the downtown area. Tentative approval had been given to a site in front of the old Queen's Avenue School on 104th Avenue, between 99th and 100th streets. No further action, however, was taken on this question. Again, in November 1933, a site for the museum was discussed by the finance committee of the City Council. A third attempt to establish an art gallery in downtown Edmonton occurred in 1947. It was one of a number of buildings in a downtown revitalization scheme proposed by Maxwell Dewar. The postwar period brought with it the acquisition of a separate building for the museum. It was the home of former Edmonton resident Richard Secord.

Finally, in 1967 the museum got a permanent home in a building especially designed for it, plus a location in the civic centre. It was the result of a bequest of more than $500,000 from Abigail and Dr. W.N. Condell. The Condells had come to Edmonton in 1907 from Spencerville, Ontario, where Dr. Condell had practised. In 1910 their only child, Arthur, died at the age of five.

the valley was subdivided for residential use. A real-estate collapse and the 1915 flood save the City of Edmonton from implementing this potentially disastrous decision. The city developed Hawrelak Park in the valley, while the provincial government developed Capital City Park.

Transformation of the physical aspects of Edmonton was equalled by changes in its social and cultural life. The Walterdale Theatre, Edmonton Symphony Orchestra, Edmonton Opera Association, Edmonton Art Gallery, and Citadel Theatre with its latest addition, the Clifford E. Lee Pavilion, provided the city with cultural offerings. The Edmonton Art Gallery, a gift to Edmonton's evolving civic centre from Dr. and Mrs. W.N. Condell, opened in 1969. The Edmonton Art Club, which was formed in 1921 following the successful staging of an art display at McKay Avenue School during World War I, survives as the only club of its type in Alberta. The Edmonton Symphony Orchestra, which was disbanded in 1932, was reestablished in 1952 and performs at the Jubilee Auditorium. The arts in Edmonton also benefitted from the initiative of Joseph Shoctor, who spearheaded a campaign to raise funds for the construction of the Citadel Theatre in 1976. The postwar period also saw the formation of the first resident ballet company. It had started modestly in the 1950s as "Dance Interlude," a showcase for student dancers organized by Ruth Carse who had been a successful

Jackie Parker joined the Edmonton Eskimos in 1954, the same year he recovered a fumble to lead the Eskimos to a victorious Grey Cup game. He was also a member of the Grey Cup champions in 1955 and 1956. In 1978 he was named the most outstanding athlete of the last quarter century in the Canadian Football League. In 1983 Jackie Parker became the head coach of the Edmonton Eskimos. (PAA, Wells Studio Collection)

professional dancer in Toronto, New York, and England before an injury cut short her career in 1954. In 1960 the company became the Edmonton Ballet, and six years later it became the Alberta Ballet Company.

After nine years' absence professional football returned to Edmonton on December 28, 1948, when Ken Montgomery, Murray Montague, Bill Forester, Dr. Walter McKenzie, Joe Schoctor, Eric Duggan, Percy Daigle, Henry Singer, Walter Blake, Bob Bradburn, and Moe Lieberman formed the new Edmonton Eskimo Rugby Football Club as a public company with 20,000 shares at one dollar each. Annis Stukas was named coach in February 1949, and rugby was dropped from the name in 1952. After limited success in their first season, the Eskimos made it to the Grey Cup in 1954. Under Coach Frank "Pop" Ivy, the Eskimos won the cup when outstanding player Jackie Parker recovered a Montreal Alouette fumble and ran 95 yards for a touchdown. The team won the cup again in 1955, 1956, 1978, and 1982.

The postwar period would also eventually see Edmonton enter the National Hockey League in 1979. After watching the hockey wars at a distance, Edmonton could now cheer for its own team, the Oilers, and its own stars, such as Wayne Gretzky. The team's greatest triumph came in 1984 with the winning of the Stanley Cup. Professional baseball was also reestablished when Peter Pocklington purchased a Pacific Coast League franchise in Ogden, Utah, and moved the team to Edmonton in 1980. The Trappers play in Ducy Stadium (formerly Renfrew Park), named after John Ducy of local baseball fame. Ducy began his career in baseball as a batboy for Deacon White with the 1921-1922 Eskimos. After the war he organized another Eskimo baseball team that participated in various Western leagues between 1946 and 1960.

In addition to the organization of professional sports, Edmonton also hosted two international sporting events. The first of the events was the Commonwealth Games, which were held in 1978, and the World University Games, which took place between July 1 and 11, 1983. The University of Alberta,

THE 1978 COMMONWEALTH GAMES

The first Commonwealth Games were held in Hamilton, Ontario, in 1930. Canada hosted the games for a second time in 1954 when they were held in Vancouver. Edmonton became the third city in Canada to earn this honour in 1978.

Mayor Ivor Dent led the community in its efforts to win the bid for the event. It involved a two-step procedure in which Edmonton's bid had to be first endorsed by the British Commonwealth Games Association of Canada. In June 1970 the federal government decided not to grant a Canadian bid for the 1978 games. This decision temporarily halted the preliminary planning for Edmonton's bid. In October 1971, however, the federal government's decision was reversed. Edmonton thus had 50 frantic days to prepare its "Book of Invitation" in time for the December 6 meeting in Montreal. This document had to include a detailed socio-economic study of all implications of a games bid: a close examination of possible sites for five new facilities, documentation of the suitability of existing facilities, proposed operating and capital budgets, an outline for an organizing committee structure, and an outline of the role of the various governments and sports federations. The 94-page document was prepared on time.

On January 8, 1972, the Edmonton delegation made its presentation to a delayed meeting of the Commonwealth Association. In making its presentation the Edmonton delegation stressed what Edmonton could do for the games, rather than what the games could do for Edmonton. Edmonton's bid triumphed over the bid from Toronto.

The second and last step in the process was to win the approval of the

Graham Smith, second from left on stand, joins the other members of the Canadian Swimming Team, in raising their arms in a victory salute, after winning another gold medal at the Games. Smith is the only person to win six gold medals at the Commonwealth Games. (COE)

bid by the Commonwealth Games Association, which would be meeting in Munich, Germany, in August. The preparations for this last step took place on many fronts. Mayor Dent made extensive trips to the Caribbean and Africa to lobby delegates. Canadian high commissioners and trade officials also assisted by providing information on Edmonton's plans and progress to the 48 Commonwealth countries. And on the home front an organizing team was being created and funding arranged. Fund drives were organized, and financial assistance was received from the government of the Province of Alberta, Edmonton Football Club, and the Exhibition Association. The Commonwealth Games Canada (1978) Foundation was also officially registered in preparation for the departure of the Edmonton delegation to Munich on August 21, 1972.

The Canadian bid, over an early strong bid from Leeds, England, was

approved. The construction program, which was formed after that decision, consisted of five new facilities for the city. The largest item was the 42,900-seat Commonwealth Stadium for the opening and closing ceremonies, as well as the track and field events. The other facilities included an aquatic centre, firing range, velodrome, and bowling green. In addition to these new constructions, various facilities of the University of Alberta were also pressed into service.

Edmonton *Journal* reporter Dan Powers recorded the official opening events on August 3, 1978:

The emotion, color and historical significance of the event were so intense people talked about having misty eyes, and shivers up their backs.

It was incredible. After long years of preparation, the Games were declared open by Queen Elizabeth. Edmonton was centre-stage for a world television audience of 500 million.

The moment seemed suspended in time.

Snowbird jets leaving plumes of white exhaust against a sharp, blue sky; the sweeping beauty of a brand new stadium; the stirring entry of a Canadian Forces band and kilted pipers; the kaleidoscope march-past of some 1,900 athletes from 46 Commonwealth countries.

There was an atmosphere of quiet pride, friendship and expectation. It was a mental high that would never be repeated.

The athletic events were complemented for the first time by an arts festival. Other cultural offerings held in connection with the Commonwealth Games included a film festival, concert series, and drama.

with the support of the City of Edmonton, made its bid for the latter games, which included track and field, basketball, cycling, gymnastics, diving, fencing, swimming, tennis, water polo, and volleyball. Many of the facilities constructed for the Commonwealth Games were used, and a new field house was built at the university to accommodate the games.

The Edmonton Exhibition also returned after the war. In 1962 it was rechristened Klondike Days, and new features, such as the sourdough raft race and the promenade, were introduced. The Summerfest brought theatre and musical presentations ranging from folk to jazz to the city for two weeks in August, and at the Heritage Festival in Hawrelak Park the public could enjoy the food, dance, and music of Edmonton's diverse ethnic communities.

Postwar Edmonton was increasingly multicultural. The traditionally small population of Italians, Germans, Greeks, Ukranians, Hungarians, and Dutch were reinforced by immigration from Europe and were joined by new ethnic groups. The Portuguese began arriving in 1957 when a group came from the Azores to work on the railway, and by 1976 there were about 6,500 Portuguese in Edmonton. The first Koreans to emigrate to Alberta arrived in Edmonton in the early 1960s.

In the early 1980s Edmonton's postwar boom slowed. Lower levels of investment in the region by oil companies in such locations as the tar sands and reduced spending by the various levels of government also had their effect on such areas of economic activity as construction. Edmonton's second boom had, however, been a period of consolidation for the city. The relatively long period of prosperity from 1939 brought into existence the city that Edmontonians had glimpsed in 1912. Unlike the 1920s, Edmonton emerged into a well-established transportation system. It had also begun to emerge as a centre for medical research, northern development research, and electronics. These are important assets for a city that has consistently demonstrated a strong will to survive.

The Imperial Oil Company hit it big with Leduc Number 1 in 1947. Hundreds of people went to see the spectacular sight of these flames rising over 200 feet into the air. (COEA)

Left: *This young athlete takes a short break from a late afternoon ski trip in Capital City Park to enjoy the setting sun. The park's paths are a haven for cross-country skiers in the winter, and for cyclists in the summer. (COE)*

Facing page: *Edmontonians enjoy the quiet and beauty of the river valley from Macdonald Drive, overlooking the pyramids of the Muttart Conservatory. Courtesy, Travel Alberta*

Below: *Ice skating continues to be popular with hardy Edmontonians who use the city's lakes and parks all year. Courtesy, Chris Bruun*

Left: *A bicyclist rides by Edmonton sculptor John Weaver's bronze statue* The Trader, *depicting fur trader John A. McDougall trading with an Indian. Courtesy, Jean Beck, Canadian Government Office of Tourism*

These views of downtown show the sleek steel-and-glass Edmonton skyline. The textile sculpture, top right, captures the spirit of Universiade '83. Top left and right, courtesy, Chris Bruun; bottom, courtesy, Bob Anderson, Canadian Government Office of Tourism

Musicians entertain in downtown Edmonton. The Waltz of Spring, a mural by Toti, is visible behind them. Courtesy, Chris Bruun, Masterfile

Right: *Puppets entertain the crowd during Summerfest, 1981, at Sir Winston Churchill Square. Courtesy, Bill Brooks, Masterfile*

Below: *Rundle Park provides shady trees and a cool waterside spot to gather. Courtesy, Chris Bruun*

INDUSTRY • INTEGRITY • PROGRESS

CHAPTER IX

PARTNERS

IN

PROGRESS

What is the business sector of any community, large or small? Not the central point of community life; nor the nerve centre of city, town, village; nor its geographic heart.

But all of these and more. The city of Edmonton owes its being to a group of businessmen and investors—a group composed of individuals who lived an ocean and a continent away from the upper reaches of the North Saskatchewan River. Members of this group called themselves "a company of gentleman adventurers," men who had the courage, initiative, and determination to become part of a force we know as the private sector of the economy.

These men came together to form the Hudson's Bay Company—a business very much alive in Edmonton 314 years after its founding on May 2, 1670. From remote trading post to fort, to village, town, city, and provincial capital, Edmonton has done little but march forward since it was given birth by its founders, that gentleman company of adventurers trading into Hudson Bay in 1795.

This march has not been consistent, nor has it been without intermittent reversal and change of pace. The fact remains that whatever progress this city made in its first 100-odd years was through the drive of the leaders of its business community.

Take the city of Edmonton's first 50 years: Business leaders such as Alex Taylor, Frank Oliver, Richard Secord, John McDougall, Matt McCauley, David McQueen, and John Walters built their community into a force that was recognized as one of enduring qualities. Their faith attracted not one, but three railways to make tracks into Edmonton, along with settlers, immigrants, professionals, laborers, clergymen, members of religious orders, and skilled tradespeople, all anxious and ready to build where there was nothing but forest and bush. Their faith had much to do with their city's selection as the capital of the two-year-old Province of Alberta; it had everything to do with the foundation of the University of Alberta and of Edmonton's growth from an outpost settlement to a metropolis.

Where these pioneer builders left off, others followed and still others followed them. World wars, recessions, real-estate booms, and the discovery of oil and natural gas riches in Edmonton's backyard—all have contributed to the fame and fortune of this city. All of these came about because city and district businessmen, at work forging their futures on the anvil of private enterprise, at the same time forged the futures of their community and their neighbours.

It was not by accident that Edmonton has achieved the stature it enjoys today. This eminence is the bottom line of contributions of the city's businessmen over 75 and more years.

The following chapter is dedicated to the business community of Edmonton, past and present. In a small way it delineates the result of its entrepreneurs' faith in a great city.

HISTORICAL SOCIETY OF ALBERTA
Amisk Waskahegan Chapter

Edmonton was founded in 1795 as a Hudson's Bay Company trading post. This 1912 photo shows the old fort with the Parliament buildings in the background. Courtesy of the Provincial Archives of Alberta.

The sponsor of this book is the Amisk Waskahegan Chapter of the Historical Society of Alberta. "Amisk Waskahegan" is Cree for "Beaver Hills House," a name selected to reflect Edmonton's origin as a Hudson's Bay Company trading post known as Edmonton House that was founded in 1795. Later Fort Edmonton, as the post came to be known, was designated as the headquarters for the Saskatchewan District of the company.

The Historical Society was founded by a group of influential citizens and incorporated by an Act of the Alberta Legislature in 1907. Its founders included the Honourable Alexander Cameron Rutherford, first premier of the province of Alberta; Dr. Henry Marshall Tory, first president of the University of Alberta; and Balmer Watt, later editor of *The Edmonton Journal*.

Maintaining the interests of these pioneers in the movement to record and preserve the records of Alberta's early days, the Amisk Waskahegan Chapter of the Historical Society encourages citizens of the province to participate in its work. It sponsors two annual awards. One is to the University of Alberta undergraduate whose essay on Western Canadian history is judged to be the best submitted during each academic year, and one is to a person who has made outstanding contributions to the histo-

ry of Northern Alberta through writings, art, teaching, or the preservation of historic artifacts or documents. The Chapter also appoints a representative to the Edmonton Historical Board, which advises the Edmonton City Council on historical matters, and is in close liaison with SPARE (The Society for the Preservation of the Architectural Resources of Edmonton).

The Chapter is active over a wide area. Today its area of special interest includes that in Alberta from Red Deer to the Northwest Territories border. Chapter members meet on the first Wednesday of each month, October through March, to hear papers presented on Northern Alberta history, and gather for the annual John Rowand Night in April. This latter

event recalls John Rowand, chief factor of Edmonton House, who was instrumental in establishing his Saskatchewan District as the wealthiest in the Hudson's Bay Company's jurisdiction. The Chapter's winter meetings are held in the lecture room of the Provincial Museum of Alberta. Summer meetings take the form of field trips to nearby communities and other points of historical interest.

It is our sincere hope that this book will further interest in the broad and rich heritage that is Northern Alberta's. We thank all those individuals and firms who have contributed to it.

The Honourable Alexander Cameron Rutherford (right), first premier of the province of Alberta and one of the founders of the Historical Society of Alberta, poses here with Lieutenant Governor Bulyer (left) and Lord Strathcona. Courtesy of the Provincial Archives of Alberta.

ALBERTA GOVERNMENT TELEPHONES

Alberta Government Telephones (AGT) began in 1906 when the provincial government entered the telephone business as a direct competitor of the Bell Telephone Company. A number of AGT's forerunners had already been in business for 20 years. First was the line established by Alexander Taylor from the Dominion Government Telegraph Office near Fort Edmonton to the H.W. McKenney store at St. Albert, 288 poles northwest of Edmonton. Calgary installed the first telephone exchange as early as 1887. The ensuing years saw much telephone expansion in several other communities as the pioneers determined the telephone was more a necessity than a convenience.

The importance of the telephone in the development of Alberta was not lost on the province's first government, which set aside a sum of $25,000 in its first budget for preliminary work to establish a government telephone system. While Manitoba proved to be the first to declare a government telephone system, it remained for Alberta's government to be the first in North America to build and operate phone lines.

AGT's first line, from Calgary to Banff, was completed in 1907, the same year the government decided to compete in earnest with the powerful Bell interests. One year later, after months of sometimes bitter negotia-tions, the province authorized the purchase of the Alberta Bell assets. The sale was completed in 1908.

AGT's early years were ones of expansion, a healthy condition that was later severely limited by the demands and the restrictions of World War I.

The '20s saw AGT concentrate on extending its rural lines over vast distances of prairie and parklands, to link early settlers as the province surged to what appeared to be a great agricultural and resource-filled potential. By 1925 Albertans were able to talk across North America, and by 1927 even to the British Isles. In 1932 AGT joined other telephone companies across Canada to form the TransCanada Telephone System, giving Canada its own coast-to-coast telephone network.

But the '30s also brought the Great Depression. And with it came drought and storms that left the provincial government and AGT economies near bankruptcy. AGT was forced to sell its extensive, but unprofitable, rural phones and transmission lines to farmer-owned/mutual telephone companies for salvage value. It was in a much-reduced state that AGT survived the Depression and prepared to meet the problems of the World War II years.

With defence contracts to meet, AGT was faced with providing services to more customers than it could handle with its hopelessly depleted facilities and manpower. The war years were hectic ones for AGT, and the increased demands did not cease with peace.

Contributing to the surge was the discovery of oil at Leduc and the establishment of the oil exploration industry. This new rush to Alberta's remote areas led to AGT's entry into the field of mobile radio communications.

Microwave transmission of long-distance communications came to Alberta in the '50s. AGT completed its portion of the TransCanada Microwave System in 1958.

AGT returned to the rural telephone business in the '60s when it realized the individual farmer/mutual companies could not cope with the costs of providing telecommunications' new technologies to update their systems. In 1963 AGT undertook to integrate approximately 1,100 mutual companies with its systems.

In the '70s AGT introduced several exceptional developments, among them community antenna television, electronic switching, phoneCentres, Altel Data, extended flat-rate calling, automated switchboards, and zero-

Edmonton pioneer Matt McCauley's livery stable was one of the first buildings in Edmonton to have a telephone. The site today is occupied by McCauley Plaza, dominated by the AGT Tower.

plus dialing.

When cablevision became a public issue in 1970, AGT was well under way with plans for a unique distribution system that would prove profitable for both AGT and community distributors. It was originally conceived as a 10-city plan, with AGT transmitting signals of American stations from an antenna located on Mt. Kelly in British Columbia to local distributors throughout Alberta.

In 1972 AGT's first electronic exchange went into service in Calgary. This was the first of an extensive programme to move into the electronic age.

Extended flat-rate calling was introduced in 1974 to communities with a common interest within 48 kilometres of each other. In 1978 the distance was expanded to 55 kilometres.

The phoneCentre concept was introduced by AGT in 1975 and phone stores were established throughout the system. Coincident with this was the rewiring of thousands of homes with special telephone jacks at no charge to the customer.

AGT turned up its first automated long-distance switchboard in 1976. At the same time the system began introducing zero-plus dialing in the Edmonton area.

The system returned to regional management of its operations in 1976 to streamline internal operations and improve customer service. Regional managers now guide the affairs of the company from headquarters established in Grande Prairie, Edmonton, Red Deer, Vegreville, Calgary, Lethbridge, and Medicine Hat.

In 1979 AGT pioneered another first for Western Canada with the introduction of digital switching at Wembley. Four other digital machines

This 35-story, 441-foot tower is the headquarters of Alberta Government Telephones. Rising above nearby office towers, the AGT Building looks down on the Low Level Bridge, first railway crossing connecting Edmonton with the rest of Canada. Courtesy of Con Boland, The Middle Earth Gallery.

were added that same year as AGT embarked once again on a huge upgrading programme to keep the system in the forefront of telecommunications technology.

Two significant milestones were passed in 1980. AGT removed its last remaining overhead toll line—from Stettler to Drumheller—and the last farmer-owned/mutual telephone company near Rimbey was integrated with the AGT system.

With the rapid developments in telecommunications technology making dramatic changes in the way society lives and works, AGT recognized the need to broaden its activities if it was to continue as a viable operation.

In 1982 AGT established Alberta Telecommunications International Ltd. as a wholly owned subsidiary. Its mandate is to seek opportunities outside Alberta's borders to give Albertans with telecommunications expertise greater opportunities to use their developing skills while generating

needed additional revenues for AGT.

Alta-Can Telecom Inc. was also formed in 1982 as another wholly owned subsidiary, to foster industrialization in Alberta by supporting high-technology companies in the field of telecommunications.

The growing importance of the mobile radio telephone in Alberta's development led to AGT's venture into a joint undertaking with NOVA, AN ALBERTA CORPORATION. The new undertaking, known as NovAtel, will actively pursue opportunities for marketing mobile radio systems throughout the world.

The '80s opened with a note of optimism which soon changed. Canada's economic downturn, coupled with the impact of the National Energy Plan on Alberta's petroleum exploration industry, forced cancellation of many AGT expansion and development programmes. The 40-year demand by Albertans for more and better facilities, new techniques for new needs, and ready adaptations to new technologies appeared to be over. But it isn't. The demand is still there, and it must be met. The challenge for today's generation of AGT employees is still to provide Albertans with the world's best telecommunications service. It is a challenge that AGT employees are proud to accept.

NOVA, AN ALBERTA CORPORATION

In the past 30 years NOVA, AN ALBERTA CORPORATION (formerly The Alberta Gas Trunk Line Company Limited) has become one of the largest companies in Alberta. Canadian owned and operated, NOVA is today engaged in a wide range of energy-related activities. The corporate headquarters is located in Calgary, with the Alberta Gas Transmission Division carrying out the firm's original business from an Edmonton base.

NOVA's story began in the early 1950s. With the excitement of the Leduc-inspired oil boom, people began to realize that the sedimentary basins containing petroleum held another potential source of energy wealth—natural gas. Private companies applied to the Alberta government for licences to export this fuel to markets elsewhere, especially in Central Canada, but the government was determined that any gas exported should be surplus to the needs of the province. When studies showed there were large surpluses, the concern

then was how to allow exports and at the same time see that the best interests of the people of Alberta were served.

The provincial government decided its objectives could best be met by establishing a new company, owned by private investors and responsible for the gathering and transmission of all Alberta natural gas to be exported from the province. By specifying that it would operate only in Alberta and that directors had to be Alberta residents, the government ensured that the new venture would fall exclusively under provincial regulatory jurisdiction and would work for Albertans in the future.

In 1954 royal assent was granted to a special act of the Alberta legislature, and NOVA was created. Its structure as outlined in the act was unique, giving rise to the mistaken notion that it was controlled by the government. Class "A" shareholders were to have no voting privileges; these rested exclusively with Class "B" shareholders. Class "B" shareholdings

were divided among four groups: utilities, export companies, producers, and government appointees, with the latter coming from the private sector. However, of the seven-man board of directors, only two were appointed by the government and each held one qualifying share of the total authorized 2,002 Class "B" shares.

Changes in the act have since increased membership of the board to 15. Class "A" shareholders now elect seven directors, Class "B" shareholders elect four, and the government appoints four.

A provisional board of directors appointed by the provincial government met in Calgary to arrange distribution of shares. William F. Knode, who had been instrumental in setting up the Alberta Petroleum and Natural Gas Conservation Board, was named to serve as general manager. James C. Mahaffy was appointed secretary/treasurer and NOVA's first office was established in Calgary.

By the end of 1954 the distribution of shares was complete, and an elected board of directors took charge after the first annual meeting in 1955. The board assembled a management team of seven persons in addition to Knode and Mahaffy.

It soon appeared that the move was premature, however, and that there was a good possibility the new venture might not be needed. The markets for natural gas were in Central Canada, so it was essential that the proposed cross-Canada pipeline (now TransCanada PipeLines Limited) be given approval before work could begin on the Alberta system. When satisfactory financing for the cross-Canada project proved impossible to arrange, a delay was announced.

A year later the project was still tied up and every gas producer but

Alberta Premier Ernest Manning (right) officially opened the initial section of the NOVA system in July 1957.

Pipeline construction today proceeds much as it did in 1962, when this line was laid in Alberta.

NOVA's world-scale ethylene complex at Joffre, Alberta, is a key element in the province's petrochemical development.

Waste heat from NOVA operations is harnessed and used in such innovative projects as greenhouses at the Princess compressor station site.

one had stopped calling at NOVA's office, convinced the situation was hopeless. The seven original employees were advised to look for new jobs. Then, after a solid month of acrimonious debate in the House of Commons, Trade and Commerce Minister C.D. Howe invoked closure to clear the way for construction of the TransCanada PipeLines System. This in turn meant that NOVA could proceed with its mandate.

The company started laying pipe in December 1956 and, in the spring of 1957, issued 2.5 million Class "A" common shares to pay for the construction. The *Financial Post* referred to the offering as "the biggest stock bonanza ever to hit the Prairies." Available only to Alberta residents, the shares were so popular that a rationing system was devised, with each person restricted to 20 shares. The forms required only family names, and people were eager to become involved in a provincially based company managed by Albertans. These early shareholders were almost all Albertans, but shares today are widely owned, with over 90 percent registered in Canada.

The official start-up of the Alberta gas transmission system came just seven months after the beginning of construction. At a ceremony near Cavendish in July 1957, Premier Ernest Manning opened a valve that allowed Alberta natural gas to flow eastward through the new pipeline.

At first, since NOVA moved gas only to eastern export points, the system was built by linking up gas fields close to the Saskatchewan border. Then the provincial govern-

ment authorized gas exports to British Columbia and the United States, and it became necessary to expand elsewhere in the province. In 1961 the company placed its Western System into service, and deliveries to the British Columbia and Montana borders began. Also that year the first compressor station was completed at Princess, Alberta. By 1963 NOVA, operating through three divisions, had more than 1,500 miles of pipeline moving about 1.3 billion cubic feet of gas per day.

Throughout the '60s NOVA continued to grow, gaining industry respect for developments in pipeline technology. A 173-mile line from Carstairs to Edson, built in 1965, was the first large-diameter pipeline to be installed in winter. That year a programme of automation began, allowing the entire system to be monitored

24 hours a day from a single control centre. The company was the first in Canada to practise topsoil conservation and one of the first to revegetate pipeline rights-of-way in forested areas.

NOVA employed more than 550 people by 1970 and operated a pipeline system over 3,000 miles long. Several service centres for the gas transmission division had been opened at various locations in the province. In Edmonton, the service centre was originally located in the Cameron Ironworks yard, off Calgary Trail and 51st Avenue. Then, in 1972, a site was purchased at 15810-114th Avenue and the service centre began operations from this location. An executive office was opened in 1973 in the Petroleum Plaza building at 9945-108th Street, Edmonton.

Gas transmission activities in Alberta continued to grow during the early '70s. However, the board of directors decided that, while NOVA could continue to provide the services

NOVA's facilities in Edmonton include the Alberta Gas Transmission Division head-quarters at 9888 Jasper Avenue.

of this utility franchise efficiently and economically, the firm had strengths that could be applied in other areas. The ability to obtain financing and an active management and professional staff provided a base for taking on new challenges that could serve both regional and national purposes and at the same time provide for long-term growth and security. Accordingly, the original act of incorporation was amended to allow diversification into areas not directly related to the original mandate.

The first steps toward diversification were into petrochemicals, and NOVA became involved in the manufacture of methanol, ethylene, and polyvinyl chloride, taking a leadership role in making Alberta a major centre for the manufacture of

these products. NOVA's experience in natural gas transmission was also put to use through its co-sponsorship of two large-scale pipeline projects: the Alaska Highway Gas Pipeline and the Trans Quebec & Maritimes Pipeline.

NOVA then acquired interests in valve manufacturing companies in the United States and Europe. In 1978 the concern purchased majority owner-ship of Husky Oil Ltd., a fully inte-grated Canadian company that is developing conventional and non-conventional petroleum resources.

Thus, in the 10 years prior to 1980, NOVA had changed from a pipeline utility to a diversified organization with interests in petroleum, petrochemicals, manufacturing, and consulting and research added to its gas transmission base. The original name of Alberta Gas Trunk Line no longer adequately described the com-pany's varied activities, and the change to NOVA, AN ALBERTA COR-PORATION was implemented in 1980

to better reflect diversity while still emphasizing the Alberta base.

That same year, NOVA manage-ment decided to transfer the head-quarters of the Alberta Gas Transmis-sion Division from Calgary to Edmon-ton. This new location afforded better access to both northern and southern areas of the transmission system and also served to broaden NOVA's eco-nomic impact throughout Alberta. Approximately 130 employees were relocated to a new 16-storey building at 9888 Jasper Avenue, overlooking the North Saskatchewan River Valley. The executive office was moved from Petroleum Plaza into the new division headquarters. The Edmonton service centre continued to operate in its location on 114th Avenue, and in 1982 an additional service centre was opened in Spruce Grove, just outside Edmonton.

Throughout this period of expan-sion NOVA maintained its commit-ment to purchasing goods and ser-vices from Alberta and Canadian sup-pliers whenever possible. As an exam-ple, pipe purchased from domestic steel producers was used throughout the Alberta system, and in 1980 these producers were awarded contracts to supply pipe for the Alaska Highway Gas Pipeline.

During 1982 NOVA moved into a new corporate headquarters building in Calgary, a 37-storey stainless-steel tower that stands as a major landmark in the west end of the city's downtown core. From this new headquarters, NOVA continues its work as a major independent Canadian-owned energy company.

At the end of 1983, NOVA had assets of approximately $6.8 billion, and the NOVA group of companies employed 8,600 people, about half of them in Alberta.

ALBERTA COLLEGE

Dating back to the early 1900s, this was the original archway to Alberta College, Edmonton's first higher-educational institution.

Alberta College as viewed from MacDonald Drive.

Alberta College, Edmonton's first higher-education institution, became the attainment of a goal 81 years ago. Planted as the vision of prominent local Methodist churchmen, it was rooted in soil initially tilled by the Reverend George McDougall—who some 30 years before had built the then-frontier settlement's first Protestant church.

Prophetically anticipating the day when the knot of crude buildings on the plateau overlooking the Hudson's Bay Company fort at river's edge would grow and eventually mature into a city, he claimed title to a block-long parcel of land now in the heart of Edmonton. On this property the minister built his little church—today an historic exhibit in Fort Edmonton Park—and immediately adjacent the permanent nucleus of Alberta College was erected. The college is there today, visible witness to its founders' faith and a beacon that over the years has led thousands of students to a wide spectrum of university degrees.

The founders' meeting was called on May 22, 1903, by the Reverend

T.C. Buchanan, succeeding the late Reverend McDougall (who had died in a prairie blizzard some years earlier), to fulfill his predecessor's dream of educational facilities in the city that would surely rise around his homestead site.

From the beginning, Alberta College was perceived as belonging to the community. When it was ceremonially opened in a Masonic Hall on December 3, 1903, Dr. J.H. Riddell, the school's first principal, said: "While the management is the responsibility of the Methodist Church, Alberta College is Edmonton's institution, which city now affords facilities for higher education."

On that occasion he also stated an expectation of the founding of a number of colleges that would be linked to one great university, a prediction that was realized in the years following the opening of the University of Alberta in 1908. A decision to sponsor a programme in theology resulted in the construction of Alberta College South, which in time became known as St. Stephen's College, on the university campus. In addition, the liberal arts students of Alberta College were able—through an affiliation between their school and McGill University—to move directly into the new univer-

sity, thereby forming the foundation of its first arts faculty.

During World War I, Alberta College's buildings were almost wholly taken over for hospital purposes. This situation prevailed until 1920; the flu epidemic of 1919 quickly overtaxed conventional hospital accommodations of the day. Further contributions to community service came in the "Hungry '30s," when the college farm ensured an adequate supply of staple foods for the dining room.

Since its inception the institution, with an initial registration of 313, has offered courses in the liberal arts, music, and business education. More recent additions to courses and services offered by Alberta College have included adoption of the semester system, special day-school programmes, facilities for teaching hearing-impaired adults, a performing-arts matriculation programme, and a four-day instruction week.

Current enrolments of approximately 5,000 students indicate the college, though relatively small, continues to increase in popularity in the last quarter of its first 100 years.

SUNWAPTA BROADCASTING LIMITED

The first transmitter building used by Radio Station CFRN was this frame building on 142nd Street. At the time it was almost at the city's western limit.

Sunwapta Broadcasting Limited, which takes its name from an Indian symbol that can be translated as "radiating waves," was originated in 1934. An increase from an initial 100 watts to its present 50,000 watts is a simple summarization of the 50-year history of G.R.A. "Dick" Rice's radio station—CFRN, the most consistent broadcast industry award-winner in the records of Northern Alberta electronic media.

It is valid to note that CFRN and its younger television sister, CFRN-TV, today blanket the northern two-thirds of Alberta, and beyond that as far north as radio receivers happen to be located. Given Edmonton's status as the "Gateway to the North," this

means that CFRN transmissions are regularly picked up on drilling rigs probing the bed of the Arctic Ocean.

Rice founded the venture in a tiny frame cottage that sat on a field almost at the city's western limit (his antenna a modest 200 feet high), subsequently purchasing a 20-acre site two miles outside the boundary. Today Broadcast House is on the Yellowhead Highway, the major trans-provincial artery connecting Edmonton with Pacific Ocean terminals at Prince Rupert and Vancouver, while the city limit has marched five miles west of the radio station. The operation's headquarters originally occupied a shared downtown building, then in 1935 moved into Jasper Avenue premises that had been renovated after serving as Canadian Pacific Railway offices.

In spite of difficult times spawned by the Depression, Sunwapta—with

seven employees and more than a little homemade equipment—went on the air for 13 hours daily. Rice's endeavours were rewarded by listener loyalty that guaranteed the success of

Dr. G.R.A. "Dick" Rice, founder of Sunwapta Broadcasting Limited.

his enterprise; a survey in 1937 revealed that CFRN had received 6,076 letters from listeners located in 324 out-of-town points. Between 1938 and 1961 the station increased its power in a series of leaps to its current wattage; and for several years following 1944, it was the Edmonton outlet for the Canadian Broadcasting Corporation's second Dominion Radio network.

Experimental television work began in 1949, and five years later CFRN-TV aired as Alberta's first TV outlet due to its joining the CBC-TV network as an affiliate, transmitting black-and-white kinescope programmes. On May 7, 1957, the first broadcast via a local microwave link was initiated, occasioned by the official opening of the Northern Alberta Jubilee Auditorium. The following year yet another "first" was achieved: the live coverage of the opening of the Alberta Legislature's spring session, with the transmission fed to five Alberta stations.

Meanwhile, CFRN had moved to its new site on the Yellowhead Highway, and broadcasting emitted from a 441-foot steel tower. The transmitter building—called the Annex—subsequently became the home of CFRN-FM, inaugurated in 1951, whose call letters were changed to CKXM-FM in 1979.

In 1961 a network of privately owned stations across Canada was licensed as the CTV Television Network Ltd. Although its programming initially necessitated videotaping for delayed telecasting, a later completion of a microwave hookup made possible live transmissions to the West. Steady progress by the network encompassed colour conductance by 1966, and its first such programme aired on September 1 of that year.

Further consolidation of operations relocated Sunwapta's downtown Radio Division to Broadcast House in 1964. Today the employee rolls have swelled to about 220, with many names in the 10-, 20-, and 30-year-service categories.

Between 1961 and 1979 the organization set up seven television rebroadcast stations in Central and Northern Alberta, thus observing the mandate carried in its federal licence. CFRN-TV is also carried on three additional community-sponsored rebroadcast outlets—this with considerable engineering assistance from Sunwapta.

In 1974 the company engaged in a joint venture with Edmonton Video Ltd. (CITV) and moved its television transmission centre to Looma, a few miles southeast of the city. At this location the unit's 915-foot tower carries two TV stations and CKXM-FM as well as two other Edmonton FM stations.

In 1984 CFRN Radio celebrates its 50th year of operation, while its founder's services to the community and the industry throughout these years have been widely recognized. His most recent honour at this writing came in 1983, at which time the University of Alberta presented him with a Business Leader Award for the year.

The recipient of an honorary doctor of laws degree from the university, Dr. Rice is renowned for his concern for local and national education, health, welfare, and arts and youth organizations.

Broadcast House, on Yellowhead Highway West, is the headquarters for all Sunwapta Broadcasting Limited operations. At the time of purchase the 20-acre site was two miles outside of Edmonton.

PRINCIPAL GROUP OF COMPANIES

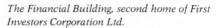

The Financial Building, second home of First Investors Corporation Ltd.

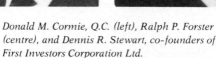

Donald M. Cormie, Q.C. (left), Ralph P. Forster (centre), and Dennis R. Stewart, co-founders of First Investors Corporation Ltd.

Edmontonians Donald M. Cormie, Ralph P. Forster, and Dennis R. Stewart spearheaded the formation of the company called First Investors Corporation Ltd. in 1954. Its head office, with a salaried staff of one person, was established in the Barry Building, a two-storey structure just off Jasper Avenue, now the site of the A.E. LePage Building. From this location the first guaranteed savings plans were issued, set up by the nucleus of the new firm's first sales/marketing team. Edmontonians were encouraged to take the first step toward financial success by forming the habit of thrift through paying themselves small amounts on a regular, monthly basis. Soon a pool of money became available for investment in the form of secured first mortgage loans and government bonds. While the savings certificate itself yielded a 4 percent compound rate of interest, at a time when bank savings rates were 2.25 to 3 percent

and the mortgage rate was 5 to 5.5 percent, the interest rate was seldom the reason why people invested. Rather, they became highly motivated by the fact that money could be put to work in small, regular amounts, until that process became a habit, and keeping a part of their income became a way of life.

Soon First Investors began to expand geographically, to Regina, Calgary, and Saskatoon. By 1957, after becoming firmly established, it made a major move and opened in Vancouver. By 1960 it was considered prudent to open in Canada's four Atlantic provinces, as well as in Seattle, Washington, where the company's U.S. affiliate, Principal Investors Corporation, was created. All this activity was still directed through the building and training of a sales group whose presentation was based entirely on the concept of thrift.

Meanwhile, First Investors had moved its head office to the Financial Building on 107th Street and had set up its first computerized systems for the benefit of the thousands of savers who now existed. As a matter of fact, the Financial Building was the only high-

rise office facility in Edmonton, towering a full 11 storeys above the city!

The company soon came to realize that it could not restrict itself to the accumulation certificate business; it had to start adding vehicles that would lead toward full financial services for its valued clients. In order to broaden its fixed-investment business, it acquired an Alberta-based firm, Associated Investors of Canada Ltd., in 1963.

That same year its first equity fund, Collective Mutual Fund Ltd., was launched. Now the firm's clients could accumulate dollars in a balanced situation—some fixed dollars, some ownership dollars. The year 1965 saw the introduction of Principal Savings and Trust Company, followed by several additional investment vehicles for further diversification. Moving ahead rapidly in the solid building of assets on behalf of a clientele that numbered in the tens of thousands, and in the building of a well-trained team in the head office and in the sales field, the company found it necessary to move to the Cambridge Building, where it had more space and an improved computer service.

Donald M. Cormie, Q.C., chairman of the board and president of the Principal Group Ltd.

Kenneth M. Marlin, director.

John M. Cormie, director.

James M. Cormie, director.

The Principal Group Ltd. was formed in 1966 to provide services to the many arms of the organization which then existed.

By the mid-1970s it became clear that people who had become faithful savers had now become potential investors as well. Dynamic measures were taken to move into the single-deposit business, in both the fixed- and equity-type of investment. This was made possible by the ongoing growth of skills of Principal people, through prestige advertising, and, to a very large extent, through a move to a spectacular on-line computer system, the GEAC Dual 8000. The system made it possible to open major Principal financial centres from St. John's, Newfoundland, to Victoria, British Columbia, and to provide its clients with accurate and instant information. Principal became the only company equipped to allow clients to buy and sell the shares of its six mutual funds across the counter of a Principal Trust office on a daily basis, or through its Cash Plus system, the automatic teller. Another part of this revolution was the elimination of a huge amount of paper; the tradi-

tional certificates became unnecessary, now that the clients could be more fully informed than ever before.

The Principal Group Ltd., with chairman of the board and president Donald M. Cormie, Q.C., one of the original visionaries, has since established itself in the prestigious Principal Plaza, a beautiful 30-storey tower standing just a half-block south of the little Barry Building where the seed of an idea had been planted 30 years earlier. With recent major moves to Scottsdale, Arizona, and to Toronto, Principal has passed the billion-dollar mark and is on its way to becoming a giant in the financial industry.

The Principal Group Ltd. continues to follow the concept of thrift, both as a responsible financial institution and on behalf of its national and international clients: Always keep part of your income, maintain a balance in the investment of that income, and above all, protection first, growth second.

Principal Plaza, the Jasper Avenue headquarters of the Principal Group Ltd. of Edmonton.

NORTH WEST MILL

The North West Mill & Feed Co. Ltd. mill was built in 1892 by Robert Ritchie and first operated as the Edmonton Milling Co. Ltd. mill. Now a designated historical landmark, the rejuvenated timber structure is still known as "Ritchie's Mill."

The "Ritchie Mill," recognized as the oldest surviving timber elevator in Western Canada, if not in all Canada, owes its current role as an Alberta provincial historic site to a prominent Edmonton family—the Cormies. The history of the mill spans almost a century.

Ritchie's Mill was built in Strathcona, Northwest Territories in 1892 on the high south bank of the North Saskatchewan River. At the time Strathcona was the end of steel for a new railway link with the CPR's main line at Calgary. Its owner-operator was Robert Ritchie, who came west from Ontario in search of business opportunity. He founded the Edmonton Milling Co. Ltd. and promptly built his plant from lumber supplied by John Walter's nearby sawmill. The new mill's power came from a steam engine whose boiler was fired by the almost limitless supply of local coal.

Robert Ritchie's family operated the mill for many years. It was sold in the 1920s, and operated under the new name of North West Mill & Feed Co. Ltd. It was bought in 1942 by George Mills Cormie, who by coincidence was born in Ontario in 1892—the year the mill was built. G.M. Cormie was the son of John Cormie and Grace Mills of Fergus, Ontario. He was the youngest of a family of six.

George Mills Cormie attended the Ontario Agricultural College, and in 1916 came to Alberta as assistant to T.A. Benson, then Dominion Government Representative for Alberta. When the latter was transferred to British Columbia, George Cormie was left in charge of the federal livestock branch, poultry division, in Alberta. Later he joined the Alberta Agriculture Department, then headed by the Honourable George Hoadley,

and in 1929 was appointed provincial poultry commissioner. Under his guidance the poultry industry grew to become a significant segment of Alberta farming operations.

Leaving the civil service in 1937, Cormie joined the staff of North West Mill & Feed Co. Ltd. In his new post he established North West's feed department. In 1938 he was appointed manager of the plant and shortly after discovered that as of 1926 the mill property was owned by Canada Biscuit Co. Ltd. of London, Ontario, and subsequently had been acquired by George Weston of Toronto. At meetings with Weston officials in 1942, George Cormie arranged for transfer to his name of the mill and shares of North West Mill & Feed Co. Ltd. Three years later Cormie bought out the Anderson Grain and Feed Company of Calgary, and changed this firm's name to Gold Medal Feeds Ltd. In 1945 his son, John Gordon, returned from overseas service as a Royal Canadian Army lieutenant and became assistant manager of the mill. Still later John G. Cormie bought his father's interest in Gold Medal Feeds.

When Cormie bought North West Mill & Feed, he had his father-in-law, Burton Mercer, bring the plant's old hammer mill back to life for use in grinding alfalfa and grain. At the time bagging and handling was done by hand, and North West Mill & Feed was kept busy filling orders for Canadian flour that poured in from around the world. Countries of destination in these wartime years included Britain, China, the Philippines, Russia, France, Italy, and Ireland. Stores throughout Northern Alberta stocked and sold North West feeds, and supplies were shipped to British Columbia, Saskatchewan, Ontario, and Hawaii.

George Cormie was deeply interested in the use of balanced rations in livestock feeding. The feed industry is basically a "conversion industry" that uses the by-products of many industries to formulate and prepare balanced rations for livestock and poultry. Cormie was a leader among agriculture experts who paved the way for the use by Alberta livestock producers of balanced-ration feeding programs.

He was the first president of the Alberta Division, Canadian Feed Manufacturers Association, and a director of the Western Flour Millers Association. Active in community affairs, George Cormie was a member of the Edmonton Chamber of Commerce, served on the Edmonton Public School Board, was president of the Edmonton branch of the Royal Overseas League, and a member of the Edmonton Rotary Club and Robertson United Church. He sold North West to his son, Donald Mercer, in 1967. George Mills Cormie died in September 1971.

In 1978 Donald Cormie merged the business with Cormie Ranch Ltd., 40 miles west of Edmonton. He sold part of the mill property to Qualico Construction Co. for high-rise development. The pioneer Edmonton Milling Co. Ltd. plant still remains on the property, and is under renovation for the old Strathcona Foundation, as a designated historical landmark.

CORMIE RANCH LTD.

Signal, a Simmental bull imported from France by Cormie Ranch Ltd., is known as one of the best bulls of his breed in North America.

Founded in 1962 by Donald M. Cormie, Q.C., Cormie Ranch owns more than 15,000 acres near Tomahawk, some 80 kilometres west of Edmonton. The property is in the watershed between Lake Wabamun and the North Saskatchewan River and consists of a drained lake bed and the surrounding highland. The combination of high ground and lake bottom is a major asset, as security for supply of internal feed requirements irrespective of dry or wet weather.

In addition to being one of the larger privately held accumulations of contiguous land in Northern Alberta actively being worked, the ranch is the largest beef seed stock breeding operation in Canada. There are separate cattle units for each of the Simmental, Maine Anjou, Hereford, and Charolais breeds, totalling between 1,500 and 2,000 registered head.

The Cormie Ranch Farming Division is responsible for land cleanup, road maintenance, haying, grain feed crops, and cash crops. A well-stocked parts bin is maintained year-round, and the shop is staffed by adaptable mechanics.

The high-priority areas are land

cleanup and crop rotation. Newly broken land is seeded to a grain crop each year until the land is cleared of all obstructions, after which it is seeded to grass for use as pasture or a hay field. If a field is seeded as pasture, it will be returned to one of the cattle groups and new land will be designated for crop rotation.

A $200,000 grain storage, handling, and mixing complex was built in 1981. This feed mill is largely automatic and can be programmed for a day's production in a few minutes and then left to run on its own. The mill has a storage capacity of 50,000 bushels of grain which are mixed with salt and minerals and then ground into prepared feed for the cattle divisions.

The ranch acquired several large registered and commercial horned Hereford herds in the early 1960s, which later were crossed with imported exotic bulls. The crossing program began with large-scale artificial insemination and later with the use of imported pasture bulls. In this way a major upgrading program started in the Charolais (1966), Simmental (1970), and the Maine Anjou (1973) breeds. In the mid-1970s the remaining Herefords were bred to polled bulls to create the Polled

Hereford Division.

From 1966 to 1976 the primary emphasis was sire testing and progeny evaluation, in order to identify the top import bulls genetically, in part resulting in the identification of one of the best Simmental bulls in North America—Signal. Imported from France and used extensively by Cormie Ranch, Signal is still the only bull to be repeatedly a four-trait genetic leader in the sire monitoring programme of the American Simmental Association. His semen, once sold at $6 per unit, is now traded at $500 per unit in Canada.

In the late 1970s the female side of the pedigree achieved a more equal importance with the male, resulting in the desire of more than one or two calves per year from the female and causing extensive embryo transplant operations in the cattle industry. Cormie Ranch started its transplant activity in 1974 and now conducts these operations both on the ranch and at four off-site locations.

With the onslaught of rising costs and decreasing sales prices, the modern cowboy has learned to slash costs that don't provide adequate return. Fertility, calving ease, growth rate, high carcass quality, and a favourable feed conversion factor remain the keys to success. Superior genetic selection based on proven performance is the Cormie Ranch solution.

Don and Eivor Cormie, operators of the Cormie Ranch Ltd. of Tomahawk, Alberta.

NORTHWESTERN UTILITIES LIMITED

The story of natural gas in Edmonton began before World War I, when a group of citizens incorporated a venture called the Edmonton Industrial Association Drilling Company Limited. They began drilling operations in the Viking area 80 miles east of the city.

The Association's drillers struck gas at a depth of 2,340 feet on November 4, 1914—a well producing in excess of nine million cubic feet daily. The Viking field was one of the largest deposits of gas discovered in Canada up to that time.

The citizenry of Edmonton, however, was not willing to risk the money needed to develop the field and build a pipeline. Three successive by-laws submitted to raise the necessary capital were defeated. A new development company was formed, but its operations were delayed by World War I. When the war was over the firm entered into franchise negotiations with the city, but was unable to raise enough money to build the necessary pipeline from Viking to Edmonton. This resulted in the formation of still another company, Northwestern Utilities Limited, incorporated on May 26, 1923, with E.G. Hill as president.

Northwestern opened its first offices in the Agency Building on Jasper Avenue, near the Capital Theatre, and contracted with a New York engineering firm—Ford Bacon and Davis Inc.—to build and operate the proposed gas system for a year.

A construction timetable was set, but it seemed almost presumptuous to hope that the pipeline would reach Edmonton before the fall freeze-up. The feat was accomplished, nevertheless, by October 27, 1923. Official inauguration ceremonies followed on November 9, when Mayor D.M. Dug-

gan lit a flare mounted on the 105th Street bridge. By year's end the utility company was supplying nature's wonder fuel to 1,830 Edmontonians.

Shortly after completion of the one-year contract with Ford Bacon and Davis, the presidency of Northwestern fell on the shoulders of C.J. Yorath, then chief commissioner for the City of Edmonton. He was persuaded by the company to resign his management position with the city in order to take on the leadership of the natural gas utility.

From its earliest beginnings Northwestern established a philosophy of service that has been its tradition ever since. The customer has always come first. This gave rise to such institutions as the customer-service and home-service departments, providing everything from free appliance adjustments to demonstrations on cooking staged for homemakers.

The Great Depression affected Northwestern as well as its customers. Coal was selling for two dollars a ton, making it fiercely competitive as a heating fuel. And there were a couple of breaks in the transmission line, causing city-wide shutdowns, but these, too, were taken in stride. A much worse setback followed on February 21, 1932, when a fire caused by a leak in the gas main levelled the Corona Hotel on Jasper Avenue.

Then came the most stunning blow of all. Several weeks after the fire, Chris Yorath, who had led the firm through its formative years, died of a heart attack at the age of 52. He was succeeded as president by H.R. Milner, K.C., who had been serving as Northwestern's chief legal counsel.

Slowly but steadily the business climbed out of the Depression. By the beginning of World War II it was

again in good shape, with a well-trained and dedicated staff. The war, of course, brought more economic belt-tightening. A large number of staff members, along with senior management, joined the Armed Forces.

After the war Northwestern's expansion resumed. The first major project was a "southern extension" from the Viking/Edmonton line, bringing service to additional towns all the way down to Red Deer. Armed Forces returnees who were put to work on this line included Brigadier J.C. "Jim" Jefferson, one of several soldiers from Northwestern Utilities, who was decorated with Distinguished Service Medals for bravery in front-line service overseas.

Then came the Leduc oil strike in the spring of 1947, which ushered in a new era of prosperity for Alberta. New gas and oil fields brought spectacular growth and unprecedented demands for service. The gas company took the lead in Western Canada in many ways, not only in the provision of service to homes and industries, but in pipe-laying operations as well. Northwestern pioneered, for example, the techniques of "plowing in" plastic pipe as an economical means of bringing natural gas to rural areas.

In the city, the company's north yard was opened in the fall of 1949, and the next year Northwestern brought gas to the Edmonton power plant via the largest-diameter transmission pipe in Canada at that time. By 1954 the company was well established as Canada's largest distributor of natural gas.

As Northwestern progressed and its staff increased over the years, it continued to move into more spacious quarters. The office staff moved to the

COOK AND HEAT WITH GAS

NATURAL GAS SERVICE

12-storey Milner Building in the spring of 1959, and on the south side the new Control Centre and No. 1 Gate Station were officially opened on October 21, 1972. The head office staff moved again, from the Milner Building to the ultra-modern, 20-storey Canadian Utilities Centre at 10035-105th Street, in the fall of 1983.

Some 15,000 additional customers were gained in the fall of 1972 when an associate company—Northland Utilities Limited—transferred its assets to Northwestern, bringing 36 northern communities into the system.

Northwestern's maximum daily demand for gas passed the billion-cubic-foot mark in 1978. In keeping with the increasing demand, one of the firm's most recent undertakings has been a $35-million salt cavern project where gas is stored under pressure for use during peak winter-consumption periods.

Today Northwestern Utilities Limited, with head office and main

A Northwestern Utilities service truck in an Edmonton residential area during the '20s. Two-man crews such as this were kept busy as new customers switched to "nature's wonder fuel."

operations base in Edmonton, is one of Canada's leading natural gas production, transmission, and distribution systems, serving more than 300,000 customers over a vast area stretching across Central and Northern Alberta and Northeastern British Columbia.

REED'S CHINA AND GIFT SHOP

A frontier town of muddy streets and plank sidewalks was an unlikely location to establish a specialty shop, particularly when the primary lines of merchandise were fine china, tea accessories, cut glass, and dinnerware. Such refinement was hardly known in Edmonton in 1905.

Nonetheless, William Henry Reed, with experience in the tea and coffee business in Ontario, saw a market in the community—whose population was barely 10,000—for lines of goods that bespoke the finer things of life. Thus the entrepreneur originated Reed's Tea and Bazaar Store on November 26 of that year, at the corner of Second Street and Jasper Avenue. Although the location was just one block from the intersection of Edmonton's two main streets, a crew of workmen had to clear the site of brush, shrub growth, and small trees before the building's foundations could be laid.

Undaunted, Reed and his store manager and brother-in-law, Russell Francis Clarke, lined their counters, shelves, and display tables with quality wares whose very textures, colours, and shapes made greater the contrast with their primitive surroundings. Reed's Bazaar specialized in tin- and enamel-ware, cutlery, fine china, silverware, cut-glass dinner services, tea and coffee—plus homesteaders' supplies down to the ubiquitous tin "airtight" heater.

Reed's later added a branch store at 101st Street and 101A Avenue, then another—designated The Fair—between 99th and 100th streets on Jasper Avenue. When a fire badly damaged the original Bazaar in 1913, it was reopened as Reed's Fair. That same year the 101st Street establishment was closed, and the next year the Bazaar was again instituted—this

William Henry Reed, owner and founder of Reed's Tea and Bazaar Store.

Russell Francis Clarke, co-founder and later owner (1945) of Reed's China and Gift Shop.

time farther west between 103rd and 104th streets. Further expansion came in 1927, when Reed's Bazaar changed its name to Reed's China and Gift Shop and opened at 10325 Jasper Avenue with an entirely new array of stock and fixtures.

An early employee at The Fair, Miss Pauline Maloy (a newcomer from England), was eventually given a partnership. The founder retired in 1945 and sold his interest in the business to his former manager, whose son, Robert M. Clarke (after serving with the Canadian Navy overseas for six years), rejoined the firm and became manager. He was accorded a partnership in the company simultaneously with Miss Maloy.

In 1955, to celebrate Reed's 50th anniversary, the main store was reno-

vated and a dinnerware salon added. The following year it was incorporated with R.M. Clarke as president; R.F. Clarke, vice-president; and Miss Maloy, secretary/treasurer and sales manager. In 1983 R.M. Clarke was named Edmonton's Small Businessman of the Year during the annual observance of Small Business Week.

Reed's today has the distinction of being the second-oldest retail firm in Edmonton—exceeded in seniority only by the Hudson's Bay Company. As well as maintaining a downtown location on 101st Street, the firm has opened branches in five suburban shopping malls; the newest is in West Edmonton Mall, the largest shopping centre in North America.

STANLEY ASSOCIATES ENGINEERING LTD.

The Stanley organization has played a major role in the development of Edmonton. Shown here is the Edmonton Rossdale Water Treatment Plant. As prime consultants, Stanley professionals have been responsible for the five-year upgrading programme.

In 1954 Dr. Donald R. Stanley, an Edmonton native and a graduate of the University of Alberta and Harvard University, formed a one-man municipal engineering firm. By 1982 Stanley Associates Engineering Ltd. had grown to a multidisciplinary group of companies employing some 700 personnel and offering a full range of civil, electrical, and mechanical engineering services worldwide.

The employee-owned company operates offices throughout Western and Northern Canada and overseas and provides planning, design, and construction management services to all levels of government and industry. In the field of municipal engineering, Stanley has been involved in more than 400 urban municipalities in Canada and around the world.

The firm also provides services to many industrial clients in the sectors of petroleum, petrochemicals, agricultural, pulp and paper, coal, electrical power, manufacturing, land development, railroads, and commer-

cial development.

Throughout its history the company has played a prominent role in the orderly development of Edmonton in areas of water supply and treatment, sewage collection and treatment, storm water management, transportation, structures, and land development.

Recently Stanley has been involved in the design of the community's LRT facilities; the Northlands Agri-Com facility; the upgrading of the Rossdale water treatment plant; the 97th Street and the 82nd Street grade separations on the Yellowhead Trail; and infrastructure development for the Genesee Power Project, including environmental impact assessments.

Since its inception, Stanley has aggressively pursued international engineering assignments. The firm, which has ongoing operations in eight countries abroad, is proud of its reputation as one of the largest exporters of engineering services in Canada. A few of the major projects undertaken include a master plan for water and sewerage for Barbados; a master plan and management of a comprehensive solid-waste system for Trinidad and Tobago; the design and construction management of 600 kilometres of rural roads in Zambia, Africa; the design and construction

supervision for water supply and sewerage facilities for the country of Belize, in Central America; regional water-supply and -treatment systems to serve a population of more than eight million, and waste treatment and disposal facilities for another 64 communities in South Korea; a sewerage system for the city of Ipoh, and a waer-treatment plant for the city of Alor Setar, both in Malaysia; and a master plan for water and sewerage for the city of Lilongwe, Malawi.

Stanley's achievements in international engineering have been recognized through the presentation of several Export Achievement Awards by the provincial government.

Among the company's extensive client list are many developing countries—as well as international aid and loan agencies such as CIDA, the World Bank, the World Health Organization, the Asian and Interamerican Development banks, and the United Nations Development Programme.

Keeping abreast of the latest technologies, the Stanley group of companies is proud of its staff—and of its worldwide reputation for quality engineering services.

Dr. Donald R. Stanley, founder of Stanley Associates Engineering Ltd.

WOODWARD'S

The development, growth, and progress of a province are directly related to the growth and development of its businesses and industries. Woodward's and Alberta are no exception to this maxim.

In 1926 Alberta was in her infancy; "Fanny Flapper" was the rage; newspapers cost five cents; Alberta was planning 1,000 miles of good roads; and Mayor K.A. Blotchford proclaimed "the streets of Edmonton safe." It was then, on May 4, 1926, that Charles Woodward, MLA—risk-taker, scrupulously honest, intuitive businessman, and founder of a retail dynasty—announced that he would be building an Edmonton store costing approximately $100,000. The site at 101st Street and 102nd Avenue would subsequently become the city centre.

Construction was begun in August 1926 by Carter Halls, Aldinger Company, and established a record in Edmonton construction circles, having been completed in 88 days. With 60,000 square feet of retail space, it was as much as possible a product of Edmonton's materials, construction

The original C. Woodward Company store opened on October 15, 1928, at the corner of 101st Street and 102nd Avenue, and featured 60,000 square feet of retail space. Courtesy of the Glenbow Archives, Calgary, Alberta.

skill, and design expertise. For its period it boasted every possible up-to-date department store feature.

On opening day, October 15, 1926, Charles Woodward stood on the main floor of the C. Woodward Company greeting customers and ready to give second-to-none service in piece goods, men's and boys' wear, carpets and linoleum, groceries and provisions, kitchenware, shoes, ladies' and children's ready-to-wear, "all for small profit with quick and easy returns if not satisfactory."

The first man hired was George Plowman; the second was Jack Barbour, a recent Scots immigrant and 36-year-old former log cutter.

As Edmonton grew and prospered, so did Woodward's. In October 1929 a three-storey extension was added to the northeast corner at a cost of $227,710.

In 1930 John Ferguson of Vancouver was named secretary/treasurer. While Woodward decided to retain the position of general manager in order to keep a watchful eye on his latest enterprise, for the next decade Ferguson ran the store.

The establishment was a monument to its owner's outstanding business acumen and showed tremendous growth. In the first year of operation, Woodward's doubled the expectations

with one million dollars in sales; by the third year this figure had increased by one-half.

Charles Woodward died in 1937 and was succeeded by his son, W.C. Woodward—who led the company through even greater development and expansion. He founded many of the staff benefits, including a retirement plan, sick pay, hospitalization, group insurance, staff discounts, and profit sharing.

In July 1939 John Ferguson resigned his position and returned to the Vancouver store. His successor was John Butterfield, a native of Yorkshire, England, who had 13 years' retail experience in Edmonton prior to joining Woodward's in Vancouver.

The C. Woodward Company in 1940 announced it would build its fourth and fifth floors within the next two years.

The organization has a history of employee loyalty, community participation, and historical firsts. Many of its shareholder employees served the firm for more than 40 years—and during the war years these same employees, after having worked a full day in the store, freely assisted local farmers. Then, as now, Woodward's never refused any reasonable charitable request, many of which came directly from people on the street.

Butterfield's outstanding work in Edmonton was recognized in 1943 with a promotion to Vancouver as general manager of the corporation.

In 1947 The C. Woodward Company became Woodward's, and added its sixth and final floor. The discovery of the Leduc oil field that year immediately and dramatically changed Alberta's economy, and with it, Woodward's. For the next 25 years the firm's expansion paralleled the

province's growth, continuing to endorse its owner's vision.

T.K. Campbell became general manager in 1949, then director of Alberta operations, and finally executive vice-president.

While it was decided in 1950 to expand the Edmonton operation, Woodward's was restricted from further additions to its downtown property. The idea of a shopping centre emerged when a New York corporation approached Woodward's with the idea of leasing space in northwest Edmonton, resulting in the new Westmount project. The endeavour, opened on a blazing August day in 1955, began on a note of cautious optimism, but achieved the phenomenal success of operating profitably in the first year.

That year as well a large addition was made to the South Edmonton Distribution Centre.

Northgate, now Northwood, opened in 1965, followed five years later by Southgate. The store manager for both was Alexander Weir, who started with the company in 1934. Both centres were built on the outskirts of Edmonton, where at the time there was little housing other than a few farms in a vast expanse of bushland.

Following the revival in 1969 of a 19-year-old proposal to rejuvenate the downtown area, Woodward's together with the Oxford Development Group and the Toronto Dominion

Woodward's, 1984. This facility, built on the site of the original courthouse, was part of the Edmonton Centre project, a 10-year, $100-million undertaking. Courtesy of the Glenbow Archives, Calgary, Alberta.

Bank formed a partnership with assets of $400 million. Their goal was to provide Edmonton with an integrated office development and retail complex that would "emphasize the creation of a city centre in the heart of the city."

The ambitious Edmonton Centre project—completed after 10 years at a cost of $100 million—hosted Woodward's as the major tenant.

The first phase of the centre, which opened in 1974, was comprised of a five-storey Woodward's store, a three-level shopping mall with more than 50 retail establishments, restaurants, specialty shops, and the first of three office towers. The new Woodward's outlet was opened on what was the site of the original Edmonton Courthouse. Expectedly, the new endeavour necessitated the emotional demolition of the old store, a 50-year edifice of many proud moments. According to some employees, "The old building was so structurally sound that the wrecking ball bounced off the bricks without making an impression." In keeping with Woodward's efficiency, the move from the old premises to the new was completed in a mere two days.

In October 1975 Woodward's celebrated both its 49th anniversary in Alberta and the first-time trading of its shares on the Alberta Stock Exchange. From 1976 to 1980 J.O. Moxon, vice-president and director, guided the company through a period of growth and high profitability. Edmonton Centre, a mecca for weary shoppers, continued to expand with the addition of a 332-room hotel, second and third office towers, and another car park.

Moxon was succeeded by Edmonton-born P.C. (Phil) McComb, who is in his 36th year with Woodward's; he is also active in the business community. C.N. (Chunky) Woodward, son of W.C. Woodward, is presently chairman of the board and chief executive officer. His leadership and foresight, in conjunction with the astute merchandising reputation of the current president and chief operating officer, G.W. (Woody) McLaren, have guided the company through tremendous expansion: The original six retail stores in 1975 have quadrupled, and two Furniture Fair stores were organized.

C.N. Woodward—active in planning, development, and merchandising—maintains a keen interest in Woodward's staff. Believing, as his father did, that a store can be no better than its employees, he takes great pride in Woodward's reputation for having a pleasant, helpful, and courteous staff.

THE EDMONTON JOURNAL

John Mills Imrie, vice-president, and managing director of The Edmonton Journal, 1921-1941.

Walter A. Macdonald, vice-president and managing director, 1941; publisher, 1942-1962.

Basil Dean, publisher, 1962-1967.

Ross Munro, publisher, 1968-1976.

One of the largest and most widely read daily newspapers in Western Canada is *The Edmonton Journal*. It is also the most colourful and most widely quoted paper in the West—if not all of Canada.

The Journal clattered to life on November 11, 1903, on a ramshackle, hastily assembled hand-me-down press newly arrived from the East and hauled by wagon from the cross-river town of Strathcona. Offices and plant were in the back room of a fruit store on the east side of First (101st) Street, a few yards north of Jasper Avenue.

It was by no means the first paper to burst into print in the determined, aggressive community on the North Saskatchewan River; both Edmonton and Strathcona had been periodically served by papers for 20 years. However, Frank Oliver's *Edmonton Bulletin* was destined to survive the trials of frontier economics of those often-parlous days. While determination and confidence were two important keys to a new publication's future, they weren't sufficient to clear

obstacles from the path toward success. With the first criterion being to fill a need, the essential ingredients were—and still are—integrity, aggressiveness, and the ability to see beyond the flamboyant, ready-made facade, as well as the ability to speak out clearly, forcefully, and without fear. It was the lack of one or more of these essentials that led to the demise of the early newspapers in Edmonton and Strathcona.

The Edmonton Bulletin, founded in 1881 by peppery publisher Frank Oliver (who in later years became a federal cabinet minister in the administration of Sir Wilfrid Laurier), was of a stripe that set it apart from those earlier competitors. Advocating the Liberal persuasion, forcefully so, its abrasive stance in political matters commanded a considerable, if not always compliant, readership. Within these perimeters the newspaper survived as part of the Edmonton community until 1951, at which time difficulties spawned by labour problems and a change of ownership

brought it to the end of an honourable—albeit boisterous—half-century career.

When *The Evening Journal* appeared on the scene, seeking an audience in a Northwest Territories town of 3,500 people, the province of Alberta was still two years in the future. Politically conservative to the core, it entered the vacuum left by *The Edmonton Post*, one of the would-be competitors of *The Bulletin*. The founding fathers of *The Journal* were a triumvirate: John Macpherson, J.W. Cunningham, and Arthur Moore. Macpherson became president and manager; Cunningham was editor and secretary; and Moore headed the mechanical staff. Inadequate preliminary financing made it necessary for the partners to unpack their machinery and equipment, set it up, and produce four pages of news and advertising columns unassisted.

The newspaper's early years were never far from financial crises. On more than one occasion W. Johnstone Walker, department store owner and

J. Patrick O'Callaghan, publisher, 1976-1982.

William Newbigging, publisher since 1982.

The Edmonton Journal's multimillion-dollar Eastgate production plant, opened in May 1980.

staunch *Journal* supporter, would temporarily bankroll the paper's pay cheques. His "rich uncle" assistance was recognized in a unique way— until the 1960s the Johnstone Walker store's advertising enjoyed inviolate right to dedicated space in *The Journal.*

Cunningham, Macpherson, and Moore continued publication until 1909, by which time *The Journal* was producing two editions daily— morning and evening—and circulation stood above the 4,100 mark. During these formative years the owners had moved from their original location on the lane north of the old Empire Building to a new, one-storey building north of the east-west lane between Rice Street (101st A Avenue) and Athabasca (102nd) Avenue. The founding partners then sold their interest in the paper to Milton Robbings Jennings, who assumed the positions of both editor and general manager. Within a few weeks the new proprietor decided to double the size of his building by adding a second

storey. This structure was later absorbed into the south wall of the Tegler Building, one of downtown Edmonton's landmarks, and was in place until the Tegler itself collapsed in a heap of rubble—victim of dynamite charges set off by a demolition crew.

The next change in *The Journal's* future came about in 1912, when William Southam and Sons bought a controlling interest in the paper. The Ontario-based firm established its new western holding as a division of The Southam Company Limited, which subsequently changed its nomenclature to Southam Press Limited; it was ultimately renamed Southam, Inc. As with all divisions within the parent company, *The Journal* was known as a member of the Southam Group.

Jennings stayed with *The Journal* following this change of ownership, remaining in charge until his death in February 1921—which preceded by only 60 days the newspaper's move from the Tegler Building to its new plant at the northwest corner of

101st Street and Macdonald Drive. Six months after Jennings' death, John Mills Imrie became the publication's vice-president and managing director. Well-known for his outstanding contributions to community and business life, he served as president of the Edmonton Chamber of Commerce and as vice-president of the Canadian Chamber.

Imrie's service as publisher of *The Journal* was highlighted in 1935-1937 by the battle he fought against the Alberta government led by the late Premier William Aberhart, due to his chairmanship of an Alberta newspaper publishers' committee set up to fight press-control measures introduced by the Aberhart regime. Most of this "press gag" attempt was centered in legislation known as the Alberta Press Act—a measure eventually declared *ultra vires* by both the Supreme Court of Canada and the Judicial Committee of the British government's privy council. For its role in this historic confrontation, *The Journal* was given a Pulitzer Award, the equivalent of the American Pulitzer Prize (given only to U.S. newspapers deemed worthy of the honour), the first ever to be bestowed beyond the United States. Imrie retired due to ill health in 1941, and died in 1942.

The intrepid publisher was succeeded by Walter Augustus Macdonald, whose newspaper career began at Vancouver as an employee in the business office of a sister Southam paper, *The Vancouver Province*. Macdonald had also served in *The Journal*'s business office, and brought to his new post a wealth of experience in financial management. Familiarly known to his staff as "WAM," he had joined *The Journal* in 1937, subsequently became vice-president and managing director, and was appointed publisher on January 1, 1942. He became a director of The Southam Company in 1952, and was named a member of Southam's executive committee in 1960.

The early Macdonald years were marked by turmoil on the labour front. The International Typographical Union, one of the strongest in the ranks of organized American labour, decided to confront the Southams with a demand that all ITU contracts should carry identical hours-of-work clauses. Interminable negotiations failed to resolve the impasse created when Southam executives rejected the union's demand. During the ensuing strikes *The Journal* and *The Bulletin*, hiring experienced printers from smaller papers across Canada, began joint publication through an agreement their publishers had signed previously.

The first double-masthead *Bulletin/Journal* appeared on May 31, 1946. Gradually the two papers separated their various layouts, and for about a year published separately in the areas of news and editorial content, although they ran identical advertising and shared the revenue thus generated. However, this situation could not continue indefinitely, and came to an end when publisher Charles Campbell decided to sell *The Bulletin*. He had suggested to the Southams that they either absorb his paper into *The Journal* or convert it to a morning publication, but Southam management—fearing what could be construed as deliberate creation of a monopoly—rejected the idea.

The Bulletin's new owners, backed by Calgary oil money, set out on a course of attacking *The Journal* at every opportunity. At the time of the sale, *The Bulletin* was selling around 19,000 copies daily; it reached 30,000 in the next year or so, but never threatened *The Journal*—whose circulation in September 1950 had passed the 56,000 mark.

The final lines to this chapter of Edmonton newspaper history were dictated by *Bulletin* publisher Hal L. Straight. On January 20, 1951, he ordered this eight-column line for the top of Page 1: "*THE BULLETIN ENDS PUBLICATION TODAY.*" Despite rumours to the contrary, *The Journal* did not buy *The Bulletin* and then terminate its life. It did, however, buy its old competitor's physical assets.

Walter Macdonald's remaining years with *The Journal* were marked by his paper's expansion. The city was growing, the oil/gas boom had excited the local and provincial economies, and Edmonton's destiny as the Gateway to the North was manifesting itself. *The Journal* met these challenges through internal growth. Its building was doubled in size in 1952, and then again enlarged. High-speed rotary presses were installed and subsequently moved to a new press building fronting on 102nd Street and back-to-back with the main plant; press capacity was doubled after the move, with further expansion in 1957. While technological developments were incorporated as they came on the market, changes in the physical plant were made as the size of the paper and its staff expanded.

Macdonald retired at the end of January 1962, and was followed by Basil Dean, an English-born newspaperman who at the time was publisher of *The Calgary Herald*. His experience had been totally "news side": He had joined *The Hamilton Spectator* as a reporter in 1938, and was later posted to the Southam news bureau in London.

Basil Dean's years at *The Journal* were years of change. He designed a new front-page banner and instituted different type styles, amended make-up practices, changed editorial policies, and hired additional reporters and copy-readers for the newsroom. Moreover, the new publisher actively sought the limelight. He accepted public speaking engagements if he felt a clash of opinion were in the offing, and opened space in the paper for "The Journal of Dissent," where individuals' opinions opposing those of *The Journal* could appear in print.

Dean's years in Edmonton were all too brief. He died in his sleep, at age 52, in Toronto while on a business trip in December 1967. However, Basil Dean did live to see *The Journal* pass *The Winnipeg Free Press* to become the largest newspaper in the country between Toronto and Vancouver.

Dean's successor was Ross Munro,

another veteran newsman; beginning his career with *The Canadian Press*, the national newspaper-owned, news-gathering cooperative, he had joined The Southam Company in 1948. Munro had served as assistant to the publisher of *The Vancouver Province*, as well as editor; then as vice-president and publisher of *The Winnipeg Tribune*; and finally as publisher of *Canadian* magazine. He began his association with *The Journal* on January 1, 1968, and remained there for eight years before accepting a position in Montreal as publisher of *The Gazette*. He retired in 1979.

Ross Munro is remembered for his work as a wartime correspondent for *The Canadian Press*. He was with the Canadians at Dieppe, for the assault on Sicily, and again in Normandy for the D-Day landings. His book, *Gauntlet to Overlord*, the story of the Royal Canadian Army in World War II, won a Governor-General's Award.

His contributions to *The Journal* were legion. His term as publisher saw the introduction of major changes in newspaper-production technology. These changes were effected without cutting *The Journal* staff—all employees whose jobs became redundant were assigned to new posts without loss of pay.

Upon Munro's retirement the position as head of the newspaper was filled by J. Patrick O'Callaghan, who returned to Edmonton after serving an earlier term at *The Journal* as assistant to the publisher. He was third in a line of the publication's top executives who came up through the ranks of the news department. Born in County Cork, Ireland, O'Callaghan worked with British newspapers between 1947 and 1959, and then migrated to Canada where he worked for *The Red Deer Advocate*. Next he went

east as executive editor of Southam News Services, and later became an executive assistant in Southam's Toronto headquarters. Then came appointment as vice-president and publisher of *The Windsor Star*, and finally—in 1976—publisher of *The Journal*.

O'Callaghan's expansion program at *The Journal* was phenomenal. He built a $35-million production plant filled with state-of-the-art machinery. The new rotary offset presses first rolled in May 1980, and are capable of turning out 25,000 papers per press hourly.

During his regime *The Journal* became the number-one newspaper in Canada in terms of advertising volume and by 1984 it still ranked in the top three in this category. In addition, its new Eastgate production centre enables *The Journal* to carry more colour advertising than any other paper in North America.

William "Bill" Newbigging, formerly publisher of *The Ottawa Citizen*, followed O'Callaghan into the office of the publisher of *The Journal*. No newcomer to the operation he now heads, Newbigging in 1957 started with the newspaper as a city-side reporter, and is the fourth in a row of publishers whose newspaper training was news-centered. Educated in Edmonton, he covered a variety of beats before serving as city editor (1965), news editor (1967), and assistant to the publisher (1971) prior to going to Ottawa.

Since its earliest days *The Edmonton Journal* has contributed notably to community service projects. It has recorded the programmes of Edmonton's unique community leagues; promoted "learn-to" classes in skiing, swimming, canoeing, golf, tennis, and dancing; sponsored cultural and

artistic events in the Northern Alberta Jubilee Auditorium; advocated the 1978 Commonwealth Games and Universiade 1983 in its news columns and by seconding senior personnel to volunteer administrative posts of both events; and annually supports an international indoor track meet and the Sir Winston Churchill senior debate competition. Additionally backing the United Community Fund through its news columns, the newspaper long has held the distinction of being the UCF's largest corporate donor.

Over the years, particularly in the past 20, *The Journal* has contributed heavily to the roll of senior executives in the various Southam divisions. The list is headed by John Ward, former advertising chief who is a retired vice-president and director of Southam, Inc. Others include Fane Polley, who became *The Calgary Herald*'s secretary/treasurer; Bryson Stone, another advertising chief who advanced to become publisher of *The Prince George (British Columbia) Citizen*; Bill Peter, now advertising manager with *The Vancouver Prince*; Douglas Millroy, former city editor and presently editor of *The North Bay Nugget*; Andrew Snaddon, an editor promoted to publisher of *The Medicine Hat News*; Dona Harvey, assistant to the publisher and later managing editor of *The Province*; E.H. (Bill) Wheatley, an advertising director who rose to become managing director of *Pacific Press* and publisher of *The Province* and *The Vancouver Sun*; Gordon Bullock, assistant to the publisher who became publisher of *The Windsor Star*; J.P. O'Callaghan, publisher first of *The Journal* and then of *The Calgary Herald*; and William Newbigging, *The Journal* publisher as of 1982.

CANADIAN NATIONAL RAILWAYS

The CN Tower in downtown Edmonton, headquarters of CN Rail's Mountain Region. The building was the city's first modern-day, highrise office structure.

It was a great day for Edmonton, that very young city on the North Saskatchewan River.

Though the Hudson's Bay Company and its Fort Edmonton fur traders, missionaries, and pioneer settlers had been coming and going along this river highway for almost 200 years, that era had passed; and in the 50 years immediately preceding the great day, Edmonton had grown from fort to settlement, village, and town. Finally, on November 7, 1904, she achieved city status.

The great day arrived one year and 17 days later, on November 24, 1905: the Canadian Northern Railway completed its tracks into Edmonton, and the year-old city achieved mainline-railway status. It was little wonder that Mayor K.W. MacKenzie declared the day a half-holiday; Edmonton and its 10,000 people had good reason to celebrate — at long last, gone were the days of travois, ox cart, paddlewheel steamer, and wagon train. The day of the iron horse had arrived!

Another great day dawned on Edmonton four years later. On August 13, 1909, the Grand Trunk Pacific Railway pulled its first train into Edmonton, to the same station that the CNR had arrived at in 1905. And from that day on, Alberta's capital city was one of the few in Canada that could boast having direct access to two transcontinental railways.

The years between 1905 and 1920 saw vast expansion in Western Canada, particularly in Alberta. The open plains were being put to the plow as immigrants streamed in from overseas. The two railways added adrenalin to Edmonton's economy, giving the city divisional-point status immediately and serving as the headquarters of rail operations all the way west to the coast.

As the Canadian Northern pushed into British Columbia, its engineers chose the North Thompson and lower Fraser River valleys as their route to tidewater at Vancouver. The Grand

The Hotel Macdonald in Edmonton is one of CN Hotel's first-line hotels across Canada. The facility was closed in 1983 to make way for extensive renovation and modernization.

Trunk, on the other hand, reached the Pacific via the upper Fraser and Skeena rivers — and created a seaport out of an isolated settlement that would become Prince Rupert.

For mile upon mile west of Edmonton, the CN and GTP laid parallel tracks. Sometimes they were two or three miles apart; and at others, side by side. Not until Red Pass Junction, 70 kilometres west of Jasper, did they go their own ways. Within a few years Canada was at war and both railways were busy. Few people gave a second thought to the financial burden that came as the inevitable result of this duplication of service through a largely unopened part of Western Alberta and in the Yellowhead Pass.

As World War I ended, the two railways found themselves in an impossible situation. They had overextended and were bankrupt, as was almost every other Canadian railway — the Canadian Pacific Railway excepted. The crisis reached a point where the federal government was forced to step in so that the trains could be kept running.

A heavy CN Rail unit train of sulphur gondola cars snakes through a Rocky Mountain canyon on its way to a waiting ship at Vancouver, British Columbia.

Ottawa's answer to this threatening disaster was the Canadian National Railways Act of 1919. This legislation created the Canadian National Railways out of more than 200 separate railway companies, many of them insolvent. CN's role was to fulfill a clear national goal: to weld a number of railway companies serving the various parts of Canada into one strong and commercially competitive system that would serve the entire nation. The cost was staggering, and the government rail system had to assume the mountain of debts accrued by the merged companies.

In order to compete effectively and operate efficiently, Canadian National has had to adapt over the years. From a firm concerned mainly with moving people and goods from one point to another, CN has become a diversified transportation and communications enterprise with a number of complementary interests ranging through telecommunications, trucking, ship-

ping, resource development, real estate, hotels, and international business consulting.

Today Canadian National, first and foremost a railway, is Canada's largest, one of the world's largest, and operates some 40,000 kilometres of track. It maintains a fleet of 2,000 diesel locomotives, among the world's most powerful, and operates 87,000 freight cars of all types.

Over the years since 1919, and particularly in the period beginning with the 1950s, the demand for CN Rail services has increased, especially in Western Canada. As a result of this expansion, Edmonton became the headquarters for CN's western division, the Mountain Region, in 1961. The increase largely has been due to greater world demand for such products as coal, grain, industrial chemicals, forest products, and the fluid hydrocarbons—oil and gas.

Traffic growth accelerated in the

CN Rail's P-811 track-renewal train replaces wooden ties with concrete ties and worn rail with new, heavier continuous-welded rail in one continuous operation.

late '60s and early '70s to strain the capacity of the existing single-track rail system. CN Rail met the challenge by acquiring more powerful locomotives and larger freight cars, improved track structure, additional and longer sidings, and better traffic-control systems.

The Mountain Region, which includes all of CN Rail's activities in Alberta, British Columbia, and Western Saskatchewan, has seen the expenditure of billions of dollars worth of improvements. In 1983 a $115 million, 135-kilometre stretch of twin track from east of Jasper to Valemount, British Columbia—the longest continuous stretch of double track in Western Canada—was completed. This work eased one of CN Rail's most serious traffic bottlenecks in the West.

In 1984 Canadian National will spend $672.5 million on capital projects—one third more than in 1983. Western expansion and upgrading plans called for expenditures of $281 million. Track-renewal projects and equipment purchases throughout the system will account for $391.5 million for 1984, with the money shared between upkeep of 40,000 kilometres of mainline track and the system's rolling stock and locomotives.

Canadian National has assets totalling $6 billion. The system employs 67,000 people whose annual wages average $30,000. Total capital-works spending has reached the point where the railway is spending one million dollars a day, seven days a week, for nine months of the year.

In the Alberta sector of the Mountain Region, CN Rail employs 5,000 people, almost 3,500 of them in Edmonton alone. The employment figures represent an Alberta payroll of more than $150 million annually.

SHELL CANADA LIMITED

Shell responds to consumer buying trends: in the photograph above, the combination of food, expert lubrication, oil services, and gasoline.

Beginning operations in the area 45 years ago, the Shell Canada presence in Edmonton is the epitome of the evolving trends in the petroleum industry.

Oil exploration in Western Canada provided the thrust for the Shell Oil Company of New York to initiate such a programme in Alberta in 1939.

Earlier in the century, in 1911, Shell Company of Canada Limited—which became Shell Oil Company of Canada Limited in 1931—had been incorporated. From its Eastern Canada base the corporation had developed retail and refining operations. By 1957, when the American exploration interest was acquired, the Shell name was known from British Columbia to Newfoundland. In July 1963 the corporate name became Shell Canada Limited.

After the discovery of the Leduc oil field in 1947, much of the exploration and production part of the business moved north from Southern Alberta. Shell Oil Company of Canada opened its first Edmonton office in the Raleigh Building on Jasper Avenue in 1952, and from there directed its northern operations (seismic, exploration, and production) in the search for and development of oil and natural gas resources. The area extended from Red Deer in the south through Northern Alberta, the Northwest Territories, and later up to the Arctic. During the next decade several major oil and gas fields were discovered—Virginia Hills, Sturgeon Lake South, Simonette, and in 1963, House Mountain—in which Shell's role was either as part of the discovery or the operator of the field.

All this activity, and the attendant investments by the firm, resulted in the inevitable move to secure markets for products in Alberta. Beginning its Edmonton marketing ventures by opening four retail service stations in 1955, its operations were consolidated in Western Canada by the purchase of North Star Oil Limited in 1960, and of the Canadian Oil Company in 1962. These acquisitions gave the organiza-

tion a real commercial and retail base to serve the needs of Alberta consumers. Shell's presence in Edmonton was enhanced in the next few years by a variety of new retail investments, offering solid investment opportunities for dealers and agents and hundreds of their employees as well as providing customers with new products and services.

Also during the 1960s the company—considered the Canadian pioneer of the in-situ steam-combustion recovery process—had begun experimental drilling in the Peace River oil sands in Northern Alberta. In addition, studies were advanced for surface recovery techniques from the Athabasca oil sands area to the northeast. With support directed from the Edmonton division, exploration had also moved into offshore British Columbia and into the Mackenzie Delta in the Arctic. At their peak, Shell's exploration and production operations had between 250 and 300 people working out of the city. They were relocated to the Financial Building on 100th Avenue and then to the Milner Building on 104th Street. However, with the industry centering more of its exploration operations in the Alberta foothills and around Calgary, the facility was closed in 1972.

The company introduced self-serve gasoline retailing to the city in 1970, in the wake of pioneering this concept in Vancouver the previous year.

Today Shell Canada Products Company, a division of Shell Canada Limited, has a strong presence in greater Edmonton in both marketing and refining activities. Its district sales office—in the Weber Building on the Calgary Trail—directs the marketing operations for the city and province. These operations are sup-

ported by the Bowden refinery near Red Deer; a new lubricants- and grease-manufacturing plant in Calgary; the new Sherwood bulk products terminal east of Edmonton; and a variety of retail outlets that include full service bays, car washes, convenience food stores, "rapidlube" lubrication centres, and self-serve gas bars. In order to satisfy the gasoline, diesel, and lubricant requirements of a variety of customers (encompassing farmers and the manufacturing, mining, and transportation industries), there is a network of farm agents in Edmonton and throughout Alberta. Aviation fuel is supplied at both the international and municipal airports through Shell dealers.

While not located specifically within the city's municipal boundaries, the corporation's new $1.4-billion Scotford refinery and styrene monomer plant are its most recent evidence of investment in Alberta and Western Canada. Situated 35 kilometres north-

east of Edmonton, the refinery is the world's first designed exclusively to process synthetic crude oil. A by-product, benzene, will be produced for the adjacent styrene plant, which will provide base materials for the plastics industry. Both facilities are to begin operations in 1984. Construction began in 1981, and 3,000 employees and construction workers were on the job during the peak building period.

As part of Shell's strategy to meet future customer needs, and to gear for growth in Western Canada, marketing and manufacturing activities in Edmonton are focussed on providing specialized fuelling facilities to the transportation industry. The latest computer technology will be utilized in this project, and also will be incorporated in the company's plans for continuous upgrading of its retail operations to ensure that consumer demand is satisfied at the lowest cost.

An active member of the Edmonton community, Shell Canada has a long

The Scotford refinery and styrene monomer plant, one of Shell Canada's most recent acquisitions, is the world's first facility designed exclusively to process synthetic crude oil.

record of support for programmes related to health and welfare, education, and cultural activities.

The firm, recognizing employees' volunteer activities, provides funding through a special grant programme, the Community Service Fund, for everything from paper supplies for a Brownie Pack to a new time clock for a community arena.

The organization supports the United Way and other health and welfare agencies, universities (through scholarships, fellowships, and research and development grants), the performing and visual arts, and civic community projects.

Shell Canada's decision to relocate its corporate head office to Calgary in 1985 further enhanced the company's presence in Alberta.

GAINER'S INC.

Gainer's Inc., pioneer Northern Alberta meat-packing plant, traces its beginnings back over the years to a small meat market opened in the late 1890s by John Gainer, a newcomer to Edmonton.

Born in St. Mary's, Ontario, in 1858 to parents of Irish stock, he immigrated west shortly after his marriage in the 1870s. After a short stay in North Dakota, the newlyweds decided to return to Canada. Their first home was in Pilot Mound, Manitoba; but at that time of railway expansion, the call of the West was irresistible.

It was not long before the Gainers answered the call. John Gainer was aboard the first passenger train over the new Calgary-Edmonton line. This trip to what turned out to be Gainer's "promised land" took 18 hours.

However, by now John had a family to care for, and not much in the way of money; his bank savings totalled $250. For the time being his dream of originating a packing plant in Edmonton had to wait—that would call for capital. Instead, he took over part of his modest dwelling and

opened a retail meat market.

Like any other small-town butcher, the owner had to buy, kill, and dress livestock—and then make the rounds to sell his product. Often, out of his one-horse rig, John would trade dressed meat for livestock. In this way his business grew.

Mrs. Gainer, meantime, had to look after her home, the shop, and somehow find time to help in the meat market. She baked bread and cakes that would round out her husband's concept of a complete food shop. In these early days of the Gainers' business, many of their out-of-town customers bought as much cured meat as they could carry—some carried theirs all the way to the Klondike River in the Yukon, centre of the Great Gold Rush of the mid-1890s.

The retail meat market did well. And as the Grand Trunk Pacific and Canadian Northern railways pushed through Edmonton on their way to the Yellowhead Pass and to the Pacific, John Gainer found there were opportunities in meat wholesaling as well. Railway construction workers were trenchermen whose appetites had to be satisfied, and their cookhouses on wheels demanded vast quantities of meat.

John kept pace with this ever-increasing demand for quality meat by spending more and more time on the road, buying cattle and hogs from farms in the Edmonton area, and during this growth period built his first slaughterhouse. He located in south Edmonton, not far from the Calgary and Edmonton Railway's Strathcona Station—where his first trip from Calgary had terminated years before. He built a brick store on Whyte (82nd) Avenue and installed facilities for curing and smoking meats. The business was growing, as was the family, and before many years sons Arthur, Chester, and Clifford were busy in their father's plant.

The second Gainer's plant, circa 1930.

Again seeing an opportunity for expansion, the entrepreneur bought a piece of property near Mill Creek, a mile or so east of his slaughterhouse, and there built his first packing plant. It was a modest start; John moved his original meat market onto the site and turned it into an office.

The site was completed with corrals for cattle, hogs, and sheep, a barn for horses, and a boiler house. By today's standards this spread could hardly qualify as a packing plant, but it proudly bore the name of J. Gainer

The original Gainer's Limited store on Whyte (82nd) Avenue, Strathcona.

The new Gainer's plant is on 66th Street in north Edmonton.

The Gainer's plant, in south Edmonton, in 1978.

& Company Abbatoir. Retail markets were being operated in Edmonton, Strathcona, and Wetaskiwin; and live hogs were being shipped from the plant to the Kootenay area of British Columbia. All the while the Gainers were beginning to bring together the nucleus of an efficient staff.

The company was incorporated in 1911 as Gainer's Limited with the founder as president; he held this position until his death in 1938. His eldest son, Arthur, had been appointed managing director and served the burgeoning enterprise in that capacity until his untimely death, at 53 years of age, in 1937.

Another son, Clifford, succeeded Arthur as general manager, and retained this post until his death in 1957. Still, direction of the company remained within the family: A grandson, Harold E. Gainer (Arthur Gainer's son), became president and carried the firm into the boom years that came into being with the discovery of oil at Leduc.

The Gainer family relinquished its interest in their pioneer firm in 1972. The purchaser was Agra Industries Ltd.; and under president P.E. Gibson, Agra began a modernization and expansion programme.

In 1977 Gainer's Foods Ltd., as it became known, was bought by the Pocklington Financial Corporation, headed by Peter Pocklington—a widely known Western Canadian who owns a number of real-estate firms, financial organizations, and other enterprises. By 1980 sales passed the $100-million mark—reflecting an impressive growth of $62 million in eight years. His other interest is hockey, and in 1977 Pocklington acquired a part interest in the Edmonton Oilers Hockey Club.

The seller was another well-known entrepreneur, Nelson Skalbania. The Pocklington-Skalbania partnership was in effect for one year, after which Pocklington became sole owner. This was before the start of the 1978-1979 hockey season and was Edmonton's last full season in the old WHA.

Then, in 1979, Pocklington paid the National Hockey League six million dollars for an expansion franchise, a move that brought NHL games to Ed-

The Gainer Superior Hockey Club, Edmonton City amateur champions, 1924-1925.

monton for the first time. It goes without saying that the Oilers and their star player, Wayne Gretzky, have drawn worldwide attention and acclaim to the team's home city.

Much earlier, from the 1920s through the 1940s, Gainer's acquired a reputation for being interested in, and backing, organized sports at the amateur and professional levels. Hockey and soccer teams for decades carried the Gainer name as far as the United Kingdom and Europe.

While sports fans of the 1920s recall the exploits of Gainer's soccer teams, few records of their achievements seem to have survived. The stories of the firm's hockey clubs—Gainer's Superior Hockey Club, the

Edmonton Superiors, and Gainer's Capitals—are thoroughly recorded, and cover the years between 1924 and the 1940s. These teams, sporting black, red, and white uniforms, carried Edmonton's name and fame wherever they played—and usually won.

Gainer's Superior Hockey Club won the Duggan Cup in 1924-1925; the Superiors were city champions in 1928-1929, and city and provincial champions in 1933-1934. Earlier, in 1926-1927, the Superior Aristo Hockey Club had won the Northern

Alberta senior championship. In 1929-1930 the Superiors were Northern Alberta senior champs; in 1930-1931 were Alberta and British Columbia senior champs; and in 1935-1936 were senior city champions again.

In 1938-1939 Gainer's Capitals were western intermediate champions. The Superiors' trophy cabinet displayed the B&K City Cup, the Edmonton Championship Shield, the Jeff Dickinson Cup, an international award won in Paris, and the *Journal-Herald* Cup, emblematic of provincial championship.

Through all these years of hockey activity most of the training was handled by Ira Stuart. His team captain was the able Jimmy Graham.

EDMONTON ECONOMIC DEVELOPMENT AUTHORITY

Edmonton Economic Development Authority general manager Allan Bleiken, left, with chairman Douglas Maloney. They meet regularly to discuss and review economic development initiatives on behalf of Edmonton.

Planning and implementation of economic growth for Edmonton is the mandate of the city's new Edmonton Economic Development Authority, established on March 1, 1983, under enabling laws passed at the 1982 session of the Alberta Legislature.

The new organization—with offices in the Oxford Tower building—is headed by chairman Douglas W. Maloney, vice-chairman of the Continental Bank of Canada. Serving as general manager of the group is Allan Bleiken, while its nine-member board of directors includes three city council representatives—two council appointees and a city alderman—and six leading figures from Edmonton's business, academic, labour, and industrial circles.

Its formation pursuant to a four-year study and evaluation by both the city and the private sector, including the Spirit of Edmonton Committee, the authority has assumed and expanded on the operations of the former City of Edmonton Business Development Department. Funded by the City of Edmonton, the authority, whose 1983 budget was set at $1.4 million, operates with a staff of 16.

Spokesmen note that the group's evolving business-to-business

approach with the private sector improves the economic-development process. "This private-sector approach is being well accepted by business and government," states Maloney. (Since its foundation the authority has received a number of requests from other cities seeking data on the authority concept.) Adding that the organization aims to seek input and advice from a consensus group of senior administrators, private industry, government, and business associations, Maloney comments: "What we are looking for is a commitment from the community as a whole to support development in Edmonton. In some cases this will mean creating task forces to deal with specific projects."

According to Bleiken, the city is fortunate in having authority members who are aware of the "national and international perspectives of the business and industrial world," and who are willing to make a major personal commitment to Edmonton.

In its first 12 months of operation, the organization handled more than 16,000 business contacts and made 648 major business presentations; by year's end it had produced or updated 25 economic or industry reports to

provide the statistical data to be used in its marketing programmes. Acknowledgements of Edmonton's entries into the economic-development arena include the top North American marketing award in 1982—presented by the American Economic Development Council, and awarded to a Canadian city for the first time since it was instituted. By December 1983 the authority, or its predecessor, was the recipient of 21 national and international awards for marketing programmes.

Strategies for strengthening Edmonton's profile across the continent and overseas include an advertising campaign designed to reach corporate decision makers, and several audiovisual presentations dealing with specific industrial sectors as well as with the city's general economy. A recently acquired computer system provides the authority's researchers instant access to statistical and demographic information.

The billion-dollar skyline of downtown Edmonton. The city's new Convention Centre, opened in 1983, is at right. The skyline's various levels follow the contour of the North Saskatchewan River Valley.

OXFORD DEVELOPMENT GROUP LTD.

With the completion of the Edmonton Centre, Oxford became a North American leader in downtown redevelopment. The centre is comprised of the Royal Trust Tower, the Toronto-Dominion Tower, the Oxford Tower, and the Four Seasons Hotel.

When G. Donald Love and the Poole brothers started Oxford in Edmonton nearly a quarter-century ago, with virtually no capital, they had no idea it would be the beginning of a multibillion-dollar real estate empire with major downtown developments across North America.

Born in Calgary, Love came to Edmonton in 1955 to set up a branch of Dominion Securities. A client, the Baker Medical Clinic, wanted to redevelop its property. Love approached Ernest Poole of Poole Construction (now PCL Construction) who referred him to his sons, John and George Poole. Under the name Polo Development (Po for Poole and lo for Love), the Baker project was

the start of the development business for Love.

Based upon Polo's success, the partners formed Oxford Leaseholds Ltd. in 1960. Their first project, the Essex Building at 107th Street and 100th Avenue, was a three-storey walk-up costing $325,000. Capital was thin, so Oxford sold the building before construction began, in order to provide cash flow. This set the pattern for all Oxford's early projects.

In 1962 Clarence Elliott, then director of real estate investments for Great-West Life, told a business seminar that Oxford might someday have assets over $100 million and operations outside Edmonton. "We all had difficulty believing this," Love recalls. But 22 years later, in 1984, Oxford started construction of the $300-million Norwest Corporation headquarters in Minneapolis.

Oxford developed the Bank of Montreal building in downtown Edmonton, its first project under a programme to own the real estate, in 1964. The policy of building, owning, and managing properties for its own portfolio became the cornerstone of Oxford's philosophy, giving tenants the security of a landlord with a long-term commitment.

Over the next few years Oxford specialized in bank developments in the $3-million to $5-million range and expanded beyond Edmonton. Projects included the Bank of Commerce in Halifax, Victoria, and Windsor; and Royal Bank buildings in Edmonton, Halifax, Winnipeg, and London. These were built on land leased from the banks to limit the need for capital.

Without significant capital sources, Oxford was somewhat limited in expansion potential. Thus, Great-West Life (in 1964) and Confederation Life

Insurance Company of Toronto and Canada Trust Company of London (in 1968) became partners with Oxford to supply the capital needed for continued expansion.

In the mid-1960s Oxford shifted its focus to integrated mixed-use downtown developments. The first project was Edmonton's $15-million McCauley Plaza: an underground commercial mall and two high-rise office facilities, the Imperial Oil and AGT buildings. This development was followed by the $25-million Lombard Place in Winnipeg.

In 1972 Oxford turned sod for Edmonton Centre, which effectively shifted the commercial centre of Edmonton's downtown and became the flagship of Oxford's major integrated downtown developments. The company has since become a North Amer-

Phase 1 of the Citicorp Plaza project in Los Angeles will open in the fall of 1985.

The Toronto-Dominion Square (left) is an Oxford development project in Calgary. It is renowned for its three-level shopping concourse, its twin office towers, and the beautiful Devonian Gardens (above), a year-round park of lush green trees, bushes, and vines in a giant greenhouse of steel, aluminum, bronze, and glass.

ican leader in downtown redevelopment. On its 10th anniversary in 1984, the centre included the Royal Trust, Toronto-Dominion, Oxford, and Canadian Commercial Bank towers, the Four Seasons Hotel, the Centre Club, a three-level retail mall, two smaller retail areas, and three parkades.

Oxford then developed Toronto-Dominion Square in Calgary, incorporating a covered park, the Devonian Gardens, sponsored by the Devonian Foundation. The park concept was also incorporated into Town Square in downtown St. Paul, Minnesota.

Oxford's first U.S. project was Denver Square in 1975. The firm is now one of Denver's prominent downtown landlords, with the Anaconda Tower, Republic Plaza, and the Great-West Life Plaza.

The company's IDS Tower in Minneapolis is the city's largest. Nearby stands Oxford's Minneapolis City Center, Phase II of which will be the 66-storey headquarters for the Norwest Bank. Together with Town Square, these projects have made

Oxford a major force in the revitalization of the downtowns in the Twin Cities area. In early 1984 Oxford won the competition to develop the Minnesota World Trade Center in St. Paul.

Other U.S. developments include United Plaza in Phoenix, Arizona, and the Lake Buena Vista office plaza at Walt Disney World, Orlando, Florida. Oxford's Louisville Galleria in Kentucky opened in 1981 to revitalize the heart of that city.

Oxford started construction of the $200-million initial phase of Citicorp Plaza in downtown Los Angeles in 1983. And in early 1984 the company entered into an agreement to build the Quaker Oats world headquarters in downtown Chicago.

Oxford has also been involved in the purchase of real estate, mainly shopping centres in Canada, starting in 1975 with the purchase of Cambridge Leaseholds Ltd. Projects included the Bayshore Inn in Ottawa and the Devonshire Mall in Windsor. Chinook Shopping Centre in Calgary

and Market Square in Kitchener were developed by Oxford.

The firm gained a strong foothold in downtown Toronto in 1978 with the purchase of Y&R Properties. Oxford's Toronto holdings now include 11 buildings, among them the Richmond-Adelaide Centre, the Continental Bank Building, the National Bank Building, and the Guardian of Canada Tower.

Starting as a private company, Oxford went public with a listing on the Toronto Stock Exchange in June 1976. The company was privatized again in 1979 following a daring takeover by Love. Today the other major shareholders are the employees and the Toronto-Dominion Bank.

Oxford moved its corporate group to Denver in 1983, "mainly because of the size of our U.S. operations," Love explains. "But we will still have a major investment in Edmonton. Oxford was born, grew up, and prospered in Edmonton. It has a strong asset base in Edmonton and the company hopes to continue to expand there in the years to come."

Oxford attributes its success to a combination of timing, solid market analysis, and a sound business approach of not starting construction until financing and major tenants are in place. To this, Love says he would add "good people and patient capital."

BANISTER CONTINENTAL LTD.

Construction of a 475-metre dam, 175 metres high, undertaken by Pitts Engineering Construction division of the Edmonton firm. Some 2.3 million cubic metres of concrete were used in the $350-million project.

Banister Continental Ltd., founded in Edmonton 36 years ago, is a giant in the heavy-construction industry. The company, with some 300 permanent employees and thousands of hourly paid workers hired for specific jobs, is building or has built enormous installations in North America and the Middle East.

Ronald K. Banister looks back to the discovery of oil at Leduc as the starting point of his engineering-construction empire. With the establishment of Ditching Contractors — the forerunner of today's firm — and a secondhand truck and used ditching machine, he was in business as a subcontractor in the Leduc oil patch. Assuming the name Banister Construction Ltd. in 1950, the company in 1977 moved into a new head office complex at 9910-39th Avenue.

Steadily advancing its pipeline construction capabilities, the organization expanded Canada-wide during the '50s and '60s. Entering the international pipeline building market in 1966 by undertaking work on a line in Alaska, three years later the firm became a public corporation; in 1975 it began pipelining in the Middle East. Further expansion came in 1978 when the firm acquired Pitts Engineering Construction of Toronto, a concern that had been founded in 1942. Two of its subsidiaries — Cliffside Pipelayers and McDace — added an underground utilities-construction division to Banister operations.

The Banister Construction Group today is working in a variety of areas. Civil-engineering projects, marine jobs, laying underground utilities, and pipeline building are all directed from corporate headquarters in Edmonton.

Company founder Ronald K. Banister was born in Okotoks, Alberta, in 1917. He flew with the Royal Canadian Air Force from 1941 to 1945, and was awarded the Distinguished Flying Cross in 1943. Serving as company president in the '50s and '60s and as chairman of the board after incorporation in 1969, Banister directed expansion into the Middle East in the '70s, and became president of the corporation's international division. Continuing to serve as a director of Banister Continental Ltd. during the '70s, he returned in 1981 as chairman of the board and chief executive officer. A founding director of the Canadian Pipeline Contractors' Association, and its president in 1957, Banister in 1978 became a director of the International Pipeline Contractors' Association — and was the first Canadian to serve on its board.

Over the years the Banister name has come to be best known for its innovation of techniques for construction of pipelines under adverse conditions. The firm has developed a series of unique wheel-mounted ditchers capable of excavating frozen ditches more economically than conventional machinery; the patented devices, through rigorous on-site testing and use, are recognized as the finest Arctic ditching units in the world. Their development and use,

Banister equipment, bearing the familiar diamond logo, working on a major pipeline project in Northern Ontario.

plus a programme of continual adaptation of construction methods and equipment, have maintained Banister's reputation as a leader in Canada's pipeline-construction industry.

While that division of the company has concentrated on large-diameter-pipeline projects in Canada, it also offers specialized ditching services for pipeline construction in the Arctic. A recent contract in this category was for a job on Melville Island, north of the Arctic Circle, as part of the Arctic Pilot Project. A second endeavour successfully completed involved construction of 190 kilometres (118 miles) of natural gas pipeline near Ottawa, Ontario, for TransCanada PipeLines.

Banister Pipelines America has built large-diameter lines in Alaska and the lower 48 states. One such effort was the construction of sections of the American prebuild of the Alaska Highway natural-gas pipeline in Oregon. This division of the corporation first entered the U.S. pipeline-construction market in 1966, and has since completed contracts from Alaska to Louisiana.

Three years after the organization's pipeline-construction activity outside North America began in 1975, Banister Pipelines International, Inc., a wholly owned subsidiary, was formed to direct operations in parts of the Middle East. In 1981 the corporation concluded disposal of its equipment assets in Iraq; however, it is again actively exploring and bidding on projects in the more stable areas of the Middle East.

The Pitts Engineering Construction division, with capabilities for both land and marine work, conducts civil-construction operations across Canada. During 1983 nine major proj-

ects were finished or under way at locations ranging from Revelstoke, British Columbia, to St. John's, Newfoundland, and from Ontario's Niagara Peninsula to Whitehorse, Yukon Territory.

Among the efforts completed were the expansion of a powerhouse on the Yukon River in Whitehorse; in Edmonton an underpass for the city, and a rail bypass for Canadian National Railway; two overpasses in Calgary, as part of the Crowchild Trail upgrading project; the "Syncrolift" ship-repair facility in St. John's harbour, built for Newfoundland Dockyard, a division of Canadian National Railway; and the Bay of Quinte Bridge near Belleville, Ontario, a contract awarded by the Ontario Ministry of Transportation and Communications.

Still another major Pitts contract calls for construction of a $350-million concrete gravity dam and hydroelectric powerhouse near Revelstoke. The firm is sponsor and 50-percent partner in the project, scheduled for completion in August 1984. The job, awarded to Dalcan Constructors (a consortium sponsored by Pitts), is the largest heavy-

Saint Mary's Generating Station in Sault Ste. Marie, Ontario, was completed in 1982. In the background is the International Bridge, built by Pitts Engineering Construction in the early 1960s.

construction contract ever to be publicly tendered in Canada. An earlier joint venture sponsored by Pitts constructed a tunnel 13 metres in diameter to divert the Columbia River during the Revelstoke Dam construction period.

As a result of its drive to excel, Banister Continental Ltd. has matured from a one-man ditching subcontractor to one of the largest pipeline and civil-engineering contractors in the nation.

In 1960 founder R.K. Banister was the proud owner of a then-new International transport unit.

UPRIGHT BROS. LTD.

A family-owned enterprise that has specialized in heating and air conditioning, Upright Bros. Ltd. has been active in the ranks of Edmonton's retail and industrial establishments for 75 years.

The firm was originated as the Upright Hardware Company; the founder, C.H. Upright, subsequently developed a sheet metal trade out of his store and shop near 92nd Street and 118th (Alberta) Avenue. In just over a decade his six sons joined the business, and it was renamed Upright and Sons. The organization became a limited company in 1947 (Upright Bros. Ltd.), and six years later sold the original property, which included a two-storey frame structure housing suites above the ground-floor establishment.

During the building activity that followed postwar expansion, the discovery of oil at nearby Leduc, and northern development, Edmonton was in the grip of a feverish housing boom; throughout the city, and particularly in the west end, whole new subdivisions sprang up to accommodate the demand for single-family residences. Motivated by the large volume of construction, the corporation—which had been manufacturing furnaces since 1935—in 1953 erected a factory in a newly opened area in the city's northwest quarter for the production of high-quality domestic furnaces.

However, in 1969 the manufacturing phase was closed down, and Upright Bros. Ltd. concentrated on heating and air conditioning installations—again reflecting a change in direction of the local building industry. The demand for living quarters resulted in a surge in apartment-block construction, as well as office-block and industrial-plant relocation projects.

The original C.H. Upright hardware store and block, 92nd Street and 118th Avenue, Edmonton. Photo circa 1913.

L.E. Upright, one of the sons of C.H. Upright, retired from the business in 1971; two of his sons, Dave and Neil, assumed leadership of the company. Under their direction the firm, after securing the necessary patents, left the crowded heating/air conditioning field and branched into a unique product line that has proved successful: the manufacture of railway-switch heaters. The devices keep mainline switching gear ice-free through the long winter months in the Rocky Mountains, thereby eliminating a problem that frequently defied the efforts of gangs of track maintenance workers to keep the trains running. Utilizing natural gas, propane, or oil heat to melt accumulated snow—plus an air-distribution system that through temperature and velocity removes moisture from the rail bed by evaporation—the equipment, generally housed in an insulated six-foot by eight-foot trackside building, can handle switch installations up to 40 feet long. There are several models, including one that can be set up between parallel tracks and another, powered by propane gas, made for specific installations where electricity is not available.

Success of the innovation on Canadian National tracks through the Rockies and Selkirks has led to its introduction on the Burlington Northern Railroad in the northwestern United States. As well, B.C. Rail uses them, and some have gone into installations of light-rail urban transit facilities in Alberta.

Upright Bros. Ltd. now employs 10 men year-round and builds 100 switch heaters annually, with inventory and price fluctuations of component parts computer-controlled. Its office and plant are now located at 16653-113th Avenue, in a recently developed west Edmonton industrial area.

An Upright Bros. Ltd. switch heater installation at Blue River, British Columbia. Blue River is a Canadian National Railway division point noted for the heaviest annual snowfall on the main line between Edmonton and Vancouver. Courtesy of CN Rail.

NUMAC OIL & GAS LTD.

William S. McGregor, founder and president of Numac Oil & Gas Ltd.

Numac Oil & Gas Ltd. and its founder, William S. McGregor, exemplify the pioneering spirit upon which the Alberta oil and gas industry is founded. Of all the exploration companies active in this foothills province, only two are headquartered in Edmonton. Numac is one of them.

The Numac story begins with and is largely built around the entrepreneurial spirit of Bill McGregor. When Turner Valley's Royalite No. 4 blew in more than 50 years ago, McGregor, a boy raised on a farm in the area, was struck by the excitement created when this huge wet gas well caught fire and blew wild. The flames could be seen in Calgary, 30 miles away. Before long, McGregor was involved. His first oil field job was with the old Anglo-Canadian Oil Company for

which he worked in production and development for 10 years. During this period he purchased land near Black Diamond and developed a successful farming and ranching operation.

In 1945 he resigned from Anglo-Canadian, expanded his farming and ranching operations, and founded an oil field construction company known as McGregor-Johanson Construction. With the discovery of the Leduc oil field in 1947, McGregor moved his fledgling enterprise to Edmonton. McGregor-Johanson operates out of Edmonton and remains active in Alberta oil field construction today as a wholly-owned subsidiary of Numac.

The Leduc discovery also fostered other opportunities and McGregor was soon involved in oil and gas exploration. In 1952 McGregor and some friends pooled their resources and drilled Mic Mac No. 1 near Calmar, a few miles west of Leduc. This first well was completed with an initial capacity of 250 barrels of crude per day and was followed by seven more producing wells in the same area. The result: the Mic Mac pool, a small but productive pool in the southwest corner of the Leduc oil field. The scene was set—Mic Mac Oils had been created.

In 1952 Mic Mac "went public" by raising $200,000 at 25 cents per share. Four years later the firm merged with two smaller independents, Skyline Oils and Banner Oils. The merged businesses were known as Consolidated Mic Mac Oils Ltd., with McGregor continuing as president of the larger entity. The company subsequently developed production in the prolific South Sturgeon Lake field, drilled the first well in the Deer Mountain field north of Swan Hills, and made two major Mississippian limestone discoveries in the North

and South Twining fields. The Mic Mac story ended in 1963 when the company was sold to Hudson's Bay Oil & Gas Limited for $15 million in cash or Hudson's Bay stock.

Immediately following the sale of Mic Mac, McGregor organized the concern he heads today, Numac Oil & Gas Ltd. Operating with a relatively small but dedicated staff, all of whom had been with Mic Mac, Numac has concentrated its activities in conventional oil and gas exploration, primarily in Alberta, with an enviable record of success.

In addition, Numac has diversified into other natural resource activities on its own, taking 100-percent interests in one million acres of uranium prospective acreage in Northern Saskatchewan; 120,000 acres of heavy oil properties at Surmont, north of Cold Lake, Alberta; and 270,000 acres in the Mackenzie Delta, Northwest Territories. In the mid-1960s Numac brought in Imperial Oil Limited as a partner to help explore the uranium properties which resulted in the discovery of the rich Midwest Lake uranium ore body in 1978. Further, the company brought in Gulf Canada Resources Inc. to help develop the heavy oil properties and brought in Suncor to help explore and develop the Mackenzie Delta oil and gas properties.

As well as directing Numac, Bill McGregor has found time to lend his expertise to the oil and gas industry at large, having served for several years as vice-president of the Independent Petroleum Association of Canada. He also is a trustee of the University of Alberta Hospital Foundation and is a member of the Business Advisory Council of the Faculty of Business Administration and Commerce of the University of Alberta.

McDOUGALL & SECORD, LIMITED

The oldest family-owned business in Edmonton, now known as McDougall & Secord, Limited, was founded in 1879 by John Alexander McDougall, who engaged in general merchandising and fur trading. Over the next decade the business grew and prospered. In 1892 Richard Secord was hired as fur buyer, and in 1897 he became a partner. The venture was henceforth known as McDougall & Secord and described itself as general merchants, wholesale and retail; buyers and exporters of raw furs; dealers in land scrip and Northwest lands; outfitters for survey parties, traders, trappers, miners, and others for the North; and suppliers for country stores.

In 1907, due to rapid growth, the young city of Edmonton was experiencing financial and other difficulties, so John A. McDougall was

John A. McDougall founded the forerunner of McDougall & Secord, Limited, in 1879 as a general merchandising and fur trading establishment.

drafted by the businessmen of the city and, that December, was elected mayor with no significant opposition. The building of a street railway system was far behind schedule, and the telephone system in need of replacement.

First, McDougall resolved the financial problems and next the telephone system. By April 1908 Edmonton had what was claimed to be the first automatic dialing system in use in North America. Next, the contract for the street railway, which had seen no significant progress in four years, was cancelled and the city took over. By November two street-cars were operating over what rapidly

became 12 miles of track with six cars operating. And finally, McDougall successfully negotiated an agreement between the city, the two levels of senior government, and the CPR for the financing of Edmonton's renowned High Level Bridge. He refused to serve a further term.

The firm sold its general store business in 1907 and a short time later the fur trading business. It then set up a financial concern, which in 1909 was incorporated under the name of McDougall & Secord, Limited, to operate primarily as a financial house and mortgage corporation. Much of Edmonton's business centre development during the years 1907 to 1914, including the Tegler Building, was financed by McDougall & Secord, Limited, and McDougall & Secord's Empire Block on the site of the present Empire Building housed the first offices of the province of Alberta in 1905.

It is interesting to note that in 1909 Canada was still very much influenced by English corporate practice of the day wherein the general manager of a corporation was the chief executive officer and the president, if there was one, a figurehead. It was not until 1922 that McDougall & Secord, Limited, adopted the American nomenclature for its officers.

In public life John A. McDougall was for many years a member of the aldermanic and hospital boards and, as previously mentioned, was twice mayor of Edmonton. He served a five-year term in the Alberta Legislature and was a member of the first senate of the University of Alberta. He was a promoter of the first Electric Light and Power Company to serve Edmonton in 1891 and also a promoter and director of the first Exhibition Com-

pany. He was a founding member of the Edmonton Board of Trade and an early president.

Richard Secord taught school in Edmonton for three years and served a term on the Legislative Assembly of the Northwest Territories.

As a consequence of World War I and the depression that followed it, the firm, through mortgage defaults, became a real estate holding company. Most of the real estate thus acquired was not sold until after World War II.

When John A. McDougall died in

Here buyers examine pelts in one of the firm's fur warehouses in 1905.

1928, he was succeeded in the presidency by his son John Charles and he in turn by his son John Frederick McDougall. McDougall & Secord, Limited, consolidated its holdings until 1960, when the company began development of the Empire Building as the first modern high-rise office structure in Edmonton. In 1975 McDougall & Secord entered the consulting field, establishing **DALCOR** Innoventures Ltd. which provides business systems and economic development services to clients throughout North America.

Throughout its 105-year history in Edmonton the firm has always been managed by a McDougall; John R. McDougall of the fourth generation now is vice-president and secretary/treasurer of the company. In its second century in Edmonton, McDougall & Secord, Limited, continues to operate as a family-owned and -operated business, managing its real estate properties and investment portfolio and providing management consulting assistance and specialized computer systems to a broad range of clients.

The Empire Building, the first modern high-rise office facility in Edmonton, was developed by and now serves as headquarters for McDougall & Secord, Limited.

EDMONTON NORTHLANDS

An aerial photo of the Edmonton Northlands AgriCom Building, which was completed in 1984 (above), and (right) part of the crowd attending a trade show in the AgriCom.

October 15, 1879, was a day to remember for the citizens of Edmonton Settlement and district—all 275 of them.

That was the day when Edmonton, Northwest Territories, staged its first agricultural exhibition. Livestock, grain, vegetables, and women's handiwork were displayed in the "Big House," as Hudson's Bay Company chief factor Richard Hardisty's residence was known. The Big House frowned over the North Saskatchewan River—the river-highway being the reason the HBC's Fort Edmonton had been established there almost a century before.

The sponsoring body behind that exhibition was the Edmonton Agricultural Society, whose members lived either in Edmonton Settlement, St. Albert, Fort Saskatchewan, or on the farms beginning to take shape between the three communities. The group's president was Inspector W.D. Jarvis of the North West Mounted Police, founder of Fort Saskatchewan; the vice-president and host of the exhibition was Hardisty. There were three directors: a sergeant-major of the Mounties; Tom Lamoreaux, from

the Sturgeon River area; and Donald Ross, Edmonton's first hotel operator.

Among the winners who shared the $173 offered in prize money were Malcolm Groat, pioneer west-end farmer; "English Charlie" Stevenson, an old prospector who had settled on the riverbank upstream from Fort Edmonton; and a Mr. Taber, a Hudson's Bay Company employee. Taber walked home with an astonishing one-sixth of the prize money—$31—plus the Governor's Prize, presented by the lieutenant-governor of the Northwest Territories.

One hundred years later the old Agricultural Society had been replaced by the Edmonton Exhibition Association (EXA). The association, which came into being in 1908 as successor to the original Agricultural Society, had outgrown its first "permanent" homesite on the river flats. In its new location, once a swamp known as Kirkness Lake, it soon sprawled over 126.5 acres in the northeast part of the city. From the original one-day stand in 1879, Exhibition Association-sponsored events in 1979 totalled 1,371.

Other century-spanning statistics are equally startling. The $173 in prize money in 1879 passed $225,000 for all categories 100 years later; the Northwest Territories grant of $10 in 100 years grew to $100,000 from the

province of Alberta; Edmonton's first fair raised no money, but in 1979 gross EXA revenue for the year totalled $21 million. There was no exhibition building in 1879; in 1979 the value of the exhibition plant totalled $65 million. At the first exhibition a few dozen assorted farm wagons brought spectators to Hardisty's Big House—in 1979 some 700,000 motor vehicles were counted on the exhibition grounds. There were no Agricultural Society employees in 1879; in 1979 there were 130 full-time and 1,600 part-time workers busy with the year-round functions sponsored by the EXA.

At the end of December 1983 the Exhibition Association changed its articles of association and officially became known as Edmonton Northlands. The "Northlands" logo had been in use for four years, with the parent body continuing to be known as the EXA.

Edmonton Northlands is a non-profit, limited company operating under the Agricultural Societies Act. In so doing it serves Northern Alberta communities, whose population totals 1.5 million. When the Exhibition Association was formed in 1908, it was allowed to issue 200 shares valued at five dollars each.

Over the years the size of the board of directors changed. Today 18 are elected by the shareholders, others are appointed by the Edmonton City Council, and the lieutenant-governor appoints two elected members of the Alberta Legislature. Northlands' authorized share capital is now 300 shares valued at five dollars each, and thus the company is owned by these 300 people—all volunteers who do not receive compensation as a result of ownership. An individual may hold only one share, and must be a resident of Northern Alberta.

The stated objectives of Edmonton Northlands are to provide facilities and programmes, and market these, for activities that fall within the general areas of entertainment, trade shows, agriculture, and community service; to establish programmes and policies that benefit the community; to provide its services to residents of metropolitan Edmonton and Northern Alberta generally; to contribute to the economy of metropolitan Edmonton and Northern Alberta; to contribute to the life-style of residents of metropolitan Edmonton and Northern Alberta; to cooperate with the City of Edmonton, the government of Alberta, and the federal government in providing its services; to cooperate with other organizations in delivering services to residents of Northern Alberta, such as Edmonton's Klondike Days Association and the Edmonton Convention and Tourism Authority; to ensure, through continuous dialogue with its shareholders, that the needs and expectations of the shareholders

are realized to the fullest extent possible; and to effectively provide its services so as to be as self-sufficient as possible, without unduly competing with the private sector.

Completion of the Northlands Coliseum in 1974 and the Northlands AgriCom facility in 1984 have given Northlands the ability to become more oriented to trade shows and regional economic development. The utilization of these and other facilities now show priorities in this order: entertainment, agriculture, and trade shows.

All Northlands facilities are operated on a "user pay" basis, which means that those who do not patronize events do not subsidize the operation of the facilities. These include the Grandstand, built in 1951 and

upgraded several times since; the Sportex (1963); the Golden Garter (1971); the $16-million Coliseum (1974); and the 450,000-square-foot AgriCom (1984). Total attendance at all Northlands events in 1983 totalled 3.2 million.

Under its lease agreement with the City of Edmonton, all capital loans undertaken by Northlands are guaranteed by the Province of Alberta rather than the city—and there is no direct cost to the city arising from Northlands' operations. New land for exhibition purposes is purchased by Northlands, and title transferred to the city. Prior to September 30, 1982, the city had spent $3,724,000 for this purpose, while Northlands, contributed $3,379,709. At that time the organization's balance sheet showed

The old Edmonton Gardens (top right), home ice for dozens of hockey teams over the 70-odd years when the Gardens was Edmonton's major winter sports centre. The building was retired in 1973 and replaced by the Coliseum. The Oilers' "Mighty 99," Wayne Gretsky (bottom right), as sell-out crowds see him in action in the Coliseum.

$61 million in assets, $32 million in revenues, and $3.4 million in net income. At the conclusion of, or non-renewal of, the lease between the city and Northlands, all buildings and facilities on the grounds will become the property of the city.

Direction of year-round activities at Northlands falls to the members of 46 volunteer committees. In 1981-1982, a total of 397 committee members served an average of 44 hours. The sum of estimated volunteer hours in the period was 17,468.

In the early 1960s the Edmonton Exhibition Association spearheaded a proposal to restructure its annual summer agricultural fair. The object was to involve citizens in an annual midsummer celebration that, it was hoped, would strike off with a new and challenging theme. Out of a series of meetings with downtown groups, Edmonton's Klondike Days

The agriculture parade at Edmonton's summer exhibition in 1900. The fair was held on the Exhibition Association's old Rossdale site.

were born.

The new theme was valid. In the 1890s the town of Edmonton was the supply base that outfitted hundreds of would-be prospectors heading for the fabulous gold fields along the Klondike River in the far-off Yukon. Outfitters made fortunes out of providing the gold-seekers with everything from horses to frying pans.

This Klondike Days theme offered exciting opportunities to Edmontonians. There was the matter of Gay '90s dress—colourful, voluminous (the dancing girls excepted), and for the men, dashing. There were the old songs; rousing nights in downtown barrooms; neighbourhood block parties; parades; and stagecoach rides to the downtown, by which daily winners of "Ex" draws would transport their "pokes" to the safety of a deposit book. And best of all there were raft races on the river overseen by an admiral of the (raft) fleet, and the Sunday afternoon promenade—an event that drew continent-wide atten-

tion. Klondike Days costumes were *de rigueur* for this event, even down to trimmings for the family canine. Edmonton's downtown area was cordoned off, transit buses rerouted, and people thronged the streets to watch shows staged on borrowed flatbed trailers. The first Sunday promenade was attended by well in excess of 100,000 citizens, and newspaper photos of the event showed most of them "dressed to the nines."

Every year a new "Klondike Kate" comes to town: a young woman selected for her beauty, stage presence, and vocal abilities. The Klondike Days theme has been recognized by the North American Association of Fairs and Exhibitions as the most novel and successful promotion reported in years.

One of the big winners at Northlands is the racing—thoroughbred and harness. The 1983 summer thoroughbred meet, featuring the Canadian Derby, generated gross revenues of $7.7 million, and the harness races brought in another $4.1 million. Klondike Days activities at Northlands brought $5.08 million, an increase of one million dollars over 1982.

In total, the events during 1983 drew $33.4 million in revenue, down slightly from the 1982 figure. Activities included the Canadian Rodeo finals, a "Superodeo," industrial and commercial exhibitions, concessions, banquets, curling, entertainment events, dances, receptions, and parties using Northlands facilities.

"Clearly," the Northlands president reported to his shareholders, "the utilization of Northlands facilities is entertainment, agriculture, and trade shows, with community services provided in all three."

PEAT, MARWICK, MITCHELL & CO.

From the windows of the 21st floor of the imposing Principal Plaza office tower in downtown Edmonton, partners and clients of Peat, Marwick, Mitchell & Co. can look down to a small office building at the corner of Jasper Avenue and 100th Street. It was in this former CPR Building that Peat Marwick in 1923 opened its first Edmonton office.

For 10 or more years previously, Marwick, Mitchell & Co. had served its Edmonton clients out of the Calgary office. In those days staff personnel would take the train to Edmonton, compile reports needed to complete their work, and return to Calgary; the completed reports would be sent out from that city.

Peat, Marwick, Mitchell & Co. traces its beginnings in North America to the founding of Marwick, Mitchell & Co. in New York City in 1897. The founders were two young chartered accountants recently arrived from Scotland: James Marwick and S. Roger Mitchell. In those days Edmonton was a young and very small town in the far reaches of Canada's Northwest Territories.

Early in the 20th century a number of British interests and American companies expanded into Canada. Marwick, Mitchell & Co. soon followed, opening an office in Winnipeg in 1907. Before long another office opened in Montreal; later others followed in Toronto, Calgary, and Vancouver.

As the Alberta economy picked up after World War I, new businesses expanded, and with this growth the need for professional accountants intensified. The coal industry, stockyards, packing plants, and retail stores all contributed to this need; by 1923 it had become apparent that Marwick, Mitchell & Co. could no longer handle its burgeoning business out of the Calgary office.

Around the time that the first Edmonton office was opened, the name of the firm became Peat, Marwick, Mitchell & Co. — through the amalgamation of the United Kingdom firm of W.B. Peat & Co. and the American firm of Marwick, Mitchell & Co.

For the first few years the new Edmonton office operated with a staff of three, while direction still came from Calgary. In July 1936 a full office opened in the Bank of Commerce Building. The first resident manager was Elmer Gunderson, C.A., whose staff consisted of one chartered accountant and two students. One of these students was Allan D. McTavish, who later became the executive secretary of the Institute of Chartered Accountants of Alberta, and continues to be prominent in Edmonton community life.

Business in the Edmonton area expanded rapidly following the Leduc oil discovery in 1947. All facets of professional and business life quickened, with none being more challenging than the chartered-accountancy sector.

In the fall of 1971 Peat Marwick moved into offices in the new $22-million Alberta Government Telephones tower, at the time the tallest structure west of Toronto. Shortly after this move a management consulting practice was opened as a branch office on the same floor of the AGT Building, operating under the name of Peat, Marwick and Partners. The practice continued to expand with commencement of a full-time insolvency practice in 1980, operating as Peat Marwick Limited.

Peat, Marwick, Mitchell & Co.'s practice has grown to encompass the financial activities of giant corporations, major cities, and rural corporations, as well as those of smaller individual entrepreneurs. As an integral part of the business community of Edmonton, the firm continues to offer sound advice and excellent service.

Allan McTavish (right) and the current managing partner of Peat, Marwick, Mitchell & Co., Douglas Carr, in front of the Canadian Imperial Bank of Commerce building at Jasper Avenue and 101st Street. McTavish was a new employee when the accounting firm moved into the facility in 1936.

EDMONTON GENERAL HOSPITAL
The Grey Nuns of Edmonton

The Edmonton General Hospital today. When the first unit was built in the 1890s, the only structure in sight was St. Joachim's Chapel, now replaced by the church visible in the background.

The orphanage and first hospital at St. Albert, 11 miles northwest of Edmonton, which served the Edmonton District until the first unit of the Edmonton General Hospital was built by the Grey Nuns in 1895.

During the early 1800s Fort Edmonton—commonly known to fur traders and Indians as "The Fort of the Prairies"—had no facilities to care for those settlers unfortunate enough to fall victim to serious illness or injury.

In 1864 the first hospital building in what was to become Northern Alberta was opened in the St. Albert Mission, some 11 miles northwest of Fort Edmonton. The pioneer surgeons of the area, Drs. E.A. Braithwaite, J.D. Harrison, and Aristide Blais, had to drive in their buggies or ride horseback to the mission in order to attend to patients there.

For the next 14 years St. Albert, Edmonton Settlement, the Royal Canadian Mounted Police post, and Fort Saskatchewan were the three major focal points of population in the Upper Saskatchewan River country. St. Albert was the centre of the Roman Catholic population; Edmonton was the chief trading post for the Hudson's Bay Company's Saskatchewan District; and Fort Saskatchewan was the nucleus of police activity.

The first railway to enter the district was the Calgary and Edmonton. It reached the North Saskatchewan at Strathcona, across-river from Edmonton, in 1891—and gave the latter settlement immediate advantage over its neighbours. The one-time Fort of the Prairies promptly began to outdistance the others, and by 1895 Edmonton's population was estimated at 1,200; the adjacent areas counted some 15,000 citizens in total.

On April 25, 1894, Bishop Vital J. Grandin of St. Albert received a letter from a group of Edmonton doctors supporting the construction of a general hospital in their community. This institution would be built by the Grey Nuns order and operated under their direction. The letter proposed that it would be the responsibility of the Sisters to provide necessary accommodations and sufficient space to meet the needs of the growing village. The physicians pledged to support the hospital to the exclusion of all others, provided construction started immediately. The petition was signed by Drs. H.C. Wilson, H.L. McInnis, P.S. Royal, James H. Tofield, J.D. Harrison, and E.A. Braithwaite.

Bishop Grandin placed the request before the Superior General of the

Grey Nuns in Montreal, who regarded it favourably. Soon afterwards, Sister Delphine Brassard, the superior of the orphanage at St. Albert, approached the Hudson's Bay Company and purchased 46 Edmonton lots—an entire block—for $2,300.

Next, on July 28, 1895, Sister Marie Xavier and Sister Arthemise Bergeron Gosselin arrived to prepare plans for the new facility. In October of that year, *The Edmonton Bulletin* reported: "The new public hospital being constructed in the village of Edmonton by the Sisters of Charity is nearing completion. It is near the southeast corner of the block which lies between Jasper and Victoria (now 100th) avenues and between 11th and 12th streets (today's 111th and 112th streets) on the HBC property. Its length lies east and west and the front is toward Victoria Avenue. It is carefully and well planned for the purpose for which it is intended and will no doubt answer the purpose excellently."

The reasons for selecting this loca-

Sister Simonne Chauvet of the Grey Nuns, circa 1895.

institution. On December 17, Dr. Braithwaite admitted the hospital's first patient, a Mr. S. Vandonqhuet; December 21 saw the formation of a Ladies' Aid Society, whose members at once went to work to raise funds for the facility. On Christmas Day the Sisters received many gifts, and a cheque for $322.75 — the proceeds of a concert sponsored by the Ladies' Aid. Thirty-one patients were treated during the hospital's first month of service. The official opening ceremony took place on February 5, 1896.

In 1908 it was realized that a training school for nurses was essential for the proper care of the patients. Sister Mary Ann Casey, a graduate of Notre Dame Hospital in Montreal, was in charge of the first class. It numbered six pupils, and was graduated in 1911.

Through the devastating smallpox epidemic of 1870 — which claimed almost one-third of the populace of the Edmonton district — and the chicken pox epidemic of 1901, the Sisters offered their services, free of

charge, to nurse the stricken citizens. Through good times and bad to the present day, the quiet, unassuming Grey Nuns have endured hardship, privation, and difficulty in giving the people of Edmonton and surrounding district the most efficient hospital service possible. Sister Marie Xavier, the founder and first superior of the General Hospital, gave this message to the people of Edmonton in January 1898:

It is to be clearly understood that this is a general hospital, superintended and run by the Sisters of Charity, and all have access without distinction of creed or nationality. The sole object of the Sisters is to minister to the temporal wants of suffering humanity. The rest will be left to the Lord, who watches over all.

There were six students in the 1911 graduating class. They were the first to be trained at the Edmonton General Hospital School of Nursing.

tion for the new institution, several blocks west of the then-settled area of the community, is a matter of speculation. No explanation for the decision has been found in the archives of the Grey Nuns. One suggestion, however, is that the site was close to St. Joachim's Chapel, which had been founded in 1882 by Father R.P. Leduc and has since been designated a permanent mission site.

On November 17, 1895, Bishop Grandin celebrated the first Mass in the new hospital's chapel. In December Bishop Adelard Langevin, from St. Boniface on the Red River, presided at the official blessing of the

The Youville Wing for geriatric rehabilitation was opened in 1982.

Sister Marguerite Laforce, Provincial Superior, Sisters of Charity (Grey Nuns) of Alberta, dressed in the formal habit of the Grey Nuns, 1984.

The tenets of the Order remain unchanged today.

The Edmonton General Hospital—a teaching institution affiliated with the University of Alberta's Faculty of Medicine—is approved for standardization by the American College of Surgeons and approved for general internship by the Canadian Medical Association. During the 88 years of its existence, the facility may be said to have written a noble chapter in the history of Western Canadian hospitals.

Today the General Hospital complex, which is situated in the heart of Edmonton's downtown residential district, has expanded to encompass five wings with a total capacity of 799 beds, 2,500 employees, and a staff of 165 physicians. The future holds promise of many exciting changes—changes that will not only correct the problems associated with an aging facility, but will strengthen the General's unique characteristics and help it to fulfill its philosophy and mission.

Due to the aging nature of the hospital's buildings and the shift of the expanding population to the suburban areas of Edmonton, the Edmonton General Hospital was asked by the Minister of Hospitals and Medical

The lobby of the geriatric rehabilitation facility in the Youville Wing of Edmonton General Hospital.

Care to relocate the active treatment component of its operations to the Millwoods area of the city and take over the ownership and operation of an urban hospital designed for the southeast (Millwoods) area of Edmonton.

At the same time the 280-bed Youville Wing, which is a specialized geriatric rehabilitation facility, will remain in the Jasper Avenue location, and in 1987 an additional 200 auxiliary hospital beds will be added to the Jasper Avenue location, thereby making that site the long-term care component of the Edmonton General Hospital complex.

The Edmonton General Hospital complex will have approximately 540 active treatment beds in southeast Edmonton and an additional 480 beds, 280 of which will be geriatric rehabilitation and 200 auxiliary hospital beds, on the

Jasper Avenue site. There is serious consideration presently being given to developing an emergency facility on the Jasper Avenue site to service the residents in downtown Edmonton.

The development of a multifaceted Edmonton General Hospital is another first for the Grey Nuns and reflects the needs of a contemporary medical institution developing different specialties on different sites

to service the ever-changing needs of a community. Completion of this plan will permit the Edmonton General Hospital to create a modern health care facility serving the growing demands of the Edmonton community and to make the environment a stimulating one for patients and staff.

Model of the Edmonton General Hospital Millwoods location, to be completed May 1987.

MELCOR DEVELOPMENTS LTD.

Tim Melton, the third generation of the family to be president of Melcor Developments Ltd., the present-day successor to the Stanley Investment Company.

L.T. (Tim) Melton founded Stanley Investment Company of Edmonton, the first of a series of Melton real estate firms, in 1923.

Melcor Developments Ltd., headed by three generations of the same family, was formed in 1923 by Louis Timothy Melton. His reputation and service were the keystones to the new firm's growth.

First known as Stanley Investment Company, the enterprise opened offices in a small house on the site of today's downtown Woodward's store. In 1929 the founder changed its name to L.T. Melton Real Estate Broker, relocated to the city's west end, and specialized in properties there and in Jasper Place.

In 1945 Melton's eldest son, Stan, joined the company as a salesman. He had recently returned from World War II service with the Loyal Edmonton Regiment. After working with his father for six years, he bought the firm and became president; he continued the same philosophy of providing the enthusiastic leadership needed to achieve growth and dominance in the real estate industry.

In the '50s, after discovery of oil at nearby Leduc precipitated a rush of development, Edmonton experienced dramatic growth. Stan Melton, responding to this opportunity, estab-

lished 16 offices throughout the city—each providing specialized service for the district in which it was located. He additionally instituted a professional management system, reorganized the company as Melton Real Estate Ltd., and offered key employees the opportunity to become shareholders.

Continued growth led to the opening of an office in Calgary in 1956, and within a few years several more were organized there. The firm became that city's leading realtor, recognized as the dominant force in the Alberta real estate brokerage business, a position its successors enjoy today.

Expansion to British Columbia followed in 1959, with the opening of several branches in Vancouver. While difficult economic times and a competitive real estate market forced the company to retreat temporarily from this market, at this time Melton's expanded into the mortgage and savings and trust industry.

In 1968 Melcor Developments became a public real-estate company, listing its shares on the Toronto Stock Exchange.

Over the next few years the company extended its real estate brokerage operation into Saskatoon, Regina,

Stan Melton, son of the founder, joined the firm in 1945 and was president prior to his death in 1973.

Winnipeg, and other centres. It also reentered the British Columbia market with the purchase of the well-known and respected Vancouver firm of A.E. Austin & Company.

The man responsible for all this growth, Stan Melton, died suddenly in 1973. The Melton board of directors appointed Cliff Willetts—a longtime friend and adviser—as chairman of the board, with Garry Holmes as president. In 1975 Stan's son, Tim, was elected president.

That same year the organization sold its real estate brokerage division; the buyer was A.E. Lepage of Toronto. Sale of the brokerage asset and the goodwill associated with the Melton name necessitated a corporate name change to Melcor Developments Ltd. These moves left Melcor management free to concentrate on development aspects of the real estate business.

Since it "went public" in 1968, Melcor's assets have grown from $6 million to $200 million. Recently completing a 400,000-square-foot office building in downtown Edmonton, the corporation plans several new projects for the future.

The firm continues to honour founder L.T. Melton by maintaining a reputation for quality of service and product.

CANADA SAFEWAY LIMITED

Canada Safeway Limited, without question the largest grocery business in Western Canada, has been a busy part of Edmonton's food market scene for 55 years.

The first Safeway outlets in the Alberta capital opened in 1929, when nine were instituted in the city. Today there are 44 stores operating in Edmonton and its metropolitan area, employing a total of 3,800 men and women to serve an area populace bordering on one million people.

Canada Safeway is headed by Bob Kinnie, a Vancouver native who joined the company as a part-time food clerk in his coast city some 27 years ago. Today president and chief executive officer, Kinnie early last year succeeded to those positions formerly held by A.G. Anselmo. He maintains his business and home bases in Calgary.

Canada Safeway Limited, so named in 1947, was incorporated as Safeway Stores Limited in Winnipeg in 1929. The company's dominion charter allowed it to "buy, sell (and) manufacture . . . at wholesale and at retail, groceries, meats, fruits (and) vegetables . . ." By the end of December 1929 Safeway Stores operated 127 markets in Canada, 16 of them in Alberta. Most of these facilities represented acquisitions of existing businesses.

Safeway evolved from a chain founded in 1915 by Marion Barton Skaggs in American Falls, Idaho. He bought his first store from his father, a Baptist minister, and by 1926 his chain had 250 outlets. In March 1926 a Maryland corporation was organized under the name Safeway Stores, Incorporated. The name "Safeway" originated in a contest held in 1925 by the Sam Seelig Company, a California firm organized in 1914. On

July 1, 1926, the Skaggs company stores merged with Safeway Stores, with Skaggs as president.

By 1954 there were 25 Canada Safeway stores in Alberta; a separate Alberta Division was set up three years later. In 1958 the Canadian company reported sales of $208 million, and its rate of growth surpassed that of the parent firm.

To ensure quality control Safeway either purchased or established supply subsidiaries. Polly Ann Bakeries Ltd. was organized as a subsidiary in 1938. The next year Empress Manufacturing Company Limited began operating as a subsidiary and provided jams, jellies, spices, and related products. In 1947 Macdonalds Consolidated Limited, a wholesale grocery business, came into the Safeway organization.

Today Canada Safeway operates bakeries in Vancouver, Calgary, and Winnipeg; fluid-milk plants in Edmonton, Oakville, Vancouver, and Winnipeg; ice cream plants in Edmonton, Vancouver, and Winnipeg; and egg-candling plants at Calgary, Vancouver, and Winnipeg. Through subsidiaries the corporation operates a coffee-roasting and tea-packing plant, while through Lucerne the firm employs 200 workers in a box beef plant in Calgary, which breaks down carcass beef for final in-store cutting in three provinces.

In addition, Safeway is active in

The interior of one of Canada Safeway Limited's newer Edmonton supermarkets. There are 44 Safeway stores operating in Edmonton, employing 3,800 people.

other countries: In 1983 the company's non-Canadian operations included 1,947 stores in the United States, 89 in England and Scotland, 25 in West Germany, and 72 in Australia. Sales in Canada at the end of 1983 totalled three billion dollars, and the organization at that time had more than 24,500 employees.

Canada Safeway Limited has formed an export-development department to facilitate the sale of Canadian food products in markets outside the country. In addition to aiding independent food processors from Western Canada, this department serves the company's Empress and Lucerne processing plants operating in British Columbia, Alberta, Manitoba, and Ontario.

In 1981 Safeway opened "no-frills" warehouse-type stores in Edmonton and Calgary under the name Food Barn. Another innovative format has now been added to the company's retailing concept: Two 70,000-square-foot stores are being built in Edmonton and one in Calgary, and will be known as Safeway Food For Less. The Edmonton units are located in Southpark Village, at the corner of 36th Avenue and the Calgary Trail, and at 137th Avenue and 133rd Street.

SYNCRUDE CANADA LTD.

Syncrude Canada Ltd. is the largest synthetic fuel producer in the world, and the second plant to commercially produce synthetic crude oil from Alberta's Athabasca oil sands.

Syncrude is an operating company employing about 4,200 people — 4,000 at the Mildred Lake operating site and head office in Fort McMurray, and the remainder at administrative offices and a research centre in Edmonton. Fort McMurray is about 430 kilometres north of Edmonton, while Mildred Lake is another 40 kilometres north of Fort McMurray.

The complex mines the oil sand, extracts the bitumen (the raw oil), and upgrades it to synthetic crude. The design capacity of the operation is 17,000 cubic metres (108,000 barrels) of oil per day. A decision was reached in 1983 to invest some $1.2 billion in the plant by 1988, in order to increase daily production by more than 20,000 barrels.

Construction of the Syncrude project began in the spring of 1974. Plans called for a world-scale, open-pit mine that would eventually cover about 26 square kilometres, a nine-storey extraction complex, a utility plant providing 260 megawatts of power and 7.5 million pounds of steam per hour (enough for a city of 300,000 residents), the largest water-treatment plant of its kind in the world, and upgrading facilities equal to a major oil refinery.

Approximately 7,500 workers were on the site during the peak construction periods in 1976 and 1977. Actual cost of the project, outside the utility plant, was approximately $2.3 billion — one of the largest single construction jobs in Canadian history.

Syncrude Canada Ltd.'s plant in Fort McMurray, Alberta. This $2.3-billion facility was one of the largest construction jobs ever undertaken in Canada.

The first oil sand was moved to the extraction plant by conveyor in February 1978, and the first oil produced was pumped into the pipeline in July of that year. The product is distributed among refineries in Edmonton, Vancouver, and Eastern Canada. The plant was officially declared open in September 1978, and in 1983 Syncrude produced more than 40 million barrels — 100 percent of design capacity.

The company has designed and built its upgrading facility to meet the stringent air-emission rates set by Alberta Environment. Four monitoring systems ensure that the factory meets environmental specifications.

In the area of social responsibility, Syncrude has worked closely with local residents to expand recreational and cultural facilities. The Alberta government has financed first-class medical and educational institutions in the area.

EDMONTON POWER

No one gives a second thought today to that most universal of all servants—electricity. At the flick of a switch, it's there, instant and unfailing.

Edmonton, now a city of a half-million, is unique in that its electrical generation and distribution systems are city-owned and provide an important revenue source that does its part in holding down municipal tax levels. More than that, Edmonton Power is the largest municipally owned electric utility in Canada with its own generating facilities. And in terms of generating capacity, Edmonton Power is Alberta's second-largest electric utility.

The story of electricity in Edmonton goes back to the 1890s. On October 23, 1891, pioneer Alex Taylor was granted the right to build and operate a power plant and distribution system. His company, Edmonton Electric Light & Power Co., was on the scene and active a scant 12 years after Thomas A. Edison had produced the first practical electric lamp.

Taylor's venture was capitalized at $10,000, made up of 1,000 shares at $10 each. Its franchise had a 10-year life span. The original plant was built on the banks of the North Saskatche-

The first steam boiler to be installed in Edmonton's Rossdale Power Station. Courtesy of the Provincial Archives.

wan River near the Low Level Bridge. Local coal was used to fire the boiler and the 450-kilowatt generator was operated on a summer/winter schedule: sunset to 1:00 a.m. in the summer and 5:30 a.m. to sunrise to provide additional service in the winter months.

Then, in 1902, the Edmonton town council decided that a municipal operation could do just as well as a private company. So Edmonton Electric Light & Power was bought out for $13,500.

At the time the town's 300 residents had nothing in the way of electrical appliances—few had even been invented. So the main use for power was for lighting homes and streets.

The town's first move was to transfer its latest acquisition beyond the reach of floodwater. The old plant's equipment was hauled upstream to the Rossdale Flats, installed in a new building, and put to work. When production began—at the site now occupied by the Rossdale Power Station—service was put on a 24-hour basis.

As town became city and demand for power increased with growth, the Edmonton plant expanded. In 1928 one of the world's first 10,000-kilowatt turbo generators was installed. In the '30s the City of Edmonton powered the plant with the largest steam boiler in Canada; by 1941 the Rossdale Power Station was

Canada's biggest thermal power producer at 60,000 kilowatts.

In the early '50s the plant was converted to burn natural gas. The abundance of gas, against the rising cost of coal, turned the tide, and in 1955 the plant banked its last coal fire. The next few years saw the installation of two new turbines that used compressed air, heated by gas, to spin the huge generators. These turbines produced 30 megawatts each—largest of their kind in Canada. Three 75-megawatt steam units were then added, bringing the Rossdale plant to its maximum capacity of 390 megawatts by 1966.

Even this wasn't enough. In 1970 Edmonton opened its new Clover Bar generating station, on the riverbank in the far northeast part of the city. By 1979 it housed four 165-megawatt generators, again fired by natural gas.

Today the utility is looking to Genesee, some 50 kilometres southwest of Edmonton, as the producer of future electricity requirements. Located in a field of coal suitable for strip mining, the $1.2-billion project went under construction in 1982. When completed, Genesee will house two 400-megawatt generators in Phase I, and the site is capable of supporting six such units in all.

In the meantime, Edmonton is studying an exciting new concept in providing heat energy—district heating. This system has been used in energy-conscious European countries for more than 50 years. It makes use of superheated water pumped from thermal plants through insulated steel pipes to nearby cities. A consultant's report on the possibilities of such a project to heat Edmonton's downtown core is now in preparation. The heat for the district heating system would be produced by the Genesee plant.

EDMONTON TELEPHONES

Edmonton's love affair with the miraculous gadget invented by Alexander Graham Bell has a 100-year-old history. Not always a love story (as in the not-so-long ago days when phones were hard to obtain) and no longer a gadget—the telephone is as much a part of Edmonton's day-to-day routine as is the rosy dawn of another day.

This love affair was kindled in the heart of pioneer Alexander Taylor. He was the dominion government telegraph operator whose brassy clickety-click was our pioneers' only source of information from the "outside," and their only means of quick communication with people in distant parts of the country. Edmonton itself was still a frontier settlement, peopled by fewer than 300 residents, a community only a short pace past its days as a stronghold of the Hudson's Bay Company in its fur-trading heyday.

Alexander Taylor, dominion telegraph agent at Edmonton, promoted the first use of the telephone locally. In 1884 he imported the first two telephones into Alberta. His inaugural call was from Fort Edmonton to the Roman Catholic mission at St. Albert, a dozen miles distant on the Sturgeon River. The date: January 3, 1885. Naturally enough it was a message containing New Year's wishes, and the call was a resounding success. As it happened St. Albert's first telephone had been mounted in a household kitchen—and above the fascination of actually hearing words coming from a hand-held receiver, the crowd around "Telephone Taylor" could hear bacon frying on the range out in the country. Conversely, the kitchen-watchers in St. Albert could hear Taylor's pencil scratching as he scribbled a message to the citizens of Edmonton. It was truly a day to remember for Taylor's Edmonton District Telephone Company.

By 1892 Alex Taylor, who was in the electric-power business as well as telephones, found he needed a switchboard for his growing telephone system. He purchased a second-hand Bell outfit and imported Arthur William Ormsby, an Ontario telephone/electricity wizard, to become his right-hand man. Ormsby installed the switchboard—and more than that, introduced his superior to a young woman looking for a part-time position. This was Jennie Lauder, the baker's daughter, who became Edmonton's first telephone operator. Jennie left school in 1893 and assumed a full-time job as a switchboard operator; she maintained her job until 1907 when she resigned to marry Edmonton alderman William Griesbach, lawyer and veteran of the Boer War. (Both Taylor and Griesbach are remembered today through buildings named after them: the Alex Taylor Elementary School and the Griesbach Canadian Forces barracks.)

Growing slowly but steadily, Taylor's company served Edmonton until it was sold to the city for

The main City Telephone System exchange in 1906-1907 housed new automatic phone equipment.

$17,000 and renamed the City Telephone System. At the takeover there were 289 subscribers in the city itself, with another 101 in the adjacent rural area.

As part of the agreement under which Edmonton and Strathcona amalgamated in 1912, the city bought Strathcona's telephone system from the Alberta government. This network, with its 673 subscribers and installations, was valued at $153,000.

The demand for phones during the early 1900s was frequently beyond Edmonton's ability to supply, from shortcomings in both manpower and technology. However, systematic purchasing and capable management kept the city's ever-expanding system abreast of the North American standard. Over the years the City Telephone System led the way in telecommunications services.

An early example was Edmonton's foresight in placing police call boxes in strategic places throughout the city in 1910. Fifty years later the community found itself in the front ranks of the innovators, with improved call boxes that gave instant access to police, ambulance, fire, and other services—a service available in only two other Canadian cities that provided police and fire service.

Further advances provided time announcements in the 1920s (a, mechanized version came into use in 1969), and the "dial 100" call that automatically connected a phone to the fire department.

The growth of the City Telephone System was such that by the mid-1930s Edmonton led the continent in the ratio of phones to residents. The city figure was 20 per 100, compared with 11 per 100 in Canada, and 13 per 100 in the United States. The Edmonton ratio has continued to climb: In 1953 it was 30 per 100; in 1959, 40 per 100; and in 1983, 87 per 100.

By the late '40s and '50s the telephone had become a necessity. Then, in the late '60s, the City Telephone System swung its emphasis from "service" orientation to "customer" orientation, resulting in the creation of Canada's first "911" service. This provided free calls from pay phones to emergency service, 411 (directory assistance), or 611 (telephone repair).

Telephone technology was making giant leaps at this time, and in 1967 Edmonton became the first city in Western Canada to install touch-tone dialing. Also in 1967, the name of the City Telephone System was changed to 'edmonton telephones.' In this era as well, the phone company was supplying data-transmission service to the University of Alberta, using phone circuits to transmit computer communications. In addition, closed-circuit television was made available for customers having security systems.

Further advances included "Centrex"—sophisticated in-house switchboard systems—and computerized directory-assistance service

Alex Taylor, founder of the Edmonton District Telephone Company, predecessor of today's edmonton telephones.

that became available in the '70s. The "Centrex" system, installed for the Alberta government in 1971, with 14,700 telephones was the world's largest; and 'edmonton telephones' was the first independent phone company in North America to set up a centralized automated loop reporting system. The CALRS repair system at 611 was installed in 1979 and it was the first of its kind in Western Canada.

Other innovations of this period include digital switching, pressurized cables (for easier detection of cable failure), and fibre optics. The latter is in a class by itself. One single glass fibre, the diameter of a human hair, can carry the same message information as a 1,200-pair cable of copper wires. The firm was the first telephone company in Canada to have a commercial (designed for customer)

fibre linking *The Edmonton Journal's* main downtown offices and its new printing plant in Strathcona in 1980.

Another step forward is facsimile service, by which photographs or documents can be transmitted by telephone. First tested in the 1920s, but rejected as too costly, facsimile has reached the point where it is a possible contender for transmission of documents now forwarded by mail.

The company made significant contributions to both the 1978 Commonwealth Games and the 1983 World University Games. Technicians served as consultants as the Games' communications services were planned, while senior department officials were loaned to both events to assist with arranging technical programmes and actually supervising their implementation.

As of July 1976 G.K. (Ken) Foster

became general manager of 'edmonton telephones.' He was vice-chairman of communications for the 1978 Commonwealth Games. A professional engineer, Foster is a graduate of Nova Scotia Technical College; serving after graduation with Maritime Telephone and Telegraph Limited, he was subsequently employed by the federal government's department of communications.

For 'edmonton telephones' present and future customers, what lies ahead? For one thing, computer phone answering. Also planned are related computer services: turning appliances and lights off/on; raising an alarm at sudden noise or smoke; rerouting incoming calls; or summoning police or a neighbour for help. There will be data banks connected to the weather office, the airport, airline ticket office, entertainment ticket counters, emergency medical data, sports scores, news reports, ad infinitum. Before too long a housewife will be able to order her week's supply of groceries through her home computer, and then drive to the market for her assembled package. She will pay for her order through a telephone "cheque," and her account will be adjusted accordingly.

The firm's first 100 years had left Alex Taylor so far behind he is out of sight, almost beyond memory. Now 'edmonton telephones' is looking at systems that will carry its subscribers into a future so sophisticated that one can't begin to imagine what the world of telephones will be like on January 3, 2085.

Jennie Lauder (center), Edmonton's first telephone operator, and Margaret Lauder (left), later Mrs. Art Ormsby, whose husband was the telephone system's first experienced technician. Photo courtesy of Miss Norine Lauder.

IMPERIAL LUMBER COMPANY LTD.

The original Imperial Lumber Company Ltd. office was in this tent in Wainwright, Alberta, in 1907.

It was a humble beginning. His first office was a tent and his first location was an Eastern Alberta town whose destiny was in the hands of a railway that had not even reached Alberta.

But to Thomas Gilbert Cook, who founded the Imperial Lumber Company in Wainwright in 1907, the promise was enough—that the Grand Trunk Pacific Railway would arrive soon. He knew that before the excitement of the first train's arrival had died down, the demand for lumber and building supplies would soar. And he was right.

Out of T.G. Cook's confidence a busy lumber empire was born—one whose operations were to extend through Northern Alberta, into Northeastern British Columbia, and east to Saskatchewan. Lumberyards, mills (a community near Lac la Biche, 150 miles north and west of Wainwright, would be named Imperial Mills), builders' supply stores, in later years a prefabricated building plant, and even a coal-distributing business were added one by one to this growing empire. Born in Fredericton, New Brunswick, Mr. Cook came West as a young man. He took the Canadian Northern train to Vermilion, and made his way south to Wainwright by buckboard—convinced that his future lay in this awakening prairie region. Within two years the railway indeed reached Wainwright and his lumberyard expanded by leaps and bounds—so much so that he needed help.

The entrepreneur was eventually joined by his two brothers, Harry and Norman, who helped him build the family business that continues today. Imperial soon expanded into communities centered around Edmonton, and in 1919 the Cooks decided to move the firm's headquarters into the city. First housed in the Adams Building, standing where Eaton's department store was built later, in 1952, the head offices were relocated across the street to the Tegler Building.

In the meantime the company had established planer mills in Rimbey and Wetaskiwin. Building-supply stores were opened in some 37 towns in Northern Alberta, Saskatchewan, and British Columbia. In all, 12 planing mills were operated—with major units located at Barrhead, High Level, Grande Prairie, and Topley. There were also numerous sawmills and logging operations under way throughout Alberta and British Columbia.

Thomas Gilbert Cook died in April 1971. Since then Imperial Lumber has been directed by his sons and daughter. In the past decade the firm has consolidated its rural operations, and today has a dozen retail outlets in larger centres in Central and Northern Alberta. In Edmonton itself, Imperial Lumber bought W.W. Arcade Ltd. in 1979; and in 1983 it opened a W.W. Arcade branch store on Stony Plain Road, with plans of opening additional locations in the future.

SHAW CABLESYSTEMS LTD.

In 13 years Capital Cable TV Ltd.—as of March 1, 1984, known as Shaw Cablesystems Ltd.—has grown from a small company serving the eastern half of Edmonton to become Canada's fourth-largest cable system, serving approximately 315,000 subscribers.

The enterprise was founded by James R. Shaw of Edmonton, who brought a sound business background and entrepreneurial skill to an industry that has undergone dramatic technological change in the past decade. Cable TV holds the unique distinction of having a major sociological impact on its customers, and of being the catalyst that brings families together again in living rooms across the nation.

In the early 1960s Shaw was living in Edmonton, involved in the family pipe-coating business. As Canada at the time had 400 cable systems with only five in Alberta, and neither Edmonton nor Calgary was on the list, he saw his opportunity and incorporated Capital Cable in 1966. The Canadian Radio-television Commission (CRTC) granted a licence in

James R. Shaw, founder and president of Capital Cable TV Ltd., now Shaw Cablesystems Ltd.

August 1970. The first subscriber was connected in Sherwood Park, Alberta, in September of the following year.

Shaw's interest in, and knowledge of, cable TV came easily. He was (and still is) president of Western Cable TV Ltd., which serves an area around Woodstock-Ingersoll, Ontario.

In discussing his holdings the owner admits to being an avowed expansionist, and firmly believes in the need for balance between "growing" and "viable" systems. The company's Colorado Cablevision, Inc., which is being built from the ground up, is an example of the "growing" system, while the purchase of Cable West TV Ltd., with systems in British Columbia and Alberta, reflects the "viable" system. The 1970s saw Capital subscriber lists expand in keeping with the growth of Edmonton and Calgary. Shaw, aware that his firm's long-range growth and investment potential lay beyond the boundaries of his licence, in 1972 acquired S.O.T.V. Holdings, which operated systems in Penticton, Kelowna, and Revelstoke, British Columbia.

Following a few years of consolidation, the farsighted businessman in 1981 bought Urban Cablevision near Victoria, British Columbia (8,500 customers); he then went across the country to buy Trans Spectrum Services Limited which operated Metrovision Limited (8,600 customers), serving the communities of Bedford and Lower Sackville, Nova Scotia. At the time Trans Spectrum owned a one-quarter share in Avalon Cablevision (28,000 subscribers) in St. John's, Newfoundland. In 1983 the company increased its interest in Avalon Cablevision of St. John's to 50 percent.

The assets of Colorado Cablevision, which serves smaller communities

around Denver, and half of Douglas County Cablevision, which operates south of the Colorado capital, had already been added to Capital holdings.

Capital Cable became a major Canadian cable system with further acquisitions in British Columbia. First came Cable West TV Ltd. (with over 100,000 subscribers). Cable West, as well as serving North and West Vancouver, also had subscribers in Trail, Nelson, Rossland, Castlegar, and Nanaimo, British Columbia, and Red Deer, Alberta. The addition of White Rock Cablevision Ltd., operating in the Lower Mainland area of British Columbia, completed this series of purchases.

From the start the corporation made its Edmonton studio facilities available to community groups and organizations, and provided coverage of major events such as the city's Klondike Days festival, the 1978 Commonwealth Games "Festival 78," and the 1983 World University Games cultural programme.

With the introduction of pay TV, Capital was ready with at least one movie channel available throughout all the systems. In Edmonton subscribers had their choice of three premium channels; with one-fifth of the company's 107,000 customers signing up almost immediately, the city became one of Canada's "hottest" markets for premium services.

While believing that entertainment will continue to be the mainstay of cable TV, Shaw looks to providing other futuristic services as they become feasible—security systems, medical service, banking, and retail buying. And, he says, more and better cable TV packages will be available to subscribers, and when they are, Shaw Cable will deliver them.

INTERPROVINCIAL PIPE LINE LIMITED

Interprovincial Pipe Line Limited (IPL), born of the oil boom stemming from the discovery of oil near Leduc, is a miracle of modern industrial technology. Built in record-breaking time beginning in 1950, Interprovincial today pumps crude oil from Edmonton all the way to Montreal, via Superior, Wisconsin; Chicago, Illinois; and Sarnia, Ontario.

After the breakthrough at Leduc in 1947, it soon became apparent that the various fields in Alberta would produce more oil than the immediate vicinity could use. As a result, IPL came into being with plans to build a large-diameter pipeline from Edmonton to Regina, thus providing a direct link between Alberta's producing fields and refining facilities in Saskatchewan. But before the project was off the drawing board, further Alberta discoveries made it plain that more was needed than an Edmonton-Regina line. To facilitate this expansion, Lakehead Pipe Line Company Inc. (LPL) was incorporated in the United States. This firm is a wholly owned IPL subsidiary. So, by late 1950, a line was built and in place all the way from Edmonton to Superior, Wisconsin, at the head of the Great Lakes.

The first stage of the IPL line was completed by the summer of 1951. Before the first snow flew that year, the line stretched from Redwater, north of Edmonton, to Lakehead.

Pipe diameter ranged from 16 to 20 inches, and Great Lakes tankers completed the flow of this western oil to Ontario's big and hungry refineries. Expansion was continuous for almost 30 years and today the Interprovincial/Lakehead system extends from Edmonton to Montreal, with connecting lines into Buffalo, New York, and Nanticoke, Ontario, while a major loop dips south to Chicago and rounds the southern tip of Lake Michigan before surfacing at Sarnia.

Construction of the 30-inch, 837-kilometre Montreal link began in the fall of 1975. This section was built to implement the federal government's announced policy of providing pipeline facilities for the supply of Western Canadian crude to Montreal refineries—the aim being to reduce dependency on foreign oil.

Regina has been a key station on the pipeline system since the Interprovincial line was built. As the headquarters for a district that extends through most of Saskatchewan and all of Manitoba, Regina also is the location of a major pumping station and tank terminal where crude oil and refined products are both delivered and received. And with the closing of several small prairie refineries in the 1970s, deliveries of crude oil in Saskatchewan began to give way to refined products from Edmonton's large block of major refineries.

During most of Interprovincial's growth period, the general scene was one of ample supplies of crude oil and an urgent need for additional markets. The producing sector of the oil industry was locked into a highly competitive buyers' market; many producing areas, including Alberta, were operating below capacity.

This hiatus came to a dramatic end in 1973, when the Arab nations clamped an embargo on crude oil exports. Almost overnight, North American crude oil supplies came to be regarded as a "depleting" resource. The per-barrel price of oil rose rapidly and all producing nations quickly revised their national oil policies, with a view to protecting domestic supplies.

Both Interprovincial and Lakehead have recently moved into operations other than expansion of the mainline system. In the United States, Lakehead is a major partner in Frontier Pipeline Company, which operates a 467-kilometre crude oil pipeline that runs from the Wyoming-Utah Overthrust Belt to Casper, Wyoming.

In Canada, Interprovincial is building the country's first modern Arctic pipeline. IPL began construction of the Norman Wells pipeline along the Mackenzie River Valley in the Northwest Territories in 1984.

Today, while not owning the oil it transports, IPL and LPL lines supply crude to 16 refineries and plants directly connected to their lines. In addition, there are 41 pipelines connected to the IPL/LPL system.

The official opening ceremony of the Interprovincial Pipe Line system in October 1950. Premier Ernest Manning of Alberta holds the valve as G.L. Stewart (left), then president of Imperial Oil Limited, and the Honourable C.D. Howe (right), Canada's Minister of Trade and Commerce at that time, look on.

REGENT DRILLING LTD.

Regent Drilling Ltd. was founded by Paul D. Bowlen in Vermilion, in East-Central Alberta, in 1943. Heavy oil from the area, used by Canadian National Railways in its steam locomotives, provided the base for the enterprise's initial operations.

With its first well—drilled to 1,800 feet—completed in the Blackfoot field in 1944, Regent thus had the benefit of five years' operating experience when Imperial Oil's Leduc No. 1 well opened development of the Leduc oil field. The discovery transformed Edmonton almost overnight into an oil capital, and the demand for drilling operators exploded.

The organization had moved into Edmonton in 1947, establishing headquarters in the former No. 1 hangar at the Edmonton Municipal Airport on Kingsway Avenue. At this time the purchase of the assets of an early competitor, Northern Development, doubled the firm's drilling capacity.

From the start Regent Drilling's policy has been to accept any challenge. While it is accurate to say that in the early days its activities were confined to oil and gas operations, the statement nonetheless is misleading. These operations were widely diversified; in the wide range of conditions encountered both above and below ground in the variety of areas where it carried out exploration and development programmes, the company had to counter diversity with diversity of capabilities.

At the same time the demand for Regent Drilling's services was increasing from beyond the oil and gas sphere, and gradually the firm expanded—all the while gaining experience in all areas of contract drilling. This experience, as well as a continual upgrading of personnel, has enabled the corporation to maintain an acceptable level of competence in a changing industry.

In 1954 Regent Drilling moved to its present location, 12912 Yellowhead Trail. This 12-acre site has been ample to provide the expansion envisioned at the time and realized today. The organization modified its administration offices and the quarters of the Fleetway Trucking Limited Division in 1980, and operates entirely from the 36,000 square feet of office, shop, and warehouse space on this site. By 1983 Regent Drilling employed a central staff of 40 administrative and 55 maintenance personnel, plus its field crews.

In addition to completed gas- and oil-drilling projects throughout Canada and the Arctic mainland, Cambridge Bay and Melville Island, and in North Dakota and Montana, the company has gained vast experience in drilling for potash and iron ore in Saskatchewan, salt-well drilling in Ontario, and disposal-well drilling in Alberta and Saskatchewan.

Eastern Canadian operations began in 1970 with drilling in Quebec; since then the corporation has operated in other locations—Anticosti Island, Nova Scotia, and Prince Edward Island. Three years later a major heavy-oil drilling programme was undertaken, an endeavour that called for expertise in modification of equipment needed for specific demands. In the Cold Lake area of Northern Alberta, Regent Drilling mounted two rigs on railway tracks and drilled 54 wells to depths of 520 metres. To reach remote areas the firm transports both rigs and equipment by truck, barge, railway, and helicopter; for work at Zama Lake, two rigs were modified sectionally into 4,000-pound "lifts" for transportation by helicopter.

Regent Drilling Ltd. was an infant,

A Regent Drilling rig, remodelled and upgraded before shipping to a Quebec well site. The rig is 144 feet high, including base.

one-rig operation in 1943. Today it is a major drilling contractor. Competent, efficient, and technologically innovative, the company is pledged to continue its role as an industry leader.

Regent's executive officers include Paul D. Bowlen, founder, who is chairman of the board; William A. (Bill) Bowlen, president (a son of Paul Bowlen); Hugh R. Hoyle, C.A., vice-president of finance; and Bud Osborne, vice-president of operations.

BOWLEN HOLDINGS LTD.

Bowlen Holdings Ltd. is an Edmonton-based company that is wholly owned by Patrick D. Bowlen. It was incorporated in Alberta in 1979.

Bowlen has been in business as an independent developer since 1970. His background includes a B.B.A. degree from the University of Oklahoma School of Business, and graduation with a J.D. degree from the same university's School of Law in 1968. After university he read law with the Calgary firm of Saucier, Jones; admitted to the Alberta Bar in 1969, the young attorney practised with Saucier, Jones until 1970.

In that year Bowlen became assistant to the president of Regent Drilling Ltd. in Edmonton, then joined Peter Batoni to form Batoni-Bowlen Enterprises Ltd., a development/construction company. Today, while still holding his position with Batoni-Bowlen, he devotes himself to Bowlen Holdings Ltd. in his capacity as president and chief executive officer. He continues to hold memberships in the Law Society of Alberta and the Canadian Bar Association.

Much of Bowlen Holdings Ltd.'s success can be attributed to the experience the founder gained during his 10 years with Batoni-Bowlen Enterprises. The two men, in a 50-50 incorporated partnership, entered the fields of property management, general contracting, and the manufacture of precast concrete.

One of Batoni-Bowlen's early projects was the Edmonton Northlands Coliseum, an $18-million, 181,500-square-foot sports facility completed in 1973 for the Edmonton Exhibition Association. The Coliseum has drawn continent-wide attention to the city as the home of the Edmonton Oilers of National Hockey League fame. Many other large-scale projects in both Ed-

monton and Calgary followed completion of the Coliseum.

Then, early in 1979, the partners decided to work individually in the areas in which each had the greatest expertise. Batoni became sole owner and operator of the company's general contracting and concrete operations, while Bowlen acquired the firm's major undeveloped properties. Batoni-Bowlen Enterprises, however, continued to own and operate the properties that had already been developed, as well as to develop residential high-rise properties.

Immediately after incorporation Bowlen Holdings Ltd. undertook several important development projects. The first was the Interprovincial Pipe Line Tower, with 200,000 square feet of office space in downtown Edmonton. The building is owned jointly by Bowlen Holdings and Interprovincial Pipe Line Limited, the primary tenant. Other downtown Edmonton endeavours include Ken-

sington Tower, a 12-storey office building with 180,000 square feet of space; and a 29-storey, 450,000-square-foot tower next to Edmonton's new convention centre.

Today Bowlen Holdings is looking increasingly toward the United States, particularly Southern California. By the end of 1983 the company had made two significant commitments there—a 500,000-square-foot twin-tower project in the Mission Valley area, built in partnership with Great-West Life; and a 600,000-square-foot tower in San Diego, again with Great-West Life as a joint-venture partner.

Other senior officers of Bowlen Holdings are Romualdo M. (Dudi) Berretti, an Italian-trained architect, who is executive vice-president, and R. Cort Smith, C.A., the secretary/treasurer.

Patrick D. Bowlen, president of Bowlen Holdings Ltd.

SCOTIABANK

The Edmonton main branch of The Bank of Nova Scotia, 1940. Courtesy of The Bank of Nova Scotia Archives.

The Bank of Nova Scotia, known as Scotiabank to its customers around the world, is Canada's second-oldest chartered bank. In 1982 the bank marked its 150th anniversary and its 100th year of operation in Canada's West.

In 1882, with broad operations in Atlantic Canada, Scotiabank embarked on what was to be a steady and solid expansion westward. The first branch west of the Great Lakes was opened in Winnipeg that year. On March 31, 1903, the bank's directors recorded in the minute book "the importance of establishing some branches in the Northwest as soon as possible." Three months later the bank set up a branch in Edmonton, which was rapidly becoming the centre of the fur trade.

Following a visit by a group of the bank's directors to the western region in 1903, branches were opened in Wetaskiwin, Fort Saskatchewan, and Calgary. The directors had described much of the province as an uncharted land, with "wolf, coyote, fox, gopher, duck, antelope, and other wildlife aplenty, but little human habitation."

The first manager, E.T. Hammett, opened the Edmonton branch for business with a staff of three: F.W. Ross, accountant; B.P. Alley, teller; and H.J. Bush, clerk. Ross later that year helped to open the bank's first branch in Calgary.

Since the opening of the Edmonton branch there have been 24 managers, among whom the most notable was G.C. Hitchman (1952-1953), who became deputy chairman of the board of Scotiabank (1974-1981).

Progressing from these humble beginnings, in 1923 the bank purchased the Merchants Bank of Canada building, at 10050 Jasper and 100A Street, from the Bank of Montreal.

This facility was the institution's home until the early 1950s, when construction on a new building began on the same site. The new structure was opened in the fall of 1958. On October 5, 1982, Scotiabank moved into its fourth and present home at Scotia Place.

In the days of the pioneers, through the Depression and World War II, Edmonton's main branch remained the only Scotiabank branch in the city. From 1948 to 1959 five more branches were opened. The next decade was a boom period, with 13 new branches followed by five branches in the 1970s and two more in 1980. Today Edmonton is served by a total of 25 Scotiabank branches.

The 1982 opening of Scotia Place in Edmonton was a highlight of Scotiabank's 150th anniversary year. An architectural gem of pink granite and glass, Scotiabank's main branch is the centrepiece between the two towers of the Scotia Place Development, in which is also located the bank's regional office for Northern Alberta. Today, as a century ago, this is the business heart of Edmonton.

Scotiabank was here with the pioneers. The first train came into Edmonton in October 1902, and within a year The Bank of Nova Scotia opened a branch on Jasper Avenue. It worked with the thousands who came into this city and province seeking new opportunity. The bank and the pioneers found that opportunity.

Today there are still new frontiers to challenge. To the north there are riches yet to be discovered and to be developed for the service of man. But today, more than in the past, the new frontiers are in Scotia Place and other business centres, in government, and in centres of learning. Man's new frontier is the better management of human and natural resources and of the economy.

The Edmonton main branch of Scotiabank was opened in 1983 to celebrate the institution's 150th anniversary. Built of pink granite and glass, the facility is the centrepiece between two towers of the Scotia Place Development.

SUNCOR INC.

Known as a curious phenomenon from the days when the first fur traders made their way into what is now Northern Alberta, the "tar sands" of the Athabasca River are far distant from the status of curiosity. Today the Athabasca oil sands stand at the head of the list of Alberta's nonrenewable natural resources.

The oil sands are the focus of a multibillion-dollar industry, an industry still feeling its way through complex oil recovery processes. At the same time, they can lay claim to responsibility for one of the most intensive research programmes ever undertaken in North America. Their story begins in reports of traders of the 18th century who noted outcroppings of bituminous sand along the Athabasca. The traders reported that the tar-laden soils were an adequate substitute for the wood gum needed to patch their canoes—and more readily available.

Not until development of the internal-combustion engine with its insatiable appetite for fuel did anyone other than scientists show much interest in Alberta's bituminous sands. Finally, in 1919, the Alberta government and the University of Alberta decided to investigate their potential; out of this interest the Alberta Research Council (ARC) was formed. In 1920 an Ontario-born research chemist, Dr. Karl A. Clark, joined the ARC and began to study the Athabasca sands. He wondered if somehow they could be used in road building. But the advent of the automobile drew his attention to another possibility—the extraction of petroleum from the sticky sands.

Dr. Clark subsequently developed an oil-sands treatment process that was successful to the point where the ARC was able to claim 90 percent recovery of relatively clean oil. But scientific achievement was a far cry from commercial success and would remain so for decades.

In the end, awareness that sources of conventional oil were limited—and dwindling—rekindled interest in the Athabasca country and its bituminous sands. By this time the petroleum industry had determined that the Athabasca sands held an estimated 159 billion cubic metres of bitumen (or heavy oil), of which one-third would be recoverable through proven extraction processes. In the meantime, several development projects had come to the sands, built small extraction plants, and gone.

Then, in 1953, a new name was added to the list of companies interested in Alberta's bituminous sands: Great Canadian Oil Sands Limited. GCOS was formed in Toronto by a group of businessmen who pinned their hopes to another on-site extraction plant.

GCOS set out in search of capital at about the same time as events on the far side of the world added impetus to the hunt for new North American oil sources. The 1956 Egyptian blockade of the Suez Canal spelled out to the petroleum industry its dependence on "offshore" oil. One Canadian oil firm, Toronto's Sun Oil Company Limited, took up the search for new domestic production. Sun Oil, a longtime operator in this country, was a wholly owned subsidiary of the Sun Oil Company of Philadelphia. The parent company was a giant in its field and had been interested in Athabasca's oil sand storehouse from the mid-1940s, to the point where it even had acquired some leases. Sun, at this time, was headed by the far-seeing J. Howard Pew who, well into his eighties, headed an executive team that made an on-site inspection of the oil sands in July 1963.

In 1962 the Alberta government issued its first oil sands production permit to GCOS. Within a year Sun Oil, through its Canadian subsidiary, Sun Oil Company Limited, Toronto, decided to help finance the GCOS plant. The plant, built 25 miles downriver from Fort McMurray, first produced synthetic crude oil in 1967. In August 1979 GCOS was merged with Sun Oil Company Limited, which held responsibility for conventional exploration, production, refining, and marketing in Canada. The result of that merger was Suncor Inc., with headquarters in Toronto.

By summer 1984 Suncor was operating a plant valued (in 1984 dollars) at $3 billion-plus. It operates on leases covering 10 square miles and its plant site alone covers 7,500 acres, of which 2,500 are occupied by production units and waste dumps. The remaining 5,000 acres are mineable and within practicable reach of two giant, $4-million bucket-wheel excavators.

Dr. Karl Clark retired from the University of Alberta in 1954 but continued to serve Great Canadian Oil Sands as an adviser almost to the time of his death in Victoria, British Columbia, in 1966—about a year before GCOS's initial plant began production. Suncor's vast operation in the heart of Athabasca's bituminous sands stands as a monument to his perseverance and ingenuity.

CITV

Dr. Charles Allard, founder of CITV, Edmonton.

Alberta owes its first independent television station to Dr. Charles Allard of Edmonton, successful surgeon-turned-businessman. Due to the far-sightedness of this well-known and respected entrepreneur, CITV came into being.

Dr. Allard's timing was perfect. In 1974 Edmonton was a thriving city with a young population—a generation of "baby boomers" with a huge appetite for trend-setting entertainment. The market was ready for innovative television programming.

On September 1, 1974, CITV's first telecast immediately provided an alternative to programmes supplied by the two national TV networks. Known as ITV, it was an independent station—created by independent individuals with new and fresh ideas.

Edmontonians took an immediate liking to their unique new station. In just three months it had captured 24 percent of the city's audience, and surpassed even the visionary expecta-tions of its originators. ITV's fresh style brought attention to the electronic media, which have through the years helped to make Edmonton one of the most exciting and competitive broadcast markets in Canada.

During its first year of operation, ITV embarked on the most ambitious project ever produced locally. More than 100 Tommy Banks shows, with guest lists of hundreds, were taped live at the studio; the "who's who" of the entertainment world paraded through Edmonton. Also in those first years, a series of concerts was produced—featuring such well-known artists as Tom Jones, Dionne Warwick, Neil Sedaka, Henry Mancini, Nana Maskouri, and Anne Murray, to name only a few. They drew international acclaim and established Edmonton as a bright spot on the world entertainment map. The series included 64 programmes and gained an industry-distribution record, reaching more than 90 markets including Great Britain, Germany,

Head office and studios of CITV, Edmonton, 1984.

France, and Japan.

The Edmonton Northlands Coliseum opened in 1975 and ITV was there, producing spectacular television specials before capacity audiences. Since the Edmonton Oilers joined the National Hockey League in 1979, ITV's mobile facilities have continued to provide local audiences with their favorite hockey telecasts.

This type of innovative production has continued. In 1980 the station again made headlines when it brought the SCTV comedy troupe to Edmonton. "SCTV Network 90" went on to become one of the first Canadian series to be scheduled by a major U.S. network, and was produced in the studios of ITV with a cast that included many local actors.

With its substantial long-term investment in facilities and personnel, ITV is today recognized as a major market-production centre and a leader in independent television programming in Canada. As a result of this independent status, producers have been able to add a distinct western perspective to news and public-affairs programming. This in turn

has helped to maintain a loyal viewing audience that has steadily increased in numbers.

In its first 10 years ITV revolutionized the standards of television production; innovative programming, creative excellence, and shrewd marketing have made it the most successful independent TV station in the country.

Over the years ITV and its parent company, Allarcom Limited, have demonstrated unparalleled growth. Since 1982, as part of the Canadian Satellite Communications System, its telecasting has extended to communities across Canada. It is now estimated the ITV signal is watched by 1.4 million viewers from coast to coast.

Then came pay televison. Launched on February 1, 1983, Superchannel provided a 24-hour pay-television service to Alberta and to Ontario (through its regional licensee, Ontario Independent Pay

Television, of which Allarcom Limited is the principal shareholder). In subsequent licensing agreements Allarcom Pay Television has expanded to serve Saskatchewan, Manitoba, the Northwest Territories, and is now part of Aim Broadcasting, which provides Superchannel service to British Columbia and the Yukon.

It was Dr. Allard's vision that brought ITV to television screens throughout Canada. One benefit of that vision is the prominence that has fallen to Edmonton as the headquarters of this outstanding company.

Edmonton's Tommy Banks and Bob McGrath of "Sesame Street" at CITV Studio in Edmonton.

Some of the world-famous entertainers who have appeared in Edmonton in live CITV productions include Anne Murray (top left), Henry Mancini (top), and Tom Jones (above).

289

CHIEFTAIN DEVELOPMENT CO. LTD.

Founded by Stanley A. Milner in 1964, Chieftain Development Co. Ltd. is one of the few Canadian independent oil companies headquartered outside of Calgary. Chieftain "went public" in 1965 and its shares were listed on the Toronto Stock Exchange in 1966.

From the outset, Chieftain focussed its exploration efforts on natural gas in east-central Alberta. Its first gas producer, at Craigend northeast of Edmonton, sent gas to market at six cents per thousand cubic feet (mcf), a far cry from the current wellhead price of approximately three dollars per mcf. Chieftain concentrated on building a strong portfolio of gas and oil rights in Alberta. By the late 1960s Chieftain was active throughout the province, making extensive use of "farmouts" in high-cost areas. In a farmout, another company conducts seismic exploration and/or drills exploration wells to earn an interest in certain acreage.

Concurrently, Milner and his board diversified Chieftain's business activity and the geographical scope of its exploration. Two contract drilling companies were acquired, one based in Alberta, the other in Ohio, and interests were acquired in automotive leasing and natural gas distribution companies. Cash flow generated by these operations helped to fund oil and gas exploration activities.

Oil and gas rights were acquired in the United States and the British and German sectors of the North Sea. Chieftain was an early Canadian entrant into U.S. exploration, where holdings were acquired in the Williston Basin and the Gulf of Mexico. By the end of 1983 Chieftain had interests in oil and gas rights covering 828,000 gross (404,000 net) acres in the United States.

The focus of Chieftain's exploration efforts changed dramatically to oil in 1981 in response to an Alberta-federal energy agreement. The agreement permitted the equivalent of the world oil price for new oil discoveries in Alberta, thus substantially improving the economics of oil exploration.

In 1982 Alberta Energy Company Ltd. acquired 56 percent of Chieftain's common shares through a tender offer to Chieftain's shareholders. An important benefit of the AEC investment was the resulting increase in Chieftain's Canadian ownership rate beyond the level required for maximum grants under the Federal/Alberta Petroleum Incentive Program.

Farther afield, Chieftain acquired interests in 17 blocks, covering 98,000 gross acres, in U.S. federal waters off the Gulf of Mexico in 1983 and initiated a multi-well exploration program. The company continues to maintain its exploration interest in the North Sea, particularly in the West Sole area of the British Sector where it has made two gas discoveries. In addition, Chieftain has a 25 percent interest in a 2.2-million-acre exploration permit in Western Australia and minor interests in the Middle East and Colombia.

While current gas production amounts to approximately 40 mcf per day, Chieftain's installed production and processing capacity exceeds 80 million cubic feet per day. Oil production has increased dramatically from 325 barrels per day in the first quarter of 1983 to 1,400 barrels per day in March 1984. In addition, the raw material for exploration—oil and gas rights—is extensive, exceeding six million acres at the end of 1983.

Chieftain's headquarters is in the Toronto Dominion Tower in Edmonton Centre. The company is a strong supporter of Edmonton's United Way and was a prominent backer of the 1978 Commonwealth Games and Universiade '83.

The firm opened this natural gas-treatment plant in September 1983. Near Hythe, Alberta, the plant has a capacity of 110 million cubic feet per day. It is Chieftain's largest production investment.

BATEMAN FOODS LIMITED

Born in the Maritimes in 1907, W. (Tubby) Bateman came to Edmonton with his parents in May 1913. As south Edmonton in those days was almost rural in life-style, the Bateman residence over the next few years was home to rabbits, chickens, hogs, and cows.

Also schooled in that community, the youngster earned his first money either from his *Edmonton Journal* delivery route or from selling Edmonton *Bulletins* to streetcar passengers riding up and down Whyte Avenue—South Edmonton's main traffic artery. Today he is retired and looks back on a business career that saw his first independent effort fail.

In the years that followed his paper-route days, the young man had taken up butchering; six years after entering the trade, he decided to branch out on his own. Purchasing a butcher business in Edson in 1929, the entrepreneur was broke and $1,500 in debt within a year.

He returned to his hometown later in 1929 and went back to work for Bell's Meat Market on 104th Street. "This experience certainly paid off in later years," Bateman relates today. "I found I wasn't half as smart as I thought I was in 1932."

Back at work in Edmonton, the former store owner was earning $25 a week (times were hard and he had taken a $10 cut in pay) and recalls selling pork shoulder roasts at 5 cents a pound, pork loin roasts at 9 cents, and T-bone, round, and sirloin steaks at 2 pounds for 49 cents.

Three years later, his debts paid in full, Bateman started a new business (with second-hand equipment and a lot of faith) on 99th Street in South Edmonton. His establishment, an old shoe repair shop that he rented for $15 per month, was tiny—a mere

8 feet wide by 33 feet deep—but it was the foundation from which Edmonton's Bateman Foods Limited grew.

Acquiring his landlord's adjoining grocery store in 1935, the expanding proprietor cut an archway between the two premises—and so entered the world of retail marketing where customers shop for groceries and meats under the same roof.

In 1937 Bateman bought another store in the Garneau area, at 111th Street and 86th Avenue, with the building, stock, and fixtures changing hands for $500 cash and the balance at $50 per month at 5 percent. The years of the Bateman Food Market chain had begun.

Within 10 years Bateman found his 99th Street facility too small, and so built a larger store at 89th Avenue and 99th Street. The next 15 years saw more stores and sites bought, and new locations developed.

In his later years in business, Bateman began obtaining properties his customers offered for sale. One of his dreams was to build a senior citizens' residence; the opportunity came when he acquired a half-block of land on 90th Avenue between 99th and 100th streets.

He applied to the city of Edmonton for permission to build such a project, but was allowed to build only a 23-suite apartment. Rather than accept, Bateman contacted the Alberta Housing Corporation, whose answer was a suggestion that he sell his property to the corporation for one dollar. This was done, and AHC built a 52-suite complex on the site. One stipulation of the land sale was that people in the community who had dealt with Bateman Foods—some as far back as 1932—would be given first option to rent suites in the new seniors' apart-

The original Bateman's Meat Market opened in 1932 on 99th Street in South Edmonton.

ment building.

Bateman Manor was opened in 1980, followed two years later by a building erected for the Catholic Social Services organization—also standing on a former Bateman property.

W. (Tubby) Bateman retired from active business in 1969. Busy for many years in community service work, he is a charter member and a past president of the South Edmonton Rotary Club; a member of the South Edmonton Businessmen's Association, the Edmonton Chamber of Commerce, and the Edmonton Better Business Bureau; a 15-year director of St. Mary's Boys' Home; a charter member and director of the Alberta Grocers' Association, and has served on the Edmonton Separate School Board, and the St. Joseph's Hospital Board.

Bateman Foods Limited is today owned by son Bob Bateman and Ivan Radostits, a son-in-law. The firm in 1984 owned and operated 17 stores in Edmonton, 6 IGA supermarkets, and 11 Red Rooster convenience stores.

LUSCAR LTD.

Luscar Ltd. is an Edmonton-based energy company that, through its predecessor and subsidiary companies, has been mining coal in Western Canada for more than 70 years. The Luscar group of companies is controlled by the Mitchell family of Bermuda. The present chairman, Mary-Jean Mitchell Green, is the third generation of the family to head the organization.

Luscar Ltd. was formed in 1967 by the amalgamation of the predecessor companies, Mountain Park Coal Company Limited, incorporated in 1911, and Luscar Collieries Limited, incorporated in 1921. The original ventures were formed to mine coal in the Coal Branch area of Alberta on the eastern slopes of the Rocky Mountains. The principal customers originally were the Canadian Northern and the Grand Trunk Pacific railways, which later merged into the Canadian National Railway. The railway required fuel for steam locomotives pulling trains over the grades of the Yellowhead Pass to the West Coast. Coal production from

The original Luscar Mine, which opened in the early 1900s to supply coal for steam locomotives working on early Western Canadian railway lines.

Luscar and Mountain Park peaked during World War II and the postwar boom.

However, by 1950 the railways as well as many other customers of the mines were converting to oil as their primary fuel, and the market demand for coal decreased as the use of diesel locomotives increased. Although forced to close the Mountain Park Mine in 1950 and the Luscar Mine in 1956, the company retained those coal leases. That decision would prove to be very prudent in future years.

In 1949, under the counsel of then future chairman and still current director, prominent Edmonton lawyer W.O. Parlee, the Luscar group purchased an operating mine near Forestburg, Alberta, and incorporated Forestburg Collieries Limited to supply the domestic market. That foresight and confidence in the future of coal on the part of Sir Harold Mitchell and his brother Alec Mitchell allowed Luscar to benefit significantly from the renewed demand for coal during the worldwide economic boom of the 1970s.

In the early 1950s Luscar became active in the acquisition, exploration, and development of oil and gas properties. In 1953 numerous oil leases were purchased in the Pembina Field,

and later substantial reserves of gas were proven in the Wilson Creek Gas Field. That base would continue to expand into a successful oil and gas operation, which today is administered from Luscar's Calgary office.

The Luscar Mine was reopened in 1969 as an equal venture of Luscar Ltd. and the Consolidation Coal Company to produce metallurgical coking coal for export. Operated by Cardinal River Coals Ltd., the new mine is on the site of the original Luscar townsite, approximately 320 kilometres west of Edmonton. The coal is transported by unit trains to Vancouver, where it is loaded onto ocean vessels at Neptune Bulk Terminals (Canada) Ltd. (of which Luscar is a shareholder).

The Coal Valley Mine is operated by a Luscar subsidiary, Luscar Sterco (1977) Ltd., on 26 square kilometres of a 103-square-kilometre coal-bearing trend for which Luscar Ltd. holds the coal rights. The Alberta Energy Company has a 25-percent minority interest in the venture. The majority of the annual production of bituminous thermal coal is shipped east to Ontario Hydro's Nanticoke generating station via unit trains to bulk-handling facilities at Thunder Bay on Lake Superior. The rail haul of 2,300 kilometres is followed by loading into lake freighters for transport 970 kilometres farther east to the generating station.

Luscar's east-central Alberta operations near Forestburg include the Diplomat Mine, which is currently being phased out, and the Paintearth Mine, both of which produce sub-bituminous coal which is delivered to the nearby Battle River power station. A new venture near Hanna, Alberta, designated as the Sheerness Mine, is now in the development stage and is

Luscar Ltd.'s Coal Valley Mine, in Alberta's Coal Branch on the eastern slope of the Rockies. The mine produces about 3.2 million tonnes of coal annually.

scheduled for production in 1988 to supply fuel to the new Sheerness power station.

Luscar's operations in Saskatchewan originated with the acquisition in 1966 of the Manitoba and Saskatchewan Coal Company Limited and its Bienfait Mine. Although most of the production from the mine, which is located in lignite coal fields near Estevan, Saskatchewan, is delivered to a generating station near Thunder Bay, Ontario, other customers include Manitoba Hydro, Winnipeg Hydro, paper producers, railways, and sodium sulphate producers. The Bienfait Mine also includes carbonization facilities, more commonly known as char plants, which produce char to be used primarily in the manufacture of barbecue briquettes. Luscar's other Saskatchewan operation, the Boundary Dam Mine, also near Estevan, produces lignite coal which is delivered to the Boundary Dam generating station of Saskatchewan Power Corporation.

Today environmental planning and reclamation programs are as integral parts of the coal industry as is mining itself. Guaranteed environmental protection and reclamation are prerequisites to receiving approval for new projects and are essential to ensure continuous production at existing mines. Luscar Ltd. devotes considerable time, attention, and capital

toward environmental protection study and implementation and it is proud of its achievements in that area. In 1981 Luscar's Diplomat Mine at Forestburg became the first coal mine in the province to receive a reclamation certificate for achieving standards under the current legislation.

The Luscar Ltd. of today bears no resemblance to the venture that com-

menced in the early decades of this century. It is now a sophisticated, technically complex, major energy company with a respected international reputation. While carrying on its strong tradition of social responsibility, Luscar strives for advancement not only within its own operations but for the benefit of the entire Canadian energy industry.

The Luscar Mine operates in Alberta's Coal Branch. Originally, the mine supplied high-grade steam coal to early railways that ran branch lines into the area from main lines farther north: hence, the name "Coal Branch."

NORTH AMERICAN CONSTRUCTION LTD.

J.Y. (Ivan) Gouin beside a huge "cat" at a construction site in Riel Park, a subdivision in St. Albert, Alberta.

The story of North American Construction Ltd. is the story of its founder and chairman, J.Y. (Ivan) Gouin.

It is also a story of Ivan Gouin's dedication to service—a dedication that in 38 years saw his one-man, one-machine operation grow to its present position as one of Western Canada's largest heavy-equipment contracting firms employing upwards of 400 people at a given time.

Ivan was born in Vimy, Alberta, a small French-speaking community 30 miles north of Edmonton. French was the language spoken at home but Ivan quickly mastered the English language while attending high school at Clyde. At the early age of 16, Ivan took over many of the responsibilities of running the home grain farm. He has been self-employed ever since, numbering grain buying, butchering, and storekeeping in his repertoire of business skills.

His interest in construction began with the purchase of a bulldozer, which he used to clear land for local farmers. Within a short time he added more equipment and men and became involved in small ditching, excavating, site clearing, and grading work. Ivan's career in construction was on the road to success.

In 1952 Ivan and his wife, Carol, moved to Edmonton, the same year that he purchased Egg Lake Coal Company. This acquisition gave his employees year-round work; in the spring and fall they were ditching, excavating, and clearing roads and construction sites; in the fall and winter months, the mine was busy.

In 1953 Ivan and his brother Bob

incorporated North American Road Ltd. The company was soon occupied with larger brushing and clearing contracts and expanded to grading and earth-moving projects. One of the larger contracts completed during these early years was the clearing and right-of-way grade construction for the Pacific Great Eastern Railway near Fort Saint John and Chetwynd, British Columbia. The company eventually concentrated its efforts in road construction and became one of Alberta's largest contractors.

Following the incorporation of North American Construction Ltd. in 1967, the companies again diversified the operations to include industrial site-preparation work for projects such as the Imperial Oil Fer-

Part of North American Construction Ltd.'s fleet of 28 heavy-duty haulers at the site of the Syncrude plant near Fort McMurray, Alberta. This project involved the removal of 15 million cubic metres of overburden.

tilizer plant at Redwater, the Procter and Gamble pulp mill at Grande Prairie, the Dow Chemical plant in Clover Bar, the Shell Oil plant at Scotford, and the City of Edmonton thermal-power plant at Genesee.

Other jobs North American has become involved in include the installing of plastic pipeline for rural gasification programmes throughout Alberta, irrigation canal work in Southern Alberta, and major overburden removal projects for Syncrude at Fort McMurray.

The Gouin companies have prospered. To provide stability and strength to their operations, Ivan and his directors have invested in office and warehouse buildings, apartment blocks, a hotel, development properties, farmland, and oil and gas interests in both Canada and the United States.

Despite the demands of developing and operating his business enterprises, Ivan has always been dedicated to supporting the community and the construction industry. He

has been active in Edmonton's civic projects and affairs as well as politics at the three levels of government. In the construction industry, he was a member of the Western Canada Roadbuilders' Association, the Alberta Roadbuilders' Association, and the Canadian Construction Association.

In the past several years Ivan's first son, Roger, has become president of the operating company and Ivan, chairman of the board. Roger's vigour and vision are noticeably fueling the Gouin companies. One example is a new venture, Meridian Fireplace Canada Ltd., which manufactures highly efficient stoves and fireplaces in Edmonton for distribution throughout Canada.

When asked to divulge the secret of his success, Ivan reveals that it was his ability to recognize the many opportunities available in Canada, his dedication to hard work, and his desire to give only high-quality service as promptly as possible. He has successfully instilled this work philosophy in his organization.

QUEEN CITY MEATS LTD.

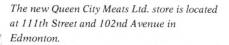

The new Queen City Meats Ltd. store is located at 111th Street and 102nd Avenue in Edmonton.

The original Queen City Meat Market, in downtown Edmonton, circa 1920.

"The most trusted name in meat" is more than a mere slogan to Albert and Bill de Vos, co-owners of Edmonton's Queen City Meats Ltd. The phrase is a personalized guarantee that this 65-year-old market stands behind every ounce of meat it sells.

Queen City was founded by Bill Noak, a British immigrant who had operated a string of six meat markets in his home city of Birmingham. Immigrating first to the United States, Noak came to Canada after trying his hand at meat-market operations in Buffalo, New York, and Seattle. Arriving in Edmonton toward the end of World War I, he opened a shop in what used to be the Bijou Theatre, on 100th Street across from Market Square. The business he founded was named Queen City Meat Market.

His establishment was unique from the start. Noak liked white paint. And he liked lots of light. Therefore, he made sure his new premises had plenty of both—and Queen City Meats shone night and day. The average Noak working day was 14 hours; and the location of his market, close to the courthouse, was soon noted by the more eminent members of Edmonton's judicial and legal circles.

One of the proprietor's whims was lavish display, and his counters were always piled high with meat—pork chops, round steaks, sausage, and chicken. There were times, however, when this enthusiasm threatened disaster: As the weekend approached, more roasts, steaks, and chops had been cut than could be sold; and by Monday these mounds of meat would have lost the freshness Noak guaranteed.

Thus, a Saturday night auction was instituted. Any cuts on hand went to the highest bidder, a practice that enabled the store to start with a clean slate on Monday morning. There were problems, even with this simple solution to the question of overstocked shelves. The city's police department, perhaps stirred by protests from Queen City competitors, acquired the habit of checking to see that the market's doors were locked at closing time on Saturday. That was easy; they were. However, the bylaws people weren't so easily satisfied; once it became known that Noak was auctioning meat behind his locked doors, fat of a different kind was in the fire. In order to make everything legal, Noak had to take out an auctioneer's licence.

The founder died in Edmonton in 1958 at the age of 89. He was in harness to the end and, though not seen as frequently at his old haunts, Noak insisted he hadn't retired—he "just hadn't been around."

Some years earlier, in 1953, Jack de Vos—young and not long out of Holland—began working for Queen City. He was a butcher, following a family tradition that reached back three generations. He took over the firm in 1963, and 10 years later the shop moved from its longtime stand in downtown Edmonton. The new location is just on the fringe of the downtown core, at 111th Street and 102nd Avenue, with ample parking beside the store.

When de Vos retired from business, Queen City Meats Ltd. was taken over by his two sons, Albert and Bill, who today operate with 36 employees. The new plant has its own smokehouse, and the market offers a full line of luncheon meats and a complete assortment of fresh meats that include pork, lamb, beef, and chicken.

The store has established an unbeatable reputation for quality and service for its freezer meats; all such orders are weighed after cutting, and fat and trim is credited for ground beef or sausage at no extra cost. The de Vos brothers and their staff take pride in the fact that Queen City Meats Ltd. is the only market in Edmonton that cuts frozen meats in this manner.

ALBERTA GLASS LIMITED

Ray Bodnar, president, Alberta Glass Limited.

Austen H. Anderton, the founder of Alberta Glass, arrived in Edmonton in 1939. He and an associate established a glass business in 1948 known as Glass and Plastics Company. It was located in a small shop on 105th Street. As well as selling auto glass and paint products, the enterprise silvered its own mirrors.

The following year the name was changed to Alberta Glass Products Limited, and in 1950 the plant moved to a new location—9641-82nd Avenue—which was designed by its owners.

In 1953 Anderton bought out his partner, and his wife, Frances Patricia, became a shareholder. Ten years later the founder saw the need for properly trained people and became actively involved in the start-up of the glassworkers' trade in the Alberta Apprenticeship Programme (1965), serving on both the local and provincial advisory committees

until 1977.

The operating portion of the firm was renamed Alberta Glass Limited in 1974, at which time a veteran employee, J.R. Schuller, purchased a 25 percent share of the organization. Two years later Anderton, planning his retirement, asked his son-in-law, Ray Bodnar, to join the operating company as general manager. Bodnar, who had a successful history of management within the construction industry, purchased Anderton's shares in 1977.

Although Bodnar has only been involved with the glass trade since 1976, he has been very influential. He continued on both the local and provincial advisory committees of the Alberta Apprenticeship Programme, became the founding president of the Glass Trades of Northern Alberta, and was named chairman of the Alberta Construction Relations Association-Glaziers Edmonton. He received a construction service award in 1978 and is a member of the Alberta Construction Association Standard and Fair Practices Committee.

Upon Schuller's retirement in 1980, contract manager Bill Flintoft purchased his shares.

While the company's plant had been expanded twice since 1950, by 1980 Alberta Glass had outgrown its facilities and moved to a new modern plant and offices at 1040-78th Avenue, off the Sherwood Park freeway.

As the glass and construction industries have advanced, Alberta Glass has kept pace. It boasts the capability to produce glass and aluminum products on a par with any of the national companies operating in Alberta, and at a rate unmatched by any other independent firm. The corporation expanded in 1983 to include

Astro-Guard security systems, and glass and brass furniture.

In April 1983 Alberta Glass celebrated its 35th anniversary with a public open house. Mayor Cec Purves and MLA Henry Woo participated in a glass-ribbon-breaking ceremony; hosts were Edmonton Oilers stars Wayne Gretzky, Kevin Lowe, and Mark Messier. Proceeds from the sale of autographed hats went to the A.C.T. Crippled Children's Fund.

Alberta Glass has expanded from its small start, with a payroll of $3,791 and four employees, to a high of 67 employees and a payroll of $1,571,688—attributing much of its success to the high quality of personnel employed. The company remains Alberta-owned and -operated. Current shareholders are R.D. (Ray) Bodnar, Wendy Bodnar (nee Anderton), W.L. (Bill) Flintoft, and Lyn I. Flintoft.

Austen H. Anderton, founder.

PRICE WATERHOUSE

The Canadian history of Price Waterhouse began in Montreal in November 1907. The accountancy practice originated with the London, England, firm, which was established in 1874 and destined to become a worldwide professional network of autonomous Price Waterhouse firms. The Canadian firm now has offices in 23 cities.

The first Alberta office of Price Waterhouse opened in Calgary in 1929. Although the office opened the same year as the stock market crash, it was well established by the onset of World War II.

In the late 1940s, when oil was discovered at Leduc and Redwater, near Edmonton, the oil boom generated a profusion of new clients for Price Waterhouse. In September 1951 the first Edmonton office was opened primarily to handle the work required at the time by two large pipeline corporations, both Price Waterhouse clients that had located their head offices in the Alberta capital.

The firm's first Edmonton office opened in the old Wilkin Building (the site of today's Empire Building). J. Wallace Beaton was sent from Montreal to be resident manager.

Growth of the Edmonton office increased significantly with the 1959 merger of the Price Waterhouse practice and that of Geddes Knebel and Beaton—a local firm founded in 1952 by University of Alberta alumnus Eric Geddes. Jack McGibbon was transferred from Calgary in 1960 to become partner-in-charge of the amalgamated firms. In 1961 Eric Geddes and Albert K. Knebel were admitted to partnership in Price Waterhouse.

The Price Waterhouse practice continued to grow, and in 1969 the office moved to the Royal Bank Building at 101st Street and Jasper Avenue. In 1976 the office again moved, this

Jack S. McGibbon (left) congratulates Eric A. Geddes as he takes over as partner-in-charge of the Price Waterhouse Edmonton office. McGibbon was transferred to the Vancouver office.

time into the new Toronto Dominion Tower in Edmonton Centre.

Meanwhile, in 1965, R.G. (Bob) Heasman was transferred to Edmonton as the office's first full-time tax staff. In 1970 McGibbon was moved to Vancouver and replaced by Geddes as partner-in-charge of the office, and Fred Barth came to the office from Windsor, Ontario. Eric Geddes retired as partner-in-charge in 1982 and was succeeded by Fred Barth.

Price Waterhouse added a full-time management consulting practice in Edmonton in 1974 headed by John Konrad. In 1981, in a merger with

Jarrett, Goold & Elliott, Price Waterhouse acquired a new office at 5240 Calgary Trail with Donald R. McPherson as partner-in-charge.

Today the two Edmonton offices have a combined total of 13 partners. Services are offered in such fields as accounting, auditing, taxation, management consulting, insolvency, and counselling owner-managed businesses. And while much of the work of the 1950s was done on hand-operated calculators, computers have now become an integral part of Price Waterhouse's professional services. Women have been welcomed into the firm in great numbers and represent almost half of the aspiring accountants these days.

Price Waterhouse's professional competence and morale will keep it active on the Edmonton scene for many years to come.

SPRAGUE DRUG LIMITED

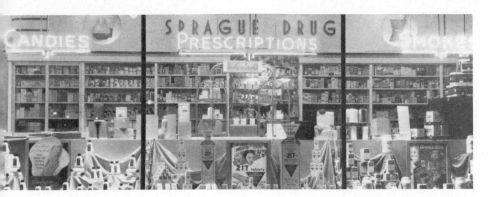

A Sprague Drug Limited store in 1938, one of the earliest in the chain.

Sprague Drug Limited celebrated its 50th anniversary in Edmonton on July 1, 1984.

Walter Sprague, company founder, graduated from the University of Alberta in 1932. He came to Edmonton in 1934 and immediately bought a small but unsuccessful professional dispensary in the McLeod Building, Edmonton's first "skyscraper," across 100th Street from the main post office on 101stA Avenue.

Operating a range of professional dispensaries, family drugstores, community stores, and smaller units established in larger office buildings, the business today is computerized and makes use of the newest products developed for the ever-changing pharmaceutical world. Although at one time the community stores featured soda fountains and lunch counters, they soon disappeared; they didn't seem to "belong" in Walter Sprague's concept of a pharmacy.

The company has a long record of service to communities in Northern Alberta and beyond, particularly to fur traders and prospectors. It also enjoyed a leading role in the so-called "American invasion" of Edmonton and the Northwest during the days of World War II, when construction of the Alaska Highway by the U.S. Army Corps of Engineers was a prime military commitment. The organization also had an important contract with the Bechtel-Price-Callahan construction consortium, builders of the Canol

Pipeline. Hundreds of rough-and-ready adventurers working on these massive projects were serviced from the main Edmonton dispensary. At this time some of the first sulpha drugs were funnelled through Sprague for distribution in the northern market.

Sprague Drug, which has always been a family concern, is presently headed by Donald H. Sprague as president. He has two sons—Robert H. and Kenneth H.—attending university; they will join the firm on completion of their studies.

From its inception, Sprague Drug Limited has been an active force in community development. The Sprague family has taken a busy role in the city's growth and welfare; Walter Sprague has been president of the Edmonton Chamber of Commerce, the Edmonton Kiwanis Club, the Edmonton Exhibition Association, and the Edmonton Eskimo Football Club. As well, he helped to establish the Canadian Derby.

Donald Sprague has been president of Jaycees, president of Mayfair Golf and Country Club, vice-president of Northlands, vice-chairman of Universiade '83, and a member of University of Alberta Hospitals Board and the Alberta Sports Council.

Founder Walter Sprague and his company have faith in Edmonton's future and look forward to being very much in the picture of the developing city of Edmonton and province of Alberta.

The Sprague family in front of Sprague Drug Limited's new Edmonton warehouse. From left they are Bob, Don, Walter, and Ken. The company was founded by Walter Sprague; Don Sprague is now president and Bob and Ken plan to join the firm when they complete their university studies.

GULF CANADA LIMITED

Gulf Canada Limited is the second-largest refiner and marketer of petroleum products in Western Canada, and its 125,000-barrel-a-day Edmonton Refinery is its largest and most efficient refinery, accounting for almost half the corporation's national refining capacity.

The enterprise was founded in Toronto in 1906 as The British American Oil Company Limited by Albert LeRoy Ellsworth, a young Canadian who had learned the basics of the oil business in the United States. Although only in his twenties, he had confidence in the future of the automobile and was able to enlist the support of businessmen, including Silas R. Parsons, a banker who became president. Ellsworth, who was secretary/treasurer initially, served as president from 1927 to 1943.

Originally incorporated in Ontario, B-A began selling kerosene and lubricants in Toronto. Soon a three-acre site on the Toronto waterfront was purchased and, in 1908, a refinery was built to serve the Ontario market. In 1909 the company obtained a federal charter and expanded into Quebec.

There were close to a half-million cars in Canada by 1920, when B-A acquired the Winnipeg Oil Company and moved into Western Canada. At that time, Canadian farmers were beginning to turn toward mechanization and B-A aimed to service their needs.

Since little oil had been found in Canada, B-A in the 1920s formed a successful U.S. exploration and producing subsidiary, and used a company-owned pipeline and rail and ship facilities to deliver U.S. oil to its Canadian refineries. In 1935 the firm extended its operations to the Maritimes and British Columbia.

The billion-dollar Gulf Canada Products Company refinery, situated a few miles east of Edmonton, opened in 1971 and was refitted in 1983 to provide facilities for processing synthetic crude oil.

Following discovery of the Turner Valley "wet" gas field near Calgary in the early 1930s, B-A supplied funds to two independent drillers, Robert A. Brown and George Bell, who proposed drilling a well away from the proven structures. The Turner Valley Royalties No. 1 well was successful, and the company became a significant Canadian oil producer in 1936. B-A's Calgary Refinery went on-stream three years later.

After World War II the Western Canada oil boom that began with the 1947 discovery of the Leduc field led to construction of the Interprovincial Pipe Line system to Eastern Canada. With western oil flowing efficiently to eastern markets, and U.S. oil no longer competitive, B-A sought to increase its Canadian reserves of crude oil to supply its refineries.

This was accomplished in 1956, when B-A acquired the assets of Gulf Oil Corporation's successful Canadian exploration-production subsidiary, Canadian Gulf Oil, for 8.3 million B-A shares. This gave Gulf Oil Corporation a majority interest in the merged Canadian company.

That same year B-A began operating a major gas conservation project in the Stettler-Nevis area southeast of Edmonton. In 1958 the company opened a major gas-processing plant at Pincher Creek, Alberta, and a refinery at Port Moody, British Columbia.

The corporation's strength in Western Canada was augmented in the mid-1960s with the acquisition of Royalite Oil Company, Anglo-Canadian Oils, and Purity 99 Limited.

In 1969 British American changed its name to Gulf Oil Canada Limited, although there was no change in the majority interest at that time.

In February 1975, by increasing the share of Syncrude oil sands project it was prepared to underwrite, Gulf Canada played a major role in helping to put together the financing necessary to build Canada's largest oil sands project at Fort McMurray.

In 1971, two decades after the firm's original Edmonton Refinery was opened, it was replaced with an 80,000-barrel-a-day plant. in 1983 a $275-million expansion was completed, including Canada's first facility specifically designed to upgrade synthetic crude oil from oil sands plants, which raised capacity to 125,000 barrels per day. The refinery now employs 320 workers, and another 70 work in the company's local marketing division. Gulf Canada has more than 400 marketing outlets in Alberta.

THE INSURANCE GROUP OF CANADA WEST LTD.

When Alberta was being settled shortly after the turn of the century, it was a great attraction for all comers—from Ontario, the West Coast, and the Maritimes. The wide-open western prairie was an irresistible lure, and "Go west, young man" was the order of the day.

Thomas Henry Connauton, of the third generation of a seafaring family, was caught up in that migration but in the reverse direction; instead of moving west, he moved east from the West Coast of the United States. His destination was the Vermilion district, a developing farm area in east-central Alberta. Ever since this migratory period of the young province's earliest years, Alberta has been the home of the Connauton family. The fourth generation now lives in Edmonton.

J.M. (Jack) Connauton was the first member of his family to be born in Alberta. He has always been thankful that his father had the foresight to break with the seafaring tradition and to venture into an area that was not only sparsely settled, but abundant in its promises for the future. However, when Jack returned from World War II, farm life was no longer an attraction. He settled in Edmonton and soon was involved with the post-war construction boom that in a few short years would catapult Edmonton from small-city status to the sprawling metropolis it is today. As the owner of Johnson Bros. Electric Ltd. he did his share of installing the lights that brighten the city's skyline, his most prominent project being the wiring of the CN Tower that stands guard over the downtown core.

The pioneering spirit that was exemplified by Jack's father stayed with the family, and by 1961 Jack, having left his mark in the construction industry, was looking for another

field of endeavour with new challenges to meet and overcome. Such an opportunity came when Canada West Insurance Company, a small Alberta-based firm, was having difficulty in competing with giants of the industry that were not only national but international in scope.

At the time, Alberta was not well represented in the insurance field. The majority of companies operating in the province had their head offices in Eastern Canada. Nonetheless, with Edmonton and Alberta experiencing tremendous growth, there appeared to be opportunity for an insurance company based in this province. To compete in this industry, such a company had to be much more than just another insurance firm; it would have to provide a wide range of services to the public.

With this in mind, the concept of The Insurance Group of Canada West was conceived. Today the organization encompasses nine companies—insurance agencies, claims adjusting, auto repair shops, finance, and travel; most are insurance-related, providing services to Albertans. It has played a significant role in the growth of the

province, and from its uncertain start in 1961, with gross sales of less than one million dollars per year, it has grown through the confidence bestowed by Albertans. Now a major player in the Alberta insurance field, The Insurance Group shows gross sales exceeding $30 million annually.

Jack is fortunate in having a son, G.T. (Gary) Connauton, to follow him into the insurance field. Also dedicated to Alberta's growth, Gary has not only grown with the firm, but has been instrumental in its growth. His has been the guiding hand that led Canada West Insurance from manual recording of all documents to a fully integrated computerized system. Working closely with dedicated employees, many of whom consider it "their company," Gary is utilizing the strong base that has been built up over the past 23 years to further expand the operations of The Insurance Group. The continuing goal is unchanged: "Growing with Alberta."

J.M. (Jack) Connauton, president and chairman of the board of The Insurance Group of Canada West Ltd. Courtesy of Miller Photography Ltd. Canada.

BLANCHETT NEON LIMITED

Edmonton's sign industry has reason to be grateful to George William Blanchett's versatility and drive, as the story behind the origin of Blanchett Neon Limited so readily demonstrates.

George was born in 1909 and came to Edmonton at the age of three with his parents, George Richard Blanchett, a painter and decorator, and Edith Rose Blanchett. (His father operated a firm, Blanchett Decorators, for many years.) George went to work for Hook Signs Ltd. when he was 15, and began learning how to apply his considerable talent to the production of commercial signs, bulletins, and pictorials.

In 1930 the young man married Elizabeth Keith (Libby) Hallock, and later a daughter, Betty, was born in Edmonton. In 1937 George toured England and the continent with the Herringay Racers, a professional hockey team. The year following found him in Vancouver, working for Neon Products of Western Canada—a job that gave him the experience and motivation to start a neon-sign business back in Edmonton. Meanwhile, in Vancouver, a son, Keith, had been born.

George returned to Edmonton in 1944 and began working for his father. His younger brother, Edward Raymond (Ted), had joined the Royal Canadian Air Force during World War II. At the time George returned to the Alberta capital, Blanchett Decorators Limited was operating from 11448 Jasper Avenue.

The beginnings of Blanchett Neon Limited date back to 1946, after Ted's discharge from the service. The brothers and their wives drove two panel trucks to Calgary, where they purchased a used neon tube-bending and pumping outfit. They brought the equipment home, where Blanchett Decorators-Neon & Sign Division was launched. The enterprise continued to function as a decorating firm during the daylight hours. During the evenings the design, manufacture, and installation of neon signs were top priority. These signs were put out on a lease basis. One of the earliest the company made was for the George Strange Auto Mart at 108th Street and Jasper Avenue; that sign is still in use today at the Automart, now located at 10252-109th Street.

In 1947 the two operations were incorporated as separate companies

with interlocking officers/directors. Management began to specialize, each brother assuming supervision of one firm. Ted still owns and operates Blanchett Decorators Limited, while ownership of the neon company (over many years) was gradually assumed by son-in-law Robert (Bud) Squair and son Keith Blanchett, who survive George as owner/partners. George died in Edmonton in November 1983.

Both organizations moved to new premises at 10224-109th Street in 1952, a structure still known as the Blanchett Building. There were tenants on the second floor and in the basement at the outset; subsequently, as the volume of business grew, the neon-sign firm assumed the entire building. A concrete-block addition was completed in the early '60s.

Again because of the growth of operation, George negotiated his purchase of Ted's half of the building—while a parent company was formed to own Blanchett Neon and the lot and building on 109th Street.

In 1969 Blanchett Neon Limited moved to its second new home, at 12850 St. Albert Trail. This facility, standing on 2.37 acres fronting the highway to St. Albert, provides 21,000 square feet of office and production space.

Early Blanchett Neon customers included the Shasta Cafe, Seven Seas restaurant, Waterloo Motors, Coles Printing, and Reliable Printing. The corporation employs 32 full-time workers, with peak periods necessitating the total rise to 50 in all categories.

Its insistence on outstanding design and production of a technically sound

The first premises of Blanchett Decorators Limited was at 11448 Jasper Avenue, Edmonton.

In 1952 Blanchett Neon Limited moved to this new facility at 10224-109th Street. It still is designated the Blanchett Building.

George Blanchett, founder of Blanchett Neon Limited.

sign developed a solid reputation for the company, and volume increased annually throughout its history until the recession of 1981 took effect. Nevertheless, its clientele and reputation have served it well in maintaining an efficient level of production.

George took the firm into membership in the Chicago-based National Electric Sign Association, and served as its director. He also joined Westarc (later World Sign Associates), which began as an alliance of independents in the Pacific Northwest—attracting Canadians from Edmonton, Calgary, and Vancouver. These connections provide constant contact with new products and methods, as well as friendships in many countries that have developed through the years.

Today the firm is located in this modern office/plant on the St. Albert Trail, just north of the CNR main line.

In 1973 Blanchett Neon Limited acquired Prairie Signs in Grande Prairie; it operated this branch for five and one-half years, developing management from local staff members. This operation never achieved its potential, in spite of the market activity, and was sold to the staff in 1978.

Blanchett Neon continues to be very much a part of Edmonton's business fabric, and for years has maintained a positive stance toward the city's emergence as an outstanding metropolitan area. Two of George's grandsons-in-law today are involved in management of the family's extensive sign-industry interests, demonstrating the influence the founder has had on the North American neon-sign industry.

FLORENCE B. HALLOCK

"A teacher affects eternity; he can never tell where his influence stops."
—Henry Brooks Adams (1838-1918)

Such could be written of Florence B. Hallock (1886-1938), an Edmonton public school teacher whose special interest and calling centered around home economics. Miss Hallock's influence lives today in the hearts of thousands of Alberta women with whom she came in contact during her 25 years with the Edmonton Public School Board.

Florence Hallock, born in the United States, was educated at the Pratt Institute, Brooklyn, New York, from which she received a certificate in household science. She later undertook postgraduate study at Teachers College, Columbia University, New York City. Other courses from which she graduated included first aid and

Florence B. Hallock (1886-1938), former home economics supervisor for the Edmonton Public School Board.

home nursing, textiles, and dress design.

Following her studies, Miss Hallock taught in Jersey City, New Jersey, and Calgary, before coming to Edmonton. Here she became supervisor of home economics in the public school system and as such was responsible for instruction in this ever-expanding field.

One of Florence Hallock's first volunteer service projects came with the postwar influenza epidemic of 1918. She supervised a 24-hour-nursing service at Victoria High School, with her own students and assistants. In another volunteer project, this one in Calgary in the early years of World War I, she organized groups of women and students to make "colours" (regimental flags) for the first Calgary regiment to be sent overseas.

During the 1930s Alberta home economists faced a challenge to develop innovations to help people cope with the difficult circumstances of the Great Depression. They re-

sponded with recipes, ideas, and often gave first-hand instruction in such subjects as nutritious and inexpensive meals, made-over clothes, homemade cleaning products and cosmetics, and inexpensive furnishings.

Consequently, in the mid-1930s, Florence Hallock organized classes for unemployed young women in the city. Hundreds responded to her call for students; many went on to obtain positions in the area. As well, she also set up a household workers' course, which later came under provincial government supervision.

Active in the community, Miss Hallock was a past president of the Edmonton Women's Teachers' Club and also of the Edmonton Home Economics Association (EHEA). Her interests extended to the Young Women's Christian Association, and she served the city branch in a variety of ways. Her days at the YWCA are remembered through the YW's "Phoebe Hallock Room," which she endowed. Miss Hallock also is remembered through the Florence Hallock Memorial Prize, instituted by the EHEA in 1951, which is awarded annually to the university student of outstanding merit in education with a home economics major.

Florence B. Hallock died in Edmonton in September 1938. She had retired a year earlier due to serious illness. The then-superintendent of schools, G.A. McKee, paid this tribute at the time of her passing: "No more enthusiastic leader in the household economics department could be found anywhere, and it was a severe loss to the service when she withdrew. In fact, the system has not even yet fully adjusted itself to her absence. . . .Miss Hallock was a fine woman and a fine teacher. We shall think of her for a long time to come."

CANADIAN PACIFIC

Canadian Pacific has been involved in Edmonton since railway steel reached the North Saskatchewan River in 1891—five years before the Klondike gold rush. But Edmonton, as Gateway to the North, was most vital to the company in the early days of CP Air.

Formed in 1942 from 10 bush airlines across the country, Canadian Pacific Air Lines really "took off" in Edmonton, flying the builders of the Alaska Highway, the Canol Pipeline, and later the DEW Line, all over the North. A duo of notable bush pilots—Punch Dickins and Wop May—were in on its birth, but it was Grant McConachie, first as general manager, western lines, in Edmonton, then as president in Vancouver, who transformed CP Air into a five-continent international flag-carrier.

Becoming a national airline meant losing its Mackenzie Valley and Saskatchewan routes to regional carriers, but CP Air still flies into Northern Alberta, British Columbia, and the Yukon from Edmonton.

Much earlier, the Edmonton area was linked to the Canadian Pacific Railway main line through completion of the Calgary & Edmonton Railway in 1891. The C&E terminated at Strathcona, across-river from Ed-monton, until completion of the High Level Bridge over the North Saskatchewan in 1913. However, by then the two communities had amalgamated to become the nucleus of the Edmonton we know today.

CP Rail operates eight freight trains and four Via Rail dayliners daily between Edmonton and Calgary, with extra freights as required. Its main yard is still in South Edmonton's Strathcona district, with a satellite yard in Lambton Park. The new Scotford Spur goes into the county of Strathcona's northeast industrial area, and an Intermodal terminal handling rail/road/container shipments was opened in October 1984, at 99th Street and 35th Avenue. CP Rail moves some 450 cars a day through Edmonton.

The 330-room Chateau Lacombe has been operated by CP Hotels since it opened in 1967. Chateau Lacombe, named for a pioneer Roman Catholic missionary who at the height of his career served for one hour as president of the Canadian Pacific Railway, commands a magnificent view of the North Saskatchewan Valley from its location at the heart of the city's downtown core.

Canadian Pacific Enterprises, headquartered in Alberta since 1982, conducts diversified international businesses through subsidiary companies involved in oil, gas, mines and minerals, forest products, iron and steel, real estate, agriproducts, financial, and other interests. Enterprises subsidiaries include PanCanadian Petroleum, Cominco, Fording Coal, Great Lakes Forest Products, CIP Inc., Pacific Forest Products, Algoma Steel, AMCA International, Marathon Realty, and Maple Leaf Mills.

Marathon Realty owns 10 office buildings in Edmonton that have a combined leasable area of 531,000 square feet. Other facilities include the 160-acre Strathcona Industrial Park, Strathcona House (a residential complex), and an aviation-related facility at Edmonton International Airport.

Maple Leaf Mills operates a 24,000-tonne feed plant producing livestock and poultry feeds under the Masterfeed brand, along with a retail outlet to serve the farm trade. The flour division operates a warehouse as a distribution centre for industrial flour.

In all, Canadian Pacific companies employ more than 800 people in Edmonton and the city's immediate district.

Grant McConachie, destined to become president of Canadian Pacific Air, flew a ski-equipped bush plane out of Edmonton in CP Air's first years.

The first Canadian Pacific passenger train to cross the North Saskatchewan River on Edmonton's High Level Bridge. The date was June 1912, a few months after the cities of Edmonton and Strathcona had amalgamated. Courtesy of the Provincial Archives of Alberta.

FOUR SEASONS HOTELS

Isadore Sharp, founder and chairman, Four Seasons Hotels.

Standing tall in the downtown area of Alberta's capital city, Edmonton's 314-room Four Seasons Hotel is a landmark among the finest of international hotels.

Opened in 1978, the lodging is operated by Four Seasons Hotels, based in Toronto, a Canadian-owned firm that in a little over 20 years has become a world leader in managing medium-size hotels of exceptional quality. It is directed by Isadore Sharp, the organization's founder, chairman, president, and chief executive officer. A Toronto-born graduate of Ryerson Polytechnical Institute, with honours in architecture, his business career began when he joined his father in Max Sharp and Son Construction Company.

Five years later the entrepreneur achieved a cherished goal when he developed the concept for a new hotel enterprise. His first unit was a Four Seasons Hotel that opened in Toronto in 1961; it was followed in two years by the Inn on the Park, also in Toron-

to. Today the corporation owns or manages 19 hotels in Canada and the United States, as well as the Inn on the Park in London, England, and is also developing substantial real estate holdings in Canada and Florida.

Aspiring "to operate the finest hotel in cities where we locate," a company mandate is excellence in service and product. The residential-style decor features antiques, original art, and fresh flowers that enhance lobbies and guest rooms, while concierge service, fine cuisine, and a host of amenities placate the most discriminating tastes of the guests.

Growth of the Four Seasons network has been meticulously planned: Opportunities for new hotels are constantly being proposed; each is carefully investigated, but only those that meet the company's high standards are considered. In a relatively few years the firm has gained the confidence of backers and financiers, and today it is associated with some of the hotel-development industry's leaders.

In 1982 Four Seasons opened hotels in Houston, Dallas, and Seattle. In Philadelphia a $150-million hotel and office tower was built in 1983 in partnership with CIGNA Corporation and Urban Investment and Development of Chicago. It is the largest privately financed development undertaken in inner-city Philadelphia. In addition, a 290-room Four Seasons hotel and a luxury condominium/apartment complex is under construction in Boston.

In the 1983 Canadian Automobile Association/American Automobile Association judging for Five Diamond Awards, the Four Seasons hotels in Toronto, Vancouver, and Montreal were among 41 properties in Canada, the United States, and Mexico to earn the prestigious Five-Diamond rat-

ing—"awarded only to those properties widely recognized for providing the finest guest facilities, services, and atmosphere," notes the CAA. Further recent recognition of Four Seasons' excellence came from the *Institutional Investor,* a magazine for financial investors, which conducted a survey among leading bankers of the world to assess the best hotels worldwide. For the second year in a row, the Four Seasons Hotel, Toronto, was named the top hotel in Canada—and the only non-United States hotel in the regional top five.

In its persistent dedication to excellence, Four Seasons Hotels is consistently praised by various publications.

Edmonton's Four Seasons Hotel is located in the City Centre Complex.

PATRONS

The following individuals, companies, and organizations have made a valuable commitment to the quality of this publication. Windsor Publications and The Historical Society of Alberta-Amisk Waskahegan Chapter gratefully acknowledge their participation in *Edmonton: Gateway to the North.*

Alberta College*
Alberta Glass Limited*
Alberta Government Telephones*
Alberta Grocers Wholesale Ltd.
Alberta Pioneer Railway Museum
Banister Continental Ltd.*
Bateman Foods Limited*
Big Axe Clearing Co. Ltd.
Blanchett Neon Limited*
Bowlen Holdings Ltd.*
Canada Safeway Limited*
Canadian National Railways*
Canadian Pacific*
Carnwood Wire Line Service Ltd.
Dr. and Mrs. John W. Chalmers
Chieftain Development Co. Ltd.*
CITV*
Cormie Ranch Ltd.*
Edmonton Economic Development
    Authority*
Edmonton General Hospital
    The Grey Nuns of Edmonton*
*The Edmonton Journal**
Edmonton Northlands*
Edmonton Power*
Edmonton Telephones*
Fabrigear Limited
George E. Failing Supply Company
    Ltd.

Four Seasons Hotels*
Gainer's Inc.*
Gulf Canada Company*
Florence B. Hallock*
June Honey
Imperial Lumber Company Ltd.*
The Insurance Group of Canada West
    Ltd.*
International Cooling Tower Inc.
Interprovincial Pipe Line Limited*
Daniel Kane
Helen LaRose
Luscar Ltd.*
McDougall & Secord, Limited*
Drs. J. Marko and M. Lieberman
Melcor Developments Ltd.*
North American Construction Ltd.*
Northwestern Utilities Limited*
North West Mill*
Nova, An Alberta Corporation*
Numac Oil & Gas Ltd.*
Oxford Development Group Ltd.*
F.R. Patrick
Peat, Marwick, Mitchell & Co.*
Ed & Susan Pohranychny
Price Waterhouse*

Principal Group of Companies*
Queen City Meats Ltd.*
Reed's China and Gift Shop*
Regent Drilling Ltd.*
Roundhouse Sales
Scotiabank*
Shaw Cablesystems Ltd.*
Shell Canada Limited*
Society for the Protection of
    Architectural Resources in
    Edmonton (S.P.A.R.E.)
Sprague Drug Limited*
Stanley Associates Engineering Ltd.*
Suncor Inc.*
Sunwapta Broadcasting Limited*
Syncrude Canada Ltd.*
Walter Szwender, M.L.A.
Upright Bros. Ltd.*
Mr. & Mrs. W.S. Watson
Woodward's*

*Partners in Progress of *Edmonton: Gateway to the North.* The histories of these companies and organizations appear in Chapter 9, beginning on page 225.

The Old Timers' Association marches up Jasper Avenue in the 1905 Inauguration Day parade. The arch was in honour of King Edward VII and Queen Alexandra. (PAA, E. Brown Collection)

HONORARY ADVISORY COMMITTEE

ACKNOWLEDGMENTS

The writing of this history of Edmonton has been made possible by the generous cooperation over many years of the City of Edmonton Archives, the Provincial Archives of Alberta, the University of Alberta Archives, the Glenbow-Alberta Institute, and the Public Archives of Canada. The author has also greatly benefitted from the conversations on the history of Alberta with Dr. John Foster of the History Department of the University of Alberta and Mr. Michael Kostek of the Edmonton Public School Board. The support and encouragement of my family, who have been a part of the history of Edmonton and Alberta, must be gratefully acknowledged.

SUGGESTIONS FOR FURTHER READING

Edmonton: A History (Edmonton, 1975) by J.G. MacGregor was the first book published to give a general overview of Edmonton's development from a fur-trade post to a city. This pioneering effort in the writing of the history of Edmonton emphasizes the role of specific individuals in its progress to metropolitan status. *The Edmonton Story: The Life and Times of Edmonton, Alberta* (Edmonton, 1956) and *More Edmonton Stories: The Life and Times of Edmonton, Alberta* (Edmonton, 1958) by Tony Cashman contain descriptions of various incidents and personalities in Edmonton's past. Pictorial overviews include *Edmonton: Portrait of a City* (Edmonton, 1981) by Carin Routledge and Dennis Person, which is distinguished by the quality of its photographs and the informational value of their captions.

Specific studies of Edmonton's physical geography include an article by William C. Wonders entitled "River Valley City—Edmonton on the North Saskatchewan" *(Canadian Geographer,* 1959). *The Atlas of Alberta* (Edmonton, 1969) and *Alberta: A Natural History* (Edmonton, 1967) are also useful in delineating regional geography.

David G. Mondelbaum discusses the native history of the Edmonton area in his study entitled *The Plains Cree: An Ethnographic, Historical and Comparative Study* (Regina, 1979). This book is of particular importance because of its information on the westward migration of the Cree from Hudson Bay to the area that would become Alberta. More detailed information on the other tribes in the Edmonton area is provided in *Indian Tribes of Alberta* (Calgary, 1979) by Hugh A. Dempsey.

The History of the Canadian West to

1870 (Toronto, 1973) by A.S. Morton and edited by Dr. L.G. Thomas is the most comprehensive account of the fur trade. It contains specific information on Edmonton's role in the trade. Secondary sources that deal specifically with Fort Edmonton include *Edmonton: Fort-House-Factory* (Edmonton, 1959) by George Heath MacDonald, *John Rowand: Czar of the Prairies* (Saskatoon, 1978) by J.G. MacGregor, *Ambition and Reality: The French Speaking Community of Edmonton, 1795-1935* (Edmonton, 1980) by E.J. Hart, and *The North West Fort: Fort Edmonton* (Edmonton, 1983) by Janice E. MacDonald. Published articles include "Chief Factor John Rowand" *(Alberta History,* 1957) by H. Rawlinson, and "Flour Mills in the Fur Trade" *(Alberta History,* 1982) by Barry Kaye. Published primary sources on the fur trade with specific reference to Fort Edmonton include the *Minutes of the Council of the Northern Department, 1821-1831* (Toronto, 1940). This is particularly important since it documents the first Bow River expedition and the reorganization of the fur trade after the amalgamation of the North West Company and the Hudson's Bay Company. "Impressions of Fort Edmonton" *(Alberta History,* 1966) by Harrison Young and "A Letter from Fort Edmonton" *(Alberta History,* 1957) by John Rowand provide glimpses of life at Fort Edmonton by two former company officials.

Unpublished sources on the fur trade in Edmonton include "Fort Assiniboine, Alberta, 1823-1914: Fur Trade Post to Settled District" (Master's Thesis, University of Alberta, 1976) by R.F. McCarty, "The Fur Trade at Lesser Slave Lake, 1815-1831" (Master's Thesis, University of

Alberta, 1967) by W.P. Baergen, and "A Study of the History of the Rocky Mountain House Area" (Master's Thesis, University of Alberta, 1952) by E.S. Gish.

The literature on the missionaries and the gold miners includes *Father Lacombe* (Edmonton, 1975) by J.G. MacGregor and *The Rundle Journals 1840-1848* (Calgary, 1977) edited by Hugh Dempsey. This edition contains an excellent introduction by Gerald M. Hutchinson who has also written an article entitled "Early Wesleyan Missions" *(Alberta History,* 1958). An excellent description of the trip of the overlanders is provided by *The Overlanders of '62* (Victoria, 1931) by M.S. Wade. A personal account of the trip by one of its participants is provided in the article "The Overlanders in Alberta, 1862" *(Alberta History,* 1966) by Thomas McMicking.

Many of the tourists and government officials who visited Fort Edmonton left accounts that comment on a variety of aspects of life at the fort. Included in these travel accounts are *Wanderings of an Artist* (Tokyo, 1968) by Paul Kane, which describes his trip through the Canadian West in 1846-1848. Others are *Ocean to Ocean* (Tokyo, 1967) by the Reverend George M. Grant, which describes Sanford Fleming's expedition through Canada in 1872, *Cheadle's Journal of Trip Across Canada 1862-1863* (Edmonton, 1971) by Walter B. Cheadle, and *The Great Lone Land* (Edmonton, 1968) by William Francis Butler.

The political, economic, and social development of the new community beyond the walls of Fort Edmonton from the 1870s to the First World War is described in various sources, including "Edmonton Civic Politics, 1891-1914" *(Urban History Review,*

1977) by John Day, *A History of the University of Alberta* (Edmonton, 1981) by Dr. Walter H. Johns, and "Edmonton's Perilous Course, 1904-1929" *(Urban History Review,* 1977) by John C. Weaver. *The Fort on the Saskatchewan* (Fort Saskatchewan, 1974) by the Reverend Peter T. Reim describes the arrival of the North West Mounted Police in the fall of 1874. *Twenty Years on the Saskatchewan* (London, 1897) is the published memoir of Edmonton's first Anglican minister, the Reverend William Newton.

The careers of Edmonton's first businessmen are described in *Edmonton Trader* (Toronto, 1963) by J.G. MacGregor, *Richard Secord 1860-1935* (Edmonton, 1981) by John McIsaac, David Leonard, and Sheilagh Jameson, and "Matthew McCauley" *(Alberta History,* 1972) by Jim Blower. Improvements in the transportation and communication system during the post-1870 period include *Steam Boats on the Saskatchewan* (Saskatoon, 1972) by Bruce Peel, "The Telegraph Line to Edmonton" *(Alberta History,* 1970) by Allen Ronaghan, "The Calgary-Edmonton Trail" *(Alberta History,* 1959) by Hugh A. Dempsey, and "Leeson and Scott" *(Alberta History,* 1976) by Donald M. Stewart, and *Edmonton's Electric Transit* (Toronto, 1983) by Colin K. Hatcher and Tom Schwartzkopf. The gold rush through Edmonton is described in *The Klondike Rush Through Edmonton, 1897-1898* (Toronto, 1970) by J.G. MacGregor.

Edmonton's theatre history during the pre-World War I era is discussed in *Fallen Empires* (Edmonton, 1981) by John Orrell, "The Pantages Theatre In Edmonton, Alberta, 1913 to 1921" (Master's Thesis, University of Alberta, 1983) by Georgina Kravetz, and "A Survey of Professional Entertainment and Theatre in Edmonton, Alberta, before 1914" (Master's Thesis, University of Alberta, 1970). The history of other recreational institutions can be found in *The Edmonton Exhibition: The First Hundred Years* (Edmonton, 1979) by Tony Cashman. *Looking Back: A Century of Education in Edmonton Public Schools* (Edmonton, 1982) by M.A. Kostek and *Edmonton's Catholic Schools: A Success Story* (Edmonton, 1977) by Tony Cashman document the development of educational institutions. The most recent study of the development of Edmonton during this period is "The Development of Urban Community in Prairie Canada: Edmonton, 1898-1921" (Ph.D. dissertation, University of Alberta, 1981) by Carl Betke.

The literature on Edmonton during and after the First World War is relatively scarce. The books already noted by Hart, Betke, Johns, and Hatcher, which cover a portion of the post-World War period, can be supplemented by *Airborne From Edmonton* (Toronto, 1959) by Eugenie L. Myles and *Uncharted Skies: Canadian Bush Pilot Stories* (Edmonton, 1983). "The Edmonton Grads: Canada's Most Succesful Team" (Master's Thesis, University of Windsor, 1976) by Cathy Macdonald discusses the 25-year history of the team. Edmonton's difficulties during the Depression are described in Keith Hart's article entitled "Military Aid to Edmonton" *(Alberta History,* 1983) and Anne B. Woywitka's article entitled "Recollections of a Union Man" *(Alberta History,* 1975). *The Dynamic Decade* (Toronto, 1958) by Eric J. Hanson, *Oil In Canada West:* *The Early Years* (Calgary, 1969) by George de Mille, and *Black Gold With Grit: The Alberta Oil Sands* (Vancouver, 1978) by J. Joseph Fitzgerald discuss the postwar development of the petroleum resources of Edmonton and the North. A discussion of other aspects of Edmonton's postwar development is to be found in *Edmonton: The Emerging Metropolitan Pattern* (Victoria, 1978) edited by P.J. Smith.

The published books and articles noted above can be supplemented with the Edmonton *Bulletin* and the Edmonton *Journal.* The former newspaper was established in 1881 by Frank Oliver and continued publishing until 1951. The Edmonton *Journal* has been published continuously since November, 12, 1903.

INDEX

TITLES IN THE WINDSOR HISTORY SERIES

Alan Rogers (1984)

California Wings: An Illustrated History of Aviation in California, by William Schoneberger (1984)

Columbia: An Illustrated History, by Alan R. Havig (1984)

We Crown Them All: An Illustrated History of Danbury, by William E. Devlin (1984)

Historic Huntsville: A City of New Beginnings, by Elise Hopkins Stephens and Sarah Newman Shouse (1984)

Jackson: An Illustrated History, by Brian C. Deming (1984)

Lincoln: The Prairie Capital, by James L. McKee (1984)

Mississippi Gulf Coast: Portrait of a People, by Charles L. Sullivan (1984)

Montana: Land of Contrast, by Harry W. Fritz (1984)

Monterey Peninsula: An Enchanted Land, by Randall A. Reinstedt (1984)

Montgomery County: Two Centuries of Change, by Jane C. Sween (1984)

Where Rivers Meet: The Story of Ottawa, by Courtney C.J. Bond (1984)

Saint John: Two Hundred Years Proud, by George W. Schuyler (1984)

International Port of Call: An Illustrated History of the Golden Gate, by Robert J. Schwendinger (1984)

Scottsdale: Oasis of Leisure and Arts, by Patricia Myers McElfresh (1984)

Spokane: City of the Falls, by William L. Stimson (1984)

Members of the Edmonton Newsboy's Band of 1924 express the exuberance of their era. (COE)